The Guinness Book of Traditional Pub Games

The Guinness Book
of Traditional
Pub Games

ARTHUR R. TAYLOR

GUINNESS PUBLISHING

Acknowledgements

I would like to thank the following publicans, sinners, games players, watchers and writers for their help – Eric Hatfield, Keith Naylor, Patrick Chaplin, David Parlett, Andrew Pennycook, Tom Payne, Guy Tunnicliffe, Alan Dean, Peter Clare, Malc Ferris, Ken Hussey, Eric Hill, Selwyn Schofield, William Ingram, Alan Lever, John Roberts, Alan Burton, Peter Brown, Peter Lambert, Barrie Pepper, Andrew Steven, Rob Magee, Liz Hauxwell, Erik de Vroede and Bob Morton. Last, but by no means least, my wife, Jean Taylor.

Editor:	Paola Simoneschi
Design:	John Mitchell
Layout:	Amanda Ward
Diagrams:	Dennis Adelman
	Sarah Goddard
Cover Design:	John Mitchell
Cover Photography:	Peter Chadwick
Picture Editor:	Alex P. Goldberg

Typeset in Great Britain by Ace Filmsetting Ltd, Frome, Somerset
Printed and bound in Great Britain by The Bath Press, Bath

A catalogue record for this book is available from the British Library

ISBN 0-85112-530-1

Picture Acknowledgements

Bartlett Jones PR Ltd
British Pétanque Association
E.A. Clare & Son
Mary Evans Picture Library
Hulton Picture Company
Henry A. Kiddy
Christine Knight
John Mills Photography Ltd
Museum of English Rural Life
J.R. Oldfield
Oldham Evening Chronicle
Pace
Popperfoto
Spectrum Colour Library
Sun

'In many societies, there is a place that constitutes a sort of neutral ground where people can meet in a public place without the strains that come from being on someone else's home ground. In West Africa, this is the space under the village's meeting tree. In England it is the pub. Its full title of public house *is significant. Although such places seem immediately natural and non-problematic to those of the English culture, an enormous amount of cultural information has to be known in order to behave properly in such a setting.'*

Native Land Nigel Barley (1989)

This one is for Tom, at last.

Reports of the demise of the British pub, and of pub games, have been greatly exaggerated; they are alive and doing as well as can be expected, in rapidly changing circumstances. The pub is, in the words of Peter Clark, one of its ablest recent historians 'quintessentially a neighbourhood theatre'. Each one has its own stage setting, its own cast of characters – and its own style of play. Despite rumours to the contrary, thousands of them still play games.

I know, because I've been searching out, playing and writing about them for over 30 years now – a taproom odyssey of epic proportions which resulted in a book in 1976 and now this one (let's call it a progress report). As any social scientist will tell you, at the end of his deliberations, what is needed is more finance and more time for research. I hope to be producing an interim report, sometime beyond the year 2000.

There is no real substitute for on-the-spot experience. Secondary sources are useful, but often misleading. There is, for instance, that standard official notice often seen hanging behind the bar, listing the games which may be played, subject to the landlord's discretion, and 'for small stakes only'. The latest edition emerged after the 1988 Licensing Act and makes interesting reading. The games listed are 'Dominoes, Cribbage, Darts, Billiards, Bagatelle, Skittles and Shove Ha'penny' – an extraordinarily narrow and limited catalogue, as this book will show. Local licensing magistrates are sometimes asked to approve other games, peculiar to their local area, but the net conclusion must be that the Authorities simply don't know what goes on.

I doubt whether the Authorities have ever been fully *au fait* with the public bar, which is why the history of pub games presents such a problem. We only know about games which, for one reason or another, were condemned by the Authorities. Peter Clark, in *The English Alehouse, A Social History 1200–1830*, mentions 'dice, tables (backgammon), card games, guile-bones or ten bones, noddy board, penny prick, shovehalfpenny or slide thrust, fox-mine host, ticktack, milking cromock, bowls, nine and ten holes, main chance, cross and pile, hide under hat and alleys (marbles)' as being indoor games played in the alehouse from 1500 to 1650.

By the 18th century even more card games were being played including 'all-fours, hotch cap, cribbage, brag and whist', and there were special rooms for some games – the boardsend room for Shove Ha'penny, the billiard room and the mississippi room (for a type of Bagatelle). There were specially built skittle alleys too – we know about them because they were frequently specified in fire insurance policies.

It all makes entertaining reading, but I'll bet it's by no means the whole story. What we have are the games which came up as detected (and punished) crimes at the assizes, quarter and petty sessions of the period.

Much the same is true of the 19th century. I have combed through the histories of pubs in this period in my local area in the Manchester connurbation and have come up with, by and large, only those games which appear in court reports, including cards, dominoes, dice, Bagatelle, Quoits, Ringing the Bull, Puff and Dart, Ratting and Lark Singing. The truth is that the Authorities never knew the whole story – and neither do we, because the taproom conversations and conventions have never been properly chronicled.

Even the developments of this century are shrouded in mystery. How many different regional dartboards were there? I've listed a dozen or so, but there were probably many more. Who invented the configuration of the standard, or London board? We don't really know, although names have been put forward, claims denied and controversy rages. Why Evesham Quoits, Northants Skittles? Why do they Push Pennies in Stamford and Shoveha'penny everywhere else? Was Dwile-flonking invented c1585 or c1965? Where does table football come from? Who was Aunt Sally? I offer solutions to some of these problems but only hazy theories and bold speculation for others. There are no easy answers because when we discuss pub games we are talking mainly about folk art and folk art defies analysis, is cheerfully oblivious to origins, follows its own house rules, changes and adapts to circumstances and is often hidden from view.

Books about pubs, although numerous are, with few exceptions (duly commended in the Bibliography) useless to the pub games devotee. They are what I call 'saloon bar books' – on architecture, licensing, history, decor, literary or artistic associations, pub signs, advice on food, drink, comfort, accommodation, the parking of cars and/or children. They are books for well-heeled, rather aloof travellers and it is assumed that all such travellers – strangers – will head for the 'best room', the saloon or the lounge, avoiding what I think of as the heart of a pub, the taproom, vault or public bar, where the locals go and where games are played.

It may be argued, with some considerable justification, that many pubs don't *have* taprooms any more. There was a story, in several of the national newspapers in 1991, to the effect that a chain of English-style 'traditional' pubs, called the Brown Bear, are soon to open across the Soviet Union, beginning with one in Moscow. This caused one Richard Littlejohn, Sage of *The Sun*, to snarl, 'Lucky old Russians. You can bet your life it won't be a *typical* English pub today. When was the last time you saw a dartboard in a public bar? When did you last see a public bar?' He frothed on entertainingly to describe the 'typical' modern British pub, serving Russian vodka made in Warrington, Czechoslovakian-sounding fizzy lager brewed in Burton-on-Trent, CD jukeboxes, traditional English food like Hungarian goulash served by traditional English wenches from New Zealand who don't understand our money. Naturally, it's an exaggerated view, coming from a journalist trapped in London.

I regard the plight of Mr Stanley House much more sympathetically. Mr House, of Bristol, cherished an admirable and lifelong ambition to get into *The Guinness Book of Records* as the man-who-had-visited-more-pubs-than-anyone-else. By 1989, when he was 72 years old, he had totted up visits to more than 3000 pubs, but at this point, gave up, claiming that things were not what they had been. Pubs, he said, were 'full of plastic and pop music and they are not for the likes of me.' Mr House abandoned the pub quest and was last heard of in the pages of the *Morning Advertiser*, the publicans' newspaper, as having taken up a new hobby – collecting the labels from vegetable tins.

There has been an appalling, relentless and prolonged blitz on pubs by teams of demented designers, with often unnecessary 'thematisation' and 'restaurantification', but, in any public house worthy of the name, a games room or a games area will remain. Indeed, in the last decade, some pubs have started to advertise their games facilities with splendidly painted signs declaring the delights within – 'Darts, Dominoes and Pool' appears to be the favourite trinity, but I'm beginning to collect esoteric pleasures such as 'Quoits in the Garden', 'Skittle Alley', 'Bagatelle Table Within' and 'Push Penny Played Here'.

On the other hand, pub games will always remain a partly submerged tradition and, even if you are following up some definite clue or useful piece of information, you can't just turn up and expect a performance. You have to get there at the right time on the right day, and possibly with the right credentials, otherwise you may easily miss the Manchester Board darts match or the nine-spot domino school. Some games, like the extraordinary and delightful Isle of Purbeck Shove Halfpenny board, are kept discreetly out of sight during the tourist season, so they don't get roughly treated by holidaymakers. Other pastimes are seasonal – it's no use searching for Aunt Sally in Oxfordshire, or steel quoits in Suffolk, in the winter, for the artifacts are removed for safe keeping and the games area is often rendered indistinguishable from the car park or back garden.

It is all too easy to panic over the dramatic decline in the number of pubs (and therefore pub games) available for inspection since the turn of the century and there are some startling and sad statistics on the pub mortality rate. Hull's High Street had 50 pubs before the First World War – now it's down to just one. In 1940, there were 445 pubs within one mile's staggering distance of St Peter's Square, Manchester; now there are 150. There were almost 600 pubs in Salford in 1900, now there are 125. In more recent times, according to *The Hotel and Catering Industry Training Board Report* of 1985, the number of pubs in Scotland, Wales and England fell, between 1977 and 1981, by 6511. Since the Monopolies and Mergers Commission and the Department of Trade and Industry decreed in 1989 that the big breweries had to rid themselves of the exclusive tie on thousands of pubs, there has been further chaos and confusion, with an estimated 11 000 houses to be sold or leased before the end of 1992. I can't recall seeing so many 'For Sale' notices, so many closed and boarded-up pubs, so much rubble on street corners where pubs once stood. As I say, it is easy to panic, but I feel that one must be courageous and not give way to blubbering nostalgia or even to alternative pleasures such as the collecting of labels from vegetable tins. There are, after all, plenty of pubs to be going on with – over 60 000 at the last count. I once worked out that even if I was able to visit five new pubs a week, every week, year in, year out, for a hundred years, I would still have covered far less than half of them.

Then there is the matter of Opening Time to consider. Since 22 August 1988, pubs have been allowed to open more or less when they like, except on Sundays, when the old rules prevail. The old rules, I should explain, for those born after 1970, were that pubs should close in the afternoons, a throwback to the Defence of the Realm Act (D.O.R.A.) of the First World War, which was designed to get workers back sober for the post-lunchtime shift. D.O.R.A.'s children, of whom I am one, were conditioned for the whole of their drinking lives, to arrive at pubs a matter of seconds after the doors opened and to be thrown out at 2.30 or 3 pm and barred until 5.30 or 6.00 pm. We had to be familiar with complicated opening and closing times throughout the country and we thrilled to extensions to normal hours, whether legal or illegal. Imagine, and sympathise with, our confusion when we are presented with a new, relaxed regime whereby some pubs are

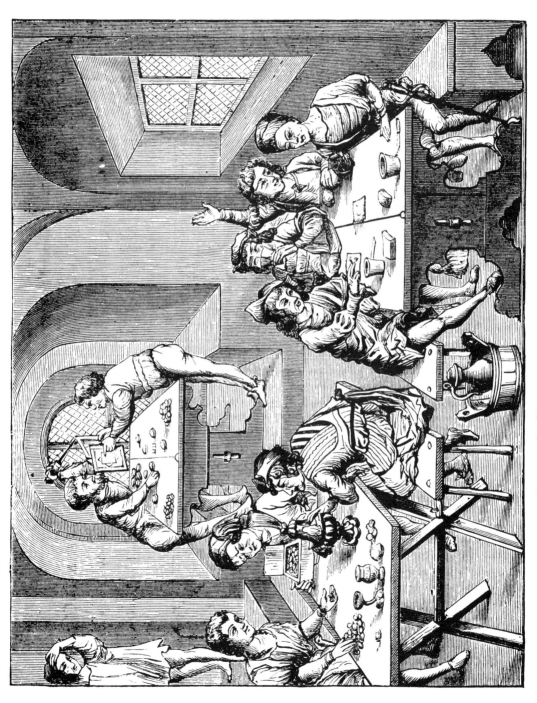

The interior of a 16th-century inn. Playing cards arrived in Britain c.1460.

apparently open all of the time, others open and close on more or less the old system and a few mavericks seem to change their hours by the day. I was left, one day – post-1988 – bewildered and frustrated, outside one of my local pubs at midday, with the door firmly locked, because Eric, the landlord, had decided to open all day, through the week, but from 2 pm onwards. I still feel a twinge of uncertainty when I see an open pub door in mid-afternoon and feel that the old Lancashire idea, as demonstrated at the Weavers' Arms, Bolton, should be revived. There, legend has it, the landlady, even in the old days, used to vary her opening hours to suit her own taste; she used to leave a mop outside the door to indicate that the pub was open for business. No mop, no beer. The Weavers' became known to all who sailed in her as T'Frizzen Mop (The Frozen Mop). Anyway, mop or no mop, if you stride courageously through the door of a pub in mid-afternoon, the chances are that games will be in progress – a new dimension has opened up.

This is a book about traditional British pub games. By that I simply mean that it is an account of games that are enjoyed regularly in British pubs but it would not do to define 'British' too strictly. We tend to pride ourselves on the Victorian achievement of the codification and export of games to the world. The cult of closely mown grass games – soccer, both rugby codes, cricket, croquet, bowls, tennis and golf – is well documented. Many traditional pub games though, drifted in from foreign parts – cards from Italy via France in the 15th century; Old English Skittles up the Thames from the Low Countries in the 17th century; dominoes from Spain or France during the Napoleonic Wars; bar billiards from Belgium and table football from Italy in the 1930s and pool from the United States via Australia in the late 1960s. The oldest game in the catalogue, Merrills, arrived courtesy of the Vikings, probably in the 8th century. The latest, at the time of writing, is Pétanque, or boules, imported from France within the last 20 years or so, although it has been played on the other side of the Channel since the early years of the century. Looked at from an economist's point of view, we've had a couple of thousand years of imports and exports and the trade deficit is against us.

Patterns change and the popularity of any game will inevitably wax and wane. Even in the comparatively short time which has elapsed between my last book and this one – a mere 16 years between publications – darts, thanks largely to television exposure, has achieved total supremacy, but peaked and is, I think, about to lose its place to Pool. Pétanque has established a firm presence remarkably quickly and, given what scientists keep saying about global warming, it is not entirely fanciful to suppose that by the turn of the century we'll all be playing under the trees in village squares, just as they do now in Provence.

There are two factors which will encourage change. As the year 2000 looms, nostalgia will become big business, which means that some of the old games may become popular again; this is already happening with Quoits and Aunt Sally. Then there is post-1992 Europe . . . I'm already hearing stories of pub trips to Belgium, Germany, Austria, France and the like, with folk coming back with a taste for European beers and in some cases, European games.

Whatever happens – and this is important – little, if anything, will be lost. It is a strange fact that games which most people think have vanished still survive somewhere. All you have to do is find them – this book is a sketch map to help you on your way.

Darts

DART COMPETITIONS.

DOGGER BANK No. 1 TEAM,
Winners of 2 Silver Cups and Several other Prizes.

The Grimsby dartboard was made by Francis Dolan (second right, back row). The numbering system went up to 28 – an unusual combination, which never strayed far from Grimsby.

Background

The dartboard is as familiar and reassuring a sight in a pub as a pint pot (imperial measure), so it is odd that we know so very little of the whys, whens and wherefores of its introduction.

I am not especially interested in the pre-history of darts, which often seems to be an endless recycling of the same few irrelevant scraps of information – Henry VIII and Anne Boleyn, the Pilgrim Fathers and First World War pilots have all been dragged in at various times, to provide some sort of long 'perspective'. What is much more important is detail of the mid-to-late 19th century, when the game actually arrived and made its home in the public bar. There is precious little to go on – my own theory, which will do until someone comes up with a better idea, is that darts was a fairground game, derived from target archery, which found its way into the Victorian domestic parlour, and the pub, in the 1850s and consolidated its hold as leisure time increased through the shortening of working hours towards the end of the century.

Gems like *Cassell's Book of Indoor Amusements, Card Games and Fireside Fun* aren't published any more, which is a shame; in the first edition of 1881, 'drawing-room archery' rated a triple entry – 'puff and dart, dart and target and dartelle', all worth looking at in some detail.

Puff and Dart, as the name suggests, involved blowing a tiny dart through a small tube 'by a puff of the breath'. The game was played by Sussex labourers in the 1880s; they used a 3ft tube, a 1in dart, and a 6in board in their local pubs. There is definite evidence of the game in the North too – in 1870, Abraham Buckley, farmer and landlord of the Beaver Inn, Crompton, near Oldham, was charged with allowing puff and dart to be played in his pub at 9.30pm on a Saturday. His offence was to offer a prize of a quart of beer for the highest score from three darts. He and his customers were at it again in 1871 and this time his licence was suspended and he was fined 20 shillings plus costs, a heavy price to pay for a couple of pints. Puff darts didn't last very long, in Sussex, Crompton or anywhere else.

For **Dart and Target** the darts were thrown rather than blown. The readers of the Cassell masterwork were encouraged to make darts from 6in-long sticks, with headless pins at one end and folded paper flights at the other. The target, to be made of soft wood, had 'three or four concentric circles of different colours, with a bull's eye in the centre'. Each circle was 'differently numbered, the outer circle counting 1, the next 2, and so on, an extra allowance being made for the bull's eye'.

Dartelle was simply the commercial toyshop version of dart and target and both were obviously modelled on outdoor archery.

Dartboards

I spent some considerable time in East Anglia in the late 1960s, on an enjoyable but fruitless quest for the **Norfolk dartboard** which, I was told, had been a familiar sight in rural pubs only 20 years before. A couple of people sketched it and described it for me – it was made of elm, a circle about 10in across, although the actual scoring area was only 5 or 6in in diameter. The bull scored 4, the next circle 3, while the third area, 'the magpie', scored 1. The outer circle was simply dead ground and didn't score anything at all. The standard game was 31 up, scored on a cribbage board. Another explorer had travelled before me; Rupert Croft-Cooke wrote the first book on darts in 1934, entitled succinctly *Darts*. In it he described a board 'with three concentric circles for the bull' – which surely sounds like the elusive target, or Norfolk board.

I did eventually manage to find a small concentric-ringed **target board** – 7in across with six concentric scoring circles. It is fixed to a thick, square-shaped piece of black wood, and it hangs on the wall of a pub called The Black Cat (*De Swarte Kat*), a loving reconstruction of a 19th-century Flemish pub in the folk museum in Bruges, Belgium. They call the game *Vogelpic* and it was apparently very popular some 70 or 80 years ago, in the bars and cafés of the city. The same eastern area of Bruges has a flourishing archery club, a cross-bow society and a workmen's café with two standard **London dartboards** – a potted history of darts within a ten minute stroll! *Vogelpic* is still played, as a casual affair, in cafés, bars and bistros along the French–Belgian border, although nowadays it is being replaced by the latest thing in that part of the world, an import called *Vogelpic Engelse* (the English dartboard).

At some stage in the late 19th-century evolution of darts in Britain, someone decided to divide the board into numbered segments, like a compass, a small sundial, or spokes in a wheel, which must certainly have made the game more interesting. An early example of this can be seen in the photograph, undated but probably of the 1890s, of the Dogger Bank No 1 Team, grouped around their fearsome-looking **Grimsby board**, which is numbered from 1 to 28, has a single bull's eye and an outer doubles ring. Until recently nothing was known about the board, the players or the game they played, other than what could be deduced from the photograph itself. In 1990, the picture appeared again in the local Grimsby newspaper and miraculously a relative recognised an ancestor and a little more information emerged. The Dogger Bank was a one room, men-only pub in Freeman Street, Grimsby, popular with local fishermen. The landlord was Francis Dolan and he designed and built the board. There are still a lot of unanswered questions. What is the significance of the twin circles and trio of lines at each corner of the backing board? Who did they play in order to win 'two Silver Cups and Several other prizes'? And why, oh why, is this the *only* photograph we have of a dartboard until the **London board** hoves into view in the 1920s? There must be dozens, if not hundreds, of dusty plate glass negatives stored away in attics, which would offer more invaluable evidence for early darts history – but no-one has bothered to look.

According to his great grandson, family legend has it that Francis Dolan also designed and built a huge board which scored up to 1000 and covered the whole of one wall of the pub. This extraordinary creation had to have water running down it constantly, to stop the wood drying out. Unfortunately, no-one recalls what the board actually looked like. The Dolan family gave up the tenancy of the pub in 1953, after some 80 years, and the pub was demolished shortly after that, so the mystery will probably never be solved.

In 1911, a traveller and writer called E. Temple Thurston produced a modest classic, a book called *The Flower of Gloster*, a compendium of lazy trips along the English canals. It is a valuable book for the canal enthusiast and contains a short passage which is fascinating – and frustrating – for the pub games connoisseur. At The Red Lion, Cropredy, in Oxfordshire, a fine pub which still functions today, Temple Thurston stumbled upon darts: 'Upon the wall opposite the open fireplace there was a board, marked out as a sundial, each division bearing the value of some number. A ring in the centre marked the highest number of all. The board was painted black, and all about the face of it were little holes where darts had entered. It was a game they played to while away a lazy hour.'

He and his boatman played against a couple of farm labourers for 'four glasses of ale' – it's a good job the Authorities weren't watching – but he doesn't tell us what the game was, or describe the board in sufficient detail for it to be recognised. Astonishingly, this is the best and only description we have of a darts match in the whole of 19th-century literature. There is one more minute but useful reference, from H.G. Wells' *Mr Britling Sees It Through*, published in 1916, describing not a pub

but a flower show: 'there were coconut shies and many ingenious prize-giving shooting and dart throwing and ring throwing stalls, each displaying a marvellous array of crockery, clocks, metal ornaments and suchlike rewards.'

It is time, perhaps, to provide some answers instead of posing so many questions. What follows is the story of the **Staffordshire**, or **Burton board**, another local oddity whose past, present and future encapsulates the development of the game.

The Burton board has a very familiar numbering system, from 1 to 20, in exactly the same sequence as the standard or London dartboard. There is a doubles ring, but no treble and no outer bull. Outside the normal scoring areas, attached to the outer ring, between the doubles 14/9 and 4/13, are two boxes, 1 in square. The boxes score 25 – the equivalent to an outer bull on a normal board.

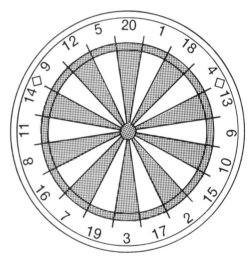

The Burton board

Some elderly people in Burton actually remember the craftsmen who used to make the boards; one pensioner wrote to me with the startling claim that Frederick Law, a publican and barber at the Oddfellows Arms in Uxbridge Street, *invented* the Burton board in the 1880s. That may or may not be true. I rather suspect that Mr Law's 'invention' may have been the addition of boxes to an existing doubles board – an ingenious bonus to an old, established pattern. What is certain is that Mr Law's son, also called Frederick, but known locally as 'Cracker', took over the barbering and board-making when he came back from the First World War. He got his elm, already cross-cut, from a small timber yard in the Peak District and, using a steel marker like a primitive pair of compasses, a pair of pliers and a soldering iron, put the 'spider' (the wires and numbers) on the wood. The board was rotated on an old piano stool, rather as a potter works his wheel. 'Cracker' Law's boards were dyed red and black. Bert Brittan was another local manufacturer; his boards were green and white and had slightly larger doubles than those on Law's – ⁵⁄₁₆-in wide instead of ¼-in. No-one seemed to mind the discrepancy. A third rival was Dusty Miller, 'the dartboard king', who made all sorts of regional boards and, according to another correspondent, was reputed to go off in the summer with a trailer full of dartboards to help pay for his holidays.

All the boards were made of elm and it was important that they were never allowed to dry out. If they did, the wires distorted and the wood became too hard to take the darts. Landlords used to keep the boards soaking, not in beer as legend had it, but in water butts or even tin baths in the backyard of the pub. They were hung up for a game dripping wet so there was often a sack on the floor beneath them, to catch the drips and protect falling darts from damage on tile or flag floors. The boards tended to last only a year because the constant soaking rusted the wires.

The Burton board was gradually squeezed out as the London board became universal. At a noisy meeting in 1976, the main league in Burton finally voted to get rid of the old board, partly to conform with the general trend in favour of the London board, partly because the last remaining local manufacturers had recently died. In nearby Tutbury though, there is still a strong league using the board. You can buy a board without trebles and an outer bull from several modern mass manufacturers for the simple reason that this is a **Yorkshire board**. In Tutbury, they used to add the distinctive Burton boxes themselves, with bits of wire and solder. Unfortunately, these do-it-yourself boxes tended to disintegrate and fall off if hit by a dart. Eventually, they stopped replacing them, although from time to time someone at a league meeting argues that they should be restored. The 'new' **Tutbury boards**, by the way, are not made from elm, but bristle, so they don't have to be put through the soaking ritual.

There is a regional board, made from elm, still in regular play – the **Manchester, Salford,** or **Lancashire, log-end board** which is used by 30 or so lively leagues roughly bounded by Altrincham, Ashton, Oldham, Cheadle and Glossop. The playing surface of the board is small, only 10in across, and the doubles are microscopic, being only ⅛in wide. As you can see from the diagram, the numbers run from 1 to 20, but in a different sequence from any other board. There is a bull ('Little Audrey') and an outer. Only the 15 and 19 segments are in the same place as they are on the London board.

Manchester board enthusiasts claim that it is very old, but there doesn't seem to be any evidence to push its history back beyond the 1880s. It was certainly very popular immediately after the Second World War, when there was an Individual Darts Championship of Manchester run by a man called Johnny Barrow – the trophy was a £200 silver cup. Many people claim that the Manchester board is a true test of a dart player's skill; they call the London board, somewhat derisively, the 'Big Girl's board'. Some pubs keep both the 'Big Girl's board' *and* 'Little Audrey' – a diplomatic solution. In parts of this Manchester dartboard world, you can play the 'Big Girl' on Mondays, then 'Little Audrey' emerges from the bath for the Tuesday league.

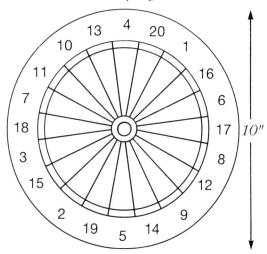

The Manchester board

The log-end board is popular in Manchester, but has reached a critical point. These are handcrafted elm boards, with intricately inlaid aluminium wire, and only a couple of people make them now. One of the Manchester men, Eddie Thompson, of Droylsden, told me that he could turn out perhaps half a dozen boards 'on a good day', which supplies demand. Eddie is reluctant to allow any detailed account of the making of a Manchester board, for fear of giving away trade secrets to a rival. On the other hand, although the craft has been in the family a long time – his mother-in-law was making boards in her 80s – there doesn't seem to be anyone willing or able to take over when Eddie decides to call it a day. At the time of writing, an unflawed, double-sided match-play Manchester board is retailing at £13.99 in local sports shops; once you have acquired one, it needs tender loving care to keep it in good condition. If the board isn't kept in soak, disaster can strike. Eddie Thompson says – with a certain quiet professional satisfaction – that the worst time is at the turn of the year. 'They play the last league match before Christmas, close the doors on the cabinet, and forget to take the board down. By the time someone remembers, the board's dried out and done for.' There are few sadder sights in the world than a dried-out Manchester board; the wires spring out of the wood, snap and distort. The damage is irreparable.

The **East London Fives board** used to be an elm board, requiring religious maintenance and regular soaking. The doubles and trebles are very narrow –

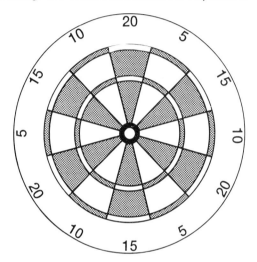

The Wide Fives board

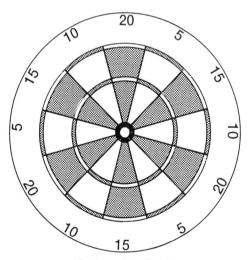

The Narrow Fives board

'the old boys who used to make 'em measured 'em out at three old pennies width', I was told by a veteran player. The board was at one time so popular that there were leagues in schools and churches as well as pubs – it must have been very strange, sitting

at school desks, or in pews, chalking the scores on a blackboard and taking tea and biscuits by way of refreshment. Nowadays, you can find Fives leagues in the pubs of places like Poplar, Bow, Canning Town, Plaistow and Plumpstead, as well as in parts of Kent and Suffolk. There's a subtle variation on the original theme too – a Fives board with wider doubles and trebles, which isn't used quite so much in league play and is known, politely this time, as the 'Ladies Board'. Both Fives boards are now made of bristle, or compressed paper.

The Yorkshire board has already been mentioned briefly. In the 1970s, Yorkshire Television launched a series called *The Indoor League* – a sort of taproom Olympics. The company made much of the fact that the local doubles board would be the one used in the darts section of the contest. By the second series, the Yorkshire board had vanished and the London board had replaced it – local pride swallowed in favour of national acceptance. The Yorkshire board has lost ground in the last decade, but several leagues cling to it, notably in Holmfirth, Hull, Goole and Bridlington.

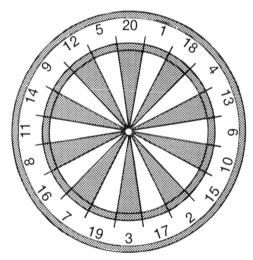

The Yorkshire board

The Yorkshire board was the subject of one of the great creation myths of darts history. In 1908, so the story goes, the landlord of the Adelphi Inn, Kirkstall Road, Leeds, was summoned to appear at the city's magistrates court for allowing a game of chance – darts – to be played in his pub. If it could be proved that darts was a game of skill, then our hero would be free and the game saved. William 'Big foot' Annakin (for that was he) threw three treble 20s while the solicitors' clerk, asked to emulate the achievement, couldn't even hit the board – case dismissed.

Variations on this story have been published through the years. Patrick Chaplin, who writes for *Darts World Magazine*, and who knows more about the history of the game than anyone, has pointed out that the Yorkshire board doesn't have trebles. He has spent years trying to find that court report, without success, but he did manage to find, in 1986, Annakin's grandson, who told him that his grandfather was not the landlord of the Adelphi, but the pub's best darts and dominoes player. The landlord brought his star performer along to prove that darts was a skilful game and this 'Big Foot' did by throwing darts into numbers selected by the magistrates. It is still a good story and certainly an important day in darts history.

The **Kent, Lincoln** and **Irish boards** are roughly the same size and pattern as the Yorkshire board, although the last two are usually all black. It is said that the Yorkshire board was taken to Kent by miners who went from the North to work in the Kent coalfields; when Yorkshiremen claim to have colonised Ireland, I would not hazard to guess. There is one of the great unresolved problems of darts wrapped up here. It would seem that the same numbering system on a doubles board appeared in several different parts of the United Kingdom – Yorkshire, Kent, Lincoln, Ireland, Staffordshire (with the addition of the Burton 'boxes') and Essex (the so-called **Corringham doubles board** had an outer bull). Why? There is no superior mathematical logic to the design – nothing that makes it better than, say, the Manchester configuration – but this pattern prevailed. And then, someone decided that it would be interesting to add trebles . . .

It may well be that somewhere, in some quiet

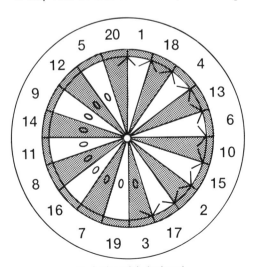

Tonbridge/Club dartboard

little pub in Kent, they are still using a **Tonbridge Sevenoaks League**, or **Trebles board**. I've never been able to find one, although from time to time, unconfirmed reports filter through of its survival. Eric Hatfield, of Chilham Darts Products in Kent, reckons that there are none left in the pubs, but he still makes the odd one – the latest a birthday present for a Tonbridge dart player exiled in Australia. The numbering system is the familiar one and there is no outer bull. The trebles occupy the outer circle normally given over to doubles, while the doubles are the curious segment shapes shown in the illustration. The difference between life or death, or at least a treble and a double, is thus a wire's breadth. No-one knows when this curious and potentially nerve-wracking board made its first appearance.

There is obviously a story to be told about the **Club, Tournament** or **No Name board**, but no-

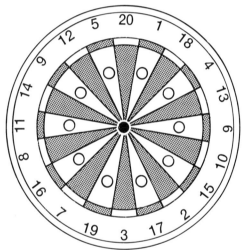

No Name board

body has yet come up with the details. Rupert Croft-Cooke described it, although he didn't disclose precisely where he saw it – the trebles were the little circles seen in each segment, like nail heads embossed around a shield. It was used, he said, in workingmen's clubs. A treble must surely have been scored more by luck than judgement.

The board which has taken over the world is the London, Standard, Clock, or Trebles board – a beautiful and intriguing design combining the ideas of the old concentric boards (with a bull, outer bull trebles and doubles) with the segmented numbering system of the Yorkshire, Burton, Irish and Lincoln boards. My feeling is that someone looked at one of the existing doubles boards and decided to spice it up with a treble that provided a fair, rather than lucky, chance of enhancing the score.

In 1979, Leighton Rees, the great Welsh darts player, had a ghosted biography published – it was called, logically enough, *Leighton Rees on Darts*. Rees's book apparently solved the mystery of the London board in two short sentences – the numbers were distributed about the board in 1896 by a 44-year-old carpenter from Bury, Lancashire, called Brian Gamlin. Poor Gamlin died in 1903 before he was able to patent his idea.

The story has been repeated, without further verification, in several subsequent histories of the game. Gamlin is an unusual name and no-one in Bury, Lancashire, has ever heard of the hero in their midst; the librarian in the Local History section has been unable to find any mention of the name or deed and suggested that he may have come from Bury St Edmunds, Suffolk. No-one in Bury St Edmunds has been able to come up with anything either, so it looks as if we have a controversy on our hands. Patrick Chaplin has several times requested evidence of the Gamlin Factor from his many readers, darts fanatics to a man (and woman). Since none has been forthcoming, the matter rests, uneasily. All I feel I can add to the debate is the obvious point that the Manchester board comes from Manchester, the Lincoln board originated in Lincolnshire, and so on.

We all call the Standard, or Trebles board, the London board, so it must in all probability have been developed in the capital, but not in the East End where they had their Fives board. In the mid-1920s, the London board began to take over the world . . .

Following a letter in the publicans' newspaper, the *Morning Advertiser*, in 1924, a group of publicans and dartboard manufacturers got together at a pub in Holborn, London, and formed the National Darts Association. Since he wrote the original letter, and was elected the first chairman of the N.D.A., Mr E.H.A. (Ted) Leggatt deserves a great deal of credit for the early codification and organisation of darts as we know it. (Mr Leggatt's other claims to fame were the invention of odourless plasticine, from which he made dartboards with his Nodor company, and the patenting, in 1932, of the helically-wound sisal board, known as the 'bristle' dartboard.)

Eventually, the National Darts Association struck gold, in the shape of sponsorship from a popular national newspaper. The first News of the World Individual Championship was set up in 1927 in the London area only, and was won in 1928 by Sammy Stone 'a Boer War veteran and father of nine', from the New South West Ham Club. By 1935, the event had spread to the Home Counties and, in 1939, took in the South of England. It was a national competition in 1947, when play was resumed after the War,

and remained a heavyweight championship of the dart player's year until its demise in 1990. This event, more than any other, unified the darts world and made the London board the icon of the public bar, often to the detriment of local boards.

The News of the World Championship, as organised by the National Darts Association, never seemed too remote from the pub. From 1948 onwards, you played a house round, a suburban round, an area round, a divisional round – four matches and you were hurled into the National Finals in London and your supporters went with you. Certainly, when I watched some of the finals in the 1960s, at the Alexandra Palace, the place seemed more like a gigantic public bar than anything else, complete with a boisterous, partisan and well-fuelled crowd. At the back, there were spartan folding wooden chairs. People used to stand on them to get a better view of the distant stage. In moments of great tension, the hall would echo with loud crashes, mingled with cheers, as the chairs collapsed under the strain.

There were other sponsored competitions – The National Team Championship, from 1938; the N.D.A. men's, women's and mixed pairs from 1958; the Nodor Fours (which grew from a regional affair in Essex in 1957 to a national event in 1961) and the Club and Institute Union Individual from 1963. Although the rules and regulations differed from organisation to organisation, they all focussed on the London board.

The London (trebles) board

When important darts matches were sponsored and televised regularly, largely under the guidance of a new, vigorous campaigning group called The

Members of the Danish and South African teams practising for the World Darts Championship, in 1975.

British Darts Organisation, in the late 1970s, the status of the London board was strengthened even further. A professional élite of players emerged, some of whom became household names. Darts heroes like John Lowe, Eric Bristow and Jocky Wilson were never seen 'on the box' throwing at anything other than a B.D.O.-approved London board. As we have seen, the regional boards, with a few exceptions, disappeared, or were relegated to the humble role of 'practice boards'.

Two new boards were developed during the 1980s; both were actually London boards in new disguises. The **Champion's Choice** was a standard board with narrower doubles and trebles than usual – the theory was that if you practised regularly within its confined spaces, then when you returned to the London board for serious match play, you would find its doubles and trebles gaping at you much more generously.

The **Manlon board** is a strange hybrid – a Manchester-sized log-end board, with a treble ring and London numbering. There is a Manlon league in Withington, Manchester, but so far it shows little sign of spreading. Again, there is a theory that experience on this board will provide good practice for anyone who aspires to greater things on the London board. Eddie Thompson makes half a dozen Manlon boards a year, diverting production from his Manchester board.

In 1991, Harrows Ltd, introduced the very latest variation on the London board design – a quadruple ring, placed between the treble and the outer bull. The 'Quadro 24D', it was claimed, would be a 'fun alternative to the traditional board' but would also be 'a state-of-the-art means of fine-tuning your game while at the same time measuring your skill level'. Time will tell, but it is worth noting that maximum score on the new board is 240 – three darts in quadruple 20.

I sense that this relentless drive towards uniformity has now been stopped, or at least checked, partly because of economic factors. *The News of the World* abruptly dropped the Individual Championship after the 1990 final and, although it was claimed that a quarter of a million players entered the preliminary stages of each year's contest, there was surprisingly little public protest. A national institution for over half a century vanished overnight and was not replaced. Slightly before that, both ITV and the BBC drew back from what had become massive saturation of darts, to emerge with much more modest coverage. The new satellite television company, British Satellite Broadcasting, promised to fill acres of empty airtime with darts, but then collapsed and was taken over by Sky Television, who showed much less interest.

There are those in the darts world who are understandably dismayed by all this. 'You have only to go into your local pub these days to see the dartboard empty in the corner', said a spokesman in *Darts World*, in early 1991 – 'The youngsters are all playing pool instead.'

There's another factor beginning to make itself felt – regionalism is coming back into fashion, partly fostered by tourism, a powerful economic growth area in Britain. It may be no bad thing that Manchester has never lost its fierce pride about its own dartboard; it might even be significant that the county of Kent boasts (quietly) that there are eight different dartboards to be played within the region – the London board, Champion's Choice, both Fives boards, the Kent (i.e. Yorkshire imported) board, the Tonbridge board, plus the **Medway** and **Rochester boards**, which are black doubles boards of slightly different sizes.

There's an illuminating tale from Hull – the Hull Individual Open Championship, begun in 1933, using a Yorkshire doubles board, succumbed to the London board in the 1970s. After initial popularity, interest declined as the same county players kept winning the title on the trebles board. The contest died. When the *News of the World* competition was abandoned, Hull Brewery and *The Hull Daily Mail* revived their local contest in 1991, reverting, amid general satisfaction, to the local board.

At the same time as the revival in Hull, Websters and Wilson Brewery, in Halifax, ran a huge and prestigious competition throughout the North, called 'The Websters 150', using the Yorkshire board. (Since there are no trebles, 150 is the maximum you can score with three darts on a Yorkshire board.)

In the summer of 1991, I travelled hotfoot to Lincoln, anxious to track down what I thought to be one of the few remaining Lincoln boards in play, at a pub called The Struggler, just behind the castle. The landlord greeted my request to see his 'rare' board with some amusement – practically *every* pub in Lincoln has one and there are Monday and Tuesday leagues with up to 40 or 50 teams involved in each. There is a London, or trebles board, league as well, on one day a week when the local board is temporarily displaced. In Lincoln, as in other places, they prefer their own doubles board and argue that the trebles circle on a board muddies an otherwise good game.

I must say I quite like the idea of enjoying different things in various parts of the country, whether it be local architecture, local accents or local food – and local pub games and local dartboards.

Darts

Wherever you go and whichever dartboard you meet, you will need a set of darts. Many pubs will have a collection of battered veterans available – they're often kept in a cracked beer mug behind the bar. They tend to have bent or blunt points, rusted shafts and subtly warped plastic flights. It is usual to put a few coins in the blind box for the dubious privilege of borrowing them for a game or two. Attempting to play with such specimens is rather like playing table tennis with pint glasses instead of bats – challenging, amusing even, but essentially futile.

Buying your own darts used to be a fairly simple affair. In Manchester, shortly before the Second World War, so I've been told, you could buy them individually from cycle shops, newsagents and sweetshops. They were in boxes on the counter, priced one penny, twopence and threepence and you picked your own set of three, weighing them one by one in your hand until you had a reasonably matched set. Some had bulbous, wooden bodies and feathered flights, while others were more sophisticated and had metal bands around the wooden hulls and weights inserted inside them – they were known as **loaded**, or **French darts** and were considered appropriate for the delicate operational skill necessary on the tiny Manchester board. There were folk tales around, when I first came across these darts more than 30 years ago, to the effect that they were made by French peasants in the Jura mountains – an idea I found almost incredible. I've since discovered that you can still buy these darts (they are easily available in Manchester and Lincoln) and they *do* actually come from France. Eric Hatfield, at Chilham Darts Products, imports them from a secret source, a village, not in the Jura, but on the French/Belgian border. He puts American turkey feathers on them before they are distributed through the trade.

A Hungarian called Frank Lowy, who was working in England in the late 1930s, is credited with providing the world with the first precision-made metal darts, sold in sets of three, smartly packaged and called 'Silver Comet'. They cost half a crown (12½ pence) and must have been considered wildly extravagant in their early days. They turned out to be a marketing triumph and Lowy's firm, Unicorn, run by his two sons, is still in the forefront of darts development and is an internationally recognised business. Mr Lowy was introduced to the game of darts for the first time in the summer of 1936, in the public bar of the New Inn (now the Clinton Arms) at Littleham, a village not far from Exmouth in Devon.

Perhaps they should put up a plaque next to the dartboard.

Darts technology took off in the 1970s with the introduction of tungsten (said to have been a discreet and unofficial spin-off from work on the Concorde supersonic airliner in the Bristol area). Tungsten alloy darts concentrate weight in a comparatively small mass – in other words, you can get a heavy dart with a thin body. Some are so slim that three of them will fit vertically in a treble.

Nowadays, the choice of darts sets is bewildering; there are specialist shops and mail order firms which take up two or three full pages of closely-typed advertisements in the darts magazines to list their stock. Would you like plain brass barrels, coloured ringed brass, faceted plain brass, faceted coloured rings, knurled tungsten or gem cut tungsten? What about flights? Standard, pear, kite, mini or slimline printed embossed foil flights perhaps? Or would you prefer Spiraline flights (as seen on TV), 2D Holograms, Eric Bristow Quadro or Reseals, personalised flights, printed in italics, scroll or large capitals on Polyester, New Dimension, Rip Stop or Embosser with a choice of colours? Then again, you might like to consider Dimplex, Vortex, Tibtex, Coalkraker Ribtex/Dimplex, Keep the World Green Dimplex – and we haven't even begun to consider flights with funny faces on them.

Once you've settled on darts, you'll need a set of point protectors, a dart sharpener, a block of grip wax and a carrying case, not to mention a cassette tape and text course in self-hypnosis to overcome nerves.

There is no useful advice to be offered to the apprentice dart buyer except to say that dart owners, unlike dog owners, do not necessarily resemble their pets – corpulent men with beer bellies sometimes use delicate, slimline, featherweight titanium/tungsten darts, while some tiny ladies heave 42g brass bull-nosed killers. I think the answer is that you make your choice and pay your money – after you've done a lot of experimenting with friends' darts, and found the combination which suits you.

Rules and Regulations

Now to some basic rules and regulations to be checked through, before moving on to some of the games that can be played. It should soon become apparent that what follows is only an outline; it is important, indeed vital, to be tolerant and flexible when you cross the threshold of an unfamiliar pub, and to fall in with the 'house rules'.

The centre of the bull should always be 5ft 8in from the floor. Some may tell you that this measurement is derived from the height of the average man. Agree with them, but bear in mind that if you are playing on an East London Fives board, the bull will be 5ft 6in from the floor, and if you play in Manchester on the local board, the height of the bull is only 5ft 4in.

There will be some sort of mark on the floor which indicates the distance from which you will throw. It may be a heavy duty rubber mat, with several distances marked on it – find out the one the house observes. It may be a brass strip nailed to the floor, or merely a crack in the lino or a nail in the parquet. The locals will call it the 'hockey' or the 'oche' (pronounced 'ockey) depending on where they read about it, or how it was pronounced by their elders. Do not put so much as a toe over the mark. If you hear someone mutter something like 'fish biting then?', or 'feet wet, are they?' it means you have trespassed over the line. In the 1930s, they used to say 'blacking back', or 'father's boots' – it meant the same thing.

The News of the World kept to an 8ft throw from 1948 until 1990, while the National Darts Association stipulated 7ft 6in for 25 years. The British Darts Organisation ruled that the distance should be 7ft 6in in 1973 but then, advised by the World Darts Federation, changed to 7ft 9¼in in 1977. The East London Leagues, throwing at the Fives boards, have always adhered to a 9ft distance. The Manchester leagues usually throw at 7ft 4in, but if you're a female, they allow you to advance to 7ft. Rupert Croft Cooke reported an incredible 10ft throw at Kingham, in Oxfordshire, in the 1930s. In Nottingham and parts of Norfolk, they used to throw at 6ft and back in the 1970s, the Watney Mann League in Norwich changed their rules to a 7ft 6in throw. For 30 years before that, they had been measuring a 9ft throw diagonally from the bull to the hockey instead of the usually accepted method of flat along the floor. You may sense confusion – and understand why house rules are so important.

On the whole, all these dimensions are fairly freely interpreted. At the Triangle Inn, Rhayader, in Powys, mid-Wales, the ceilings are very low and players have to stand in a hole to throw. I remember winning a match in a remote Oxfordshire pub with a dart which ricocheted off the ceiling into the appropriate double, much to the consternation of the locals. The grooves scratched on the ceiling, which I examined later, proved that this built-in hazard had trapped generations of strangers before me.

The rules say somewhere that the board should be adequately lit and this is usually done with some sort of directional lamp above, or to the side. The lamp switch is sometimes behind the bar counter, so that the landlord can control or stop proceedings without having to fight his way through the crowd. Here again, local rules and conditions apply. Anthony Hern, in a splendid series of anecdotes about darts games in *Punch*, told of a greasy board in Great Rissington, Oxfordshire, fitfully illuminated by 'one smoking oil lamp about six inches away from double 13'. The locals had adapted well, of course,

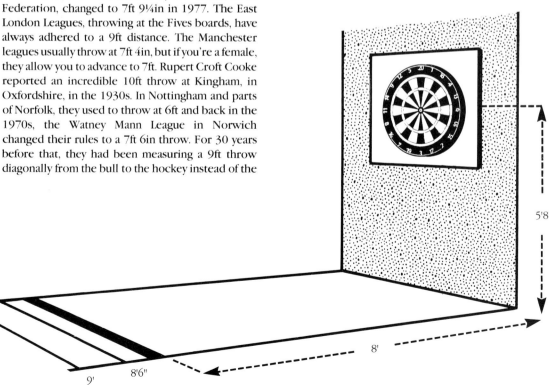

The position of the board and the toe line

but for all others 'the temptation to leave the mark and walk to the board peering for the double 19 was almost irresistible'.

There will be a scoreboard, sometimes within the doors of the cabinet enclosing the dartboard, sometimes a blackboard fixed to the wall; if you are lucky, there will also be some chalk and a duster. If someone is already playing a casual game of darts, it is custom and practice to 'take chalks' – that is, to score for them prior to taking your turn. The first test of the novice dart player is thus in mental arithmetic – there is nothing more embarrassing in a public bar than the sight of a chalker doing sums on his fingers.

Darts scoring has succumbed to a range of technology. There may be a mechanical scoreboard, which has to be preset, then worked by a series of interlocking telephone dials, or there may be an electronic board, full of flashing numbers. Either way, you will probably need practice on them. They can be utterly baffling for the beginner.

The main games you will see played in pubs will be **301** or **501**. A player may have to throw a double to begin, or he may go straight in (again, house rules apply). He will then knock off the score as quickly as possible and must finish exactly on a double. Some schools allow a bull (counting as double 25) to finish, others do not. A match, if there is time, will usually be 'best of three'. It's probably wise to watch a few games and try to grasp what's going on – in the Tutbury League, for example, playing on the Burton doubles board, a team game is three doubles matches at 605 and six singles at 405, straight off, double to finish. In Lincoln, the Monday league plays six-a-side 1501, straight off, finish on a double, best of three legs. However, in the Tuesday league, things get more complicated and they play one set of 1501 with four players to a team, two doubles matches, best of three legs, and four singles of 501. In the East End of London, with a Fives board, the current league game is 3005 (teams of eight), followed by two foursomes at 1005. The professionals, when they're not playing apparently endless games of 501 on television, have been known to get involved in 'money races', where each player bets £100 on himself on one leg of 3001 or best of three legs of 1001 – winner takes all. Best not to get involved, I think.

One thing you *can* say in favour of darts on television – it has certainly improved the level of the nation's numeracy. There can't be many in the land who haven't grasped that three darts in treble 20, a maximum score, add up to 180, a feat announced with a triumphant bellow from the caller whose peculiar cadences have passed rapidly into folk history: 'ONE hundred 'n' EIGHTY!'

The real mathematical agility, however, comes towards the end of a game of 501 (or any of the subtraction games) and you have to think of approaching the double to finish. Time was when the best tactic seemed to be to struggle to leave yourself on double 16; if you go for double 16 and miss it, but hit the single, you still have two darts left for double 8. If you need double 8 to finish, but get the single, you still have two darts to get double 4, and so on. This is amateur stuff these days and the professionals have mastered the higher mathematics of miraculous finishes – going out on 170 – treble 20, treble 20, bull for example. Vast tables have been produced, with suitable finishes deduced from impossible scores – you sometimes see them on posters in the bar, or in the form of small pocket calculators, or occupying pages of the growing library of darts textbooks. It is possible to finish 301 in 6 darts, 501 in 9 and 1001 in 17 – regular successes and near misses are published each month in *Darts World*.

This is all superhuman stuff. At a more modest, local level, the actual finish may come down to the dreaded double 1; you get a single – what happens next? Many schools will let you 'split 11' for a game, which means you have one dart to get *between* the two numerals of the number 11. Again, in some areas, if you have 111 to get, they may give you the game if you hit treble 1, with one dart. In cricket, 111 is looked upon as an unlucky or dangerous score to be on. In darts, it may cause some ribaldry – 111 is called 'Nelson', interpreted as 'one arm, one leg and one ambition', if ladies are present, and described much more vulgarly if they are not. There is also the little matter of the 'Shanghai challenge', discussed in more detail on page 26.

One final point about local peculiarities – in some areas, until recently, *aggregate* or totalled collective scores were used to decide the result of team league matches. Thus a match of, say, seven singles games of 501 could be won by the side that had won only a couple of games, but won them convincingly. Sanity prevails nowadays, and such contests are decided by individual victories and defeats.

There is no such confusion over the other darts games you might encounter in a local pub. The rest of this chapter is given over to some of them, beginning with the most popular of all.

Round the Board/Round the Clock

Round the Board is an excellent game for beginners and yet, with one or two deft adjustments to the rules, it can be a challenge for expert players too.

The simplest game demands that you go round the board in sequence from 1 to 20, doubles up to 10

By the 1930s, the London, Standard or Trebles board began to be used all over Britain. This example was in a Hastings pub, in 1935.

(but not trebles) counting, then finish on the first double you got, followed by the bull. If you hit double 1, your next target is 3, and so on. Once you get to 11, doubles are no good to you and you have to 'walk' to 20 in singles. If you didn't manage a double on your way to 20, you have to get your opponent's first double before going out on the bull. If neither of you got a double then you can either agree on one, perhaps double top, or find a simpler game to play.

When I learned the game, on a London board in Lancashire more years ago than I care to remember, if you scored with each of your three darts, it was saluted as a 'sergeant' and you had another turn straight away. There were rumours that, in certain bizarre corners of Manchester, if you scored with your last dart of three you were on again – but I put that down to malicious metropolitan gossip. We used to count two outer bulls in three arrows as a legitimate finish, but there were purists who said that only an inner bull would do.

One of the virtues of Round the Board for the beginner is that it will familiarise you with the actual layout of the board. Go into deepest Manchester and you will have to learn to cope with an entirely different numbering system on the log-end board. They play Round the Board there, too, but call the game **Slip Up**. In 1983, Phil Pickford of Eccles completed a game of Slip Up in seven darts – a feat which is still discussed in hushed tones throughout Greater Manchester and as far afield as Glossop. I'm still trying to work out how he did it. If anyone does it in ten or 11 darts, it makes the newspapers – remember, the doubles on a Manchester log-end board are only ⅛in wide and barely visible from 8ft for those of us with failing eyesight.

On the Burton board, the game was called **Slip It** and instead of the penultimate double, you had to score left-hand box, then right-hand box before finishing with the bull. (Those Burton 'boxes' were used, interestingly, to spice up several different games, as we shall see.)

Wherever you are and whatever you call the game, the most sophisticated version of it involves progressing round the board in doubles only, which certainly avoids the arguments about who got which double in the normal game.

The Killer Collection

A group of games where friendship counts for nothing and assassins stalk the public bar. Great fun, and better if several people are involved.

Killer

Each player throws 'bad handed' at the board; right-handed players throw left-handed, left-handed players right-handed, for a random number. It's important that no players have the same number and advisable that people don't have adjacent numbers. Before you are a certified 'killer', you must score exactly five times or 'lives' on your own number (doubles and trebles counting). In other words, you must score five singles, or a treble and two singles, or a treble and a double, or some such combination. Once you have achieved this, your fifth life and certification to kill is noted with the letter K; now you can go hunting victims, knocking off other players' lives – one for a single, two for a double, three for a treble.

Here's a sample scoreboard, at an intermediate stage of the game:

A (2)	B (6)	C (3)	D (19)
1	1	1	1
1	1	1	1
1		1	1
1		1	1
K		K	

Player A, on 2, has compiled his five lives and is a killer. Player C, on 3, has done the same. Player B (6) is not looking at all well and a dart in his double, or two singles, from one of the killers will see him out of the game. Player D, on 19, needs *exactly* one on his own number to become a killer – if he hits treble 19, he gains one life and loses two, if he homes in on double 19, he takes one step forward and one back, so stays in the same vulnerable position. The killers A and C can try to finish off the weaklings – or go for each other's throats.

In a variation on this Killer theme, some people will let a killer loose if he merely gets his own double: he is then allowed three (or sometimes five) lives and the game continues on doubles only. Whichever version you play, the final survivor is the winner.

Blind Killer

Bluff and counter bluff characterise this chilling game. Random numbers are drawn out of a hat, or cards drawn from a pack, so that each player knows his own number – but not his opponents'. All the numbers (but not names) are put up on the board by a neutral scorer, and then everyone throws at enemy doubles and occasionally tries a near miss at his own number, just to confuse the enemy. Three lives are given to each player – if your three lives go, you admit your identity and drop out of the game. There's a less devious form of Killer, sometimes called **Knockout**, where the numbers are chosen by the left/right-handed throw but are known to all throughout the game.

Professional Killer/Follow On/Loopy

Professional Killer was unveiled at a disastrous National Darts Show held at Olympia, London, in December 1976 - only 4000 people turned up over the ten day show. It's an interesting game for all, previously known in some circles as **Follow On**.

Each player is allowed four lives and loses one each time he fails to beat his previous opponent's score. Since professionals hit 180 with mind-numbing regularity, there was an interesting additional rule - the inner bull scored 75 instead of the usual 50, which meant that the maximum score was 225 - but that's a much more difficult maximum to achieve, of course. What it meant in practice was that a response to 180 would be two treble 20s and a heroic fling at the bull.

Another version of Follow On depends not on scores, but on specific areas of the board. Player one throws a random dart, left-handed. Player two has three darts to follow on, but must hit *exactly* the same section of the board as his predecessor. Every section of the spider counts as a separate scoring area. If the first player hits a single 20 in that section of the 20 between the double and the treble, then that is where the second player must go. The double, treble and single 20 between the treble and outer bull are no use to him. Assuming he is on target with one of his three darts, he throws one dart to provide the challenge for the next player. It has been known for a player to keep on missing the target and go out of the game immediately - death, not by a thousand cuts, but by 12 darts.

In this game, some eccentric schools allow use of parts of the board outside the usual scoring area: such fanatics would say that inside the '0' on the 10 or 20, or within the various circles of the figures 18, 6, 19, 16 and so on are legitimate targets. If you get an arrow in the circle of the 6, for example, then your opponent has three darts to follow exactly where you have been, otherwise he loses a life. In Oldham, Lancashire, this variation is known, appropriately enough, as **Loopy**.

Shanghai

From time to time, when boredom sets in with the subtraction games, like 501, 1001, etc., someone re-invents a competition embracing a combination of different games, called a **Pentathlon**. The first professional version of the compendium game surfaced in 1976 in Maidstone, Kent, and its development was credited to Sam Hawkins, a director of the British Darts Organisation. It included games of 501, 1001

and 2001, a Round the Board (in doubles, of course) and **Shanghai** and **Halve It**.

In an ordinary pub, Shanghai is a classically simple game for lots of players. Each player throws three darts in turn at each number on the board from 1-9 (some people play from 1-7, others 1-12). Doubles and trebles count, so a first throw, at 1, could produce 9 points - three in the treble. When you get to 9, it's possible to score 81 in three darts. Whoever has the highest total score at the end of the game is the winner.

However, complications can be added. Certain numbers are picked out, before the game begins, as 'Shanghai numbers' - usually 3 and 7, sometimes 5 and 9 as well. If a player fails to score on any of these previously selected numbers, he is 'Shanghaied' and immediately and ignominiously drops out of the entire game. On the other hand, if he gets a single, double and treble on one of the numbers, he has got 'Shanghai' and wins the game outright.

One of the unwritten conventions of some pubs is the 'Shanghai Challenge'; if, during the course of a friendly game of 301 or 501, you have scored a single and a double or treble of a number in two darts, you can suggest 'Shanghai for game?'. If your opponent agrees, then you must get the required double or treble with your third and last dart. If you are successful, you win the game outright. If you miss, you lose the game, no matter what stage you had actually reached. Your opponent may refuse to accept the challenge and the game will go on as usual - but you have established a subtle psychological advantage.

Halve It

When I first learned to play this game it was known as **Chinese Chequers** or **The Burma Road** - very odd names. **Halve It** is the contemporary title and describes the progress of the game exactly. A sample scoreboard is useful at this point (shown at the top of the next page).

Any number can play the game. In this example we have five players, A to E. The numbers and letter in the left-hand column are targets, arbitrarily selected, but usually including something tricky. In this case, besides a scatter of numbers there is a treble, bull and 41 - the last to be scored exactly, using three darts.

Each player is credited with 32 points to begin with, then has three darts in turn at each of the targets. (Some schools begin with 20, some with 0.) Whenever a target is hit, the player claims the appropriate score - doubles and trebles are allowed on the numbers. If the player misses with all three darts, his existing score is halved.

	A	B	C	D	E
20	16	52	112	16	132
18	8	70	184	70	222
41	4	111	92	35	263
16	2	127	140	17	327
T	1	130	70	77	87
10	11	140	100	127	407
8	5	210	50	177	457

Halve It scoreboard example

We can now follow the drama of the game illustrated. A is obviously a hopeless case and will have to go on halves (of bitter), since he has missed everything except a single 10. Player B is a steady plodder and has scored just one of the required numbers each time – we assume he got one treble one for T. Player C does well on straightforward numbers, but fails on the more tricky shots. D starts badly but gains confidence and finishes well. E is clearly the superior player and needs to be watched carefully.

Scram

In **Scram** a dart nearest the bull decides who is the 'stopper', the other player is then the 'scorer'. The stopper throws first and tries to get a dart in the three highest numbers – 20, 19, 18. Whichever numbers he hits are then 'dead' for his opponent. The scorer goes next and can aim for anything which is not dead; he scores whatever he hits, doubles and trebles counting. (Inner and outer bulls are usually ignored in this game, but I suppose there's nothing to stop experts including them – by prior agreement, of course.) When the stopper has killed off all the numbers 1–20, the roles are reversed. Whoever ends up with the larger total score is the winner.

I've come across a gambling version of Scram, called **Brag**, which the authorities would not be too pleased about. The scorer starts first and bets that he will top a specified score. The stopper, as one might expect, has to try and stop him.

Mickey Mouse

Some of these names really are extremely confusing. I was introduced to the game of **Mickey Mouse** 30 years ago, when I was industriously misspending my youth in London – it was called **London Shanghai**

in those days, although it's more like Scram, with its territorial imperatives, than the previously encountered Shanghai. Nowadays, the same game is popularly known as Mickey Mouse, or **Tactics**, while the Americans call it **Cricket**. Don't let this worry you – it is a splendid game, no matter what name it goes by.

If the patrons are very keen on this game, you may find that the pub sports a specially constructed scoreboard with little sliding panels, which reveal or close up lives. You can chalk up the layout on an ordinary scoreboard. It could look something like this:

A			B	
60 X X X	20		X X X	
19 X X X	19		X X X	
X X	18		X X X	36
	17			
	16			
	15			
	14			
	13		X X X	
	12			
	11			
	10			
	B			

Here we can see that player A has got his three 20s and 19s and has scored on both before player B managed to close him down, and has opened his account with four 18s – three to qualify, one scored so far. In trying to stop A's progress on 18, it looks as though B has had a lucky stray into treble 13 . . . Play continues until each number has been eliminated, then the final scores are added up.

Noughts and Crosses

You may remember learning to be unbeatable at **Noughts and Crosses** when you were very young. Now you might transfer those childhood skills to the dartboard. All you have to do is construct a framework along these lines:

1	2	3
4	5	6
7	8	9

Now what you have to do is get the appropriate number with one dart and then put your '0' or 'X' in its place. You could win a game by getting a line of three with your three dart turn, without giving your opponent a choice to throw.

Here's a completed game:

X	0	0
4	X	6
7	8	X

Player X has won, getting a line with 1/5/9. Player 0 got 2 and 3, but it was not enough. If this becomes too easy, simply promote the requirement to doubles rather than singles.

The figures within the framework can be altered, of course. You may eventually graduate to a more demanding variation which puts the bull in the middle and random doubles around it, as shown here:

17	12	1
4	B	20
3	16	9

Oxo

There are two versions of **Oxo** - for the first one, we return to the Burton, or Staffordshire, board and its boxes. In Burton, the winner of Oxo was the player to get the left and right-hand boxes, and bull, in the least number of darts.

The more complicated, but better known game is similar to Shanghai, and not, as one might think, to Noughts and Crosses. It is best played by a largish group. Each player throws two random darts at the same time. (If there are fewer than five players, they might throw three darts each.) The numbers with darts in them are the ones to be used. If there are two darts in one number, it will be used twice, if three, three times, and so on. Each time a dart enters off the scoring section of the board, that area will be used. The targets to be used are then chalked up on the scoreboard and thrown for in turn, with three darts aimed at each. You score 1 point each time you get a required number, 2 points for its double and 3 for its treble. So, in Oxo, a treble and double would score 5 points, while in Shanghai, the same throw would score 20.

Quoits

There are two versions of **Quoits**, both new to me, both using a rubber ring about 3in across - the same ring used in **Evesham Quoits** (see page 133).

The first is a game for two players. Player A throws a random dart at the board, then hangs the ring on the dart. Player B has to throw three darts within the quoit - he scores 1 point for a single, 2 for a double and 3 for a treble, 4 for an inner and 5 for an outer bull. The roles are then reversed. The routine continues until one player gets 31 points.

Secondly, a more complicated pastime for a larger group of players. The first dart is thrown high up on the board and the ring slung on it. The first player then has two darts to fire into the ring. If he fails, he drops out; if he succeeds, he scores whatever he hits and leaves the ring slung on his lowest dart. The second player takes over, and has three darts to attempt to score, re-slinging the ring around his lowest dart. As the game progresses, the ring slowly sinks down the board. If it drifts below the scoring area before all the players have had their turn, the ring is positioned up top again. Luck is a strong factor in this game.

Fives

This is a game for a lot of players where the aim is to achieve a number divisible by five, but all three darts must count. One point is scored for each division, so for a score of 100 ('a ton') you would tot up 20 points. If the total of your three darts is not divisible by five, then you score nothing for that throw. The 5/20 is a popular zone to aim at - the match is won when a player gets 61 points. This scoring system will seem familiar to domino players - it resembles their game of 5s and 3s. Some darts schools play points for any number divisible by 5 or 3. Therefore, 15 counts 8 points, with 5×3 plus 3×5. In Suffolk, they play this game on the Fives board and keep track of the game on a cribbage board.

Shove Ha'penny

I suppose it is quite natural for darts - the pub's most popular pastime - to absorb ideas from older pub games. It's easy to imagine a darts player watching a Shove Ha'penny match in some quiet corner and suddenly realising how easily the main elements of the game would translate onto the dartboard. The object of Shove Ha'penny is to place three discs in each of the nine beds - the first player to fill all nine beds wins the game.

The shove ha'penny board is drawn up on the chalkboard; for discs read darts. Trebles count three discs in a bed, doubles two and singles one. If your throw goes over the required three, the extra points go to your opponent. Thus needing, for example, a double to complete your three in a bed, you hit the treble - the whole treble goes to your opponent, if he needs it. You must score your final shot - you cannot receive it from your opponent.

			1			
			2			
			3			
			4			
			5			
			6			
			7			
			8			
			9			

The Shove Ha'penny scoreboard

Football

There are two versions of **Darts Football**; both games are suitable for two players.

In the first version, it is easiest to think of the bull as the ball – you have to gain possession of the ball before you can start to score. Player A goes first – let's be charitable and assume he gets a centre bull (or two outer bulls) in his first three-dart throw. He now has the ball and can aim at goal – any double. Player B has to get the ball back by hitting the bull, before he in turn goes for goal. You can play football as ten goals up, or to a time limit, say five or ten minutes, with a referee to blow the whistle for full time.

The second football game is a plod across the board from double to double. Each player throws a random dart for his number – obviously the two players can't have the same number. In order to score, each player has to start with his own double and work his way, section by section, to the bull, then out to his opponent's double. There are 11 steps to victory, as shown in the diagram. (Two darts needed in the outer bull.)

Some pubs have seasonal bursts of excessive enthusiasm for football to the exclusion of all else. When this happens, all available players are marshalled into a vast league or knockout cup competition. Each player names a team (no duplicates allowed), that team is allocated a number and the bits of paper go into the hat. Everyone draws a team and the contest commences.

Cricket

Cricket is a game for two players or two teams. After tossing a coin, or throwing for nearest to bull to decide who bats and who bowls, the bowling side chalks up ten wickets, or lives, on the board. The batsmen have first throw and always aim to score more than 40 with their three darts. Everything over 40 is credited to them as 'runs'. If they fail to get 40, a wicket is lost and crossed out on the board. The bowling side then throws for bull. An inner counts as two wickets, an outer counts as one. When all the wickets are down, the roles are switched and the bowling side bats. Whichever side scores the most runs wins the game.

There are a few cricketing refinements – if a batsman accidentally gets a bull, inner or outer, he is deemed to have 'hit wicket' and lost a life. If a bowler hits the board outside the scoring area (a considerable feat, since he is actually aiming for bull), he is penalised by 20 'extras' awarded to the batting side. Some players rule that if a bowler strays outside the

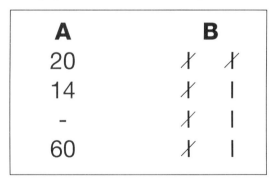

A Cricket scoreboard

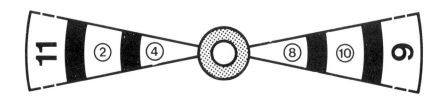

A version of Darts Football: 11 steps to goal

treble circle, whatever he 'scores' is added to the batsman's total.

One of the beauties of darts cricket is that the game's rules can be adjusted to the level of skill - or hopelessness - of the players. Reduce the number of wickets required to five and the minimum needed to score to 20 and you have a game beginners can enjoy. Insist on inner bulls only for wickets and a scoring threshold of 60 and you have a game for the experts.

Golf

The numbers 1 to 18 on the board represent the holes on a golf course. The aim is to get three of each number starting, of course, at the first 'hole' - number 1. A dart in the single counts 1, double 2, treble 3. The number of darts taken to get three units is equal to the number of strokes taken at the hole. If you get treble 1 with your first dart, for example, it is a hole in one and scores as such. If you get a double and a single in two darts, you have holed out in two strokes. If you get three singles in three darts, it's three strokes.

Par for the course for a decent player should be a score of 54 - an average of three strokes per hole. Golf is one of the few darts games you can play by yourself in the pub. If you spend a lot of time alone in the public bar, you could work out a handicap for yourself and strive to beat it.

Snooker

Numbers 1–15 represent the red balls in normal snooker and as such, count 1 point each. The other colours, their number and value are listed: Yellow, 16 (2 points); Green, 17 (3 points); Brown, 18 (4 points); Blue, 19 (5 points); Pink, 20 (6 points); Black, 25 (7 points).

The first player must pot a red by scoring 3 in one of the appropriate segments, with no more than three darts (a treble, a double plus a single, or three singles). Once one of the red numbers, from 1 to 15, is 'potted' it stays down and is no use to anyone else. If a player gets a red down in three shots, he can go for one of the colours. He must nominate which one he is going for and must score the three in a segment to pot it. The colours come back into play until all the reds have gone and then they are potted in order, from yellow down to black.

If you miss a red with all three darts, this scores 4 points to your opponent. If you miss a colour, the points valuation of the colour goes to the other side.

Bowls

Here, the bull is the jack. Each player throws his three darts as near the jack as he can. As in bowls or petanque, the player with his bowl nearest the jack wins a point and, if he has two or three darts nearer the bull than his opponent, he scores two or three points. The game is 21 points up.

Middle for Diddle

This game was invented by Noel Williamson, who wrote one of the early books on darts. You need a double to start and then everything *inside* and including the treble circle scores, 501 up and finish on a double. As Williamson says, 'This game is excellent practice for attaining accuracy in the centre of the board.'

Background

One of the most soothing and reassuring sounds that the pub has to offer is, to my mind, the muted rattle and clatter of dominoes being shuffled. Midday sun streaming through the leaded, stained glass windows, illuminating golden cream-topped pints and a domino table in thoughtful, good-humoured play – put me somewhere within that sort of picture and all is right with the world. (A vignette from the Bay Horse, Otley, West Yorkshire.)

Several friends and acquaintances, knowing of my interest, have remarked on the spread of British pub games, such as darts and dominoes, to Spanish holiday resorts on the mainland and Mediterranean and Atlantic islands. Darts on the Costa del Sol is most certainly a recent British export, but dominoes may have originally travelled the other way, from Spain to Britain, a couple of hundred years ago, on an entirely different cultural tide.

The French connection is the usual story. In 1801, Joseph Strutt, in his book *Sports and Pastimes of the People of England*, dismissed dominoes witheringly as: 'a very childish sport, imported from France a few years back with nothing but the novelty to recommend it to the notice of grown persons in this country'. Couple with this reference the fact that several museums in the South of England have collections of dominoes carved from bone by bored French prisoners of war kept here during the Revolutionary and Napoleonic Wars of 1793 to 1815, and you have the evidence for the theory of French introduction.

The most comprehensive collection of these artifacts is held in Peterborough Museum because the largest prisoner of war camp was nearby – the Barracks, or Depot, at Norman Cross – commemorated today by an obelisk beside the A1. The prison was opened for business in 1797 and by 1810 it held 6272 men, penned in wooden huts covering an area of 22 acres. Many of the prisoners were skilled craftsmen and to pass the time they made things from the materials to hand, principally straw and bone; they carved ships, guillotines, lice boxes, ornaments, automata and toys, as well as gaming chips, miniature playing cards, cribbage boards and domino sets. The Museum Services Curator at Peterborough, Mr Martin Howe, points out that the prisoners tended to make things which they hoped would sell because the object of the exercise was not merely to fill the unhappy hours, but also to make a little extra money to supplement the camp's meagre supplies and comforts. In other words, the suggestion is that there was a market for dominoes because the game was *already* known in this country. The answer could be that the game was brought here not from France, but from Spain, by British troops who were fighting their way across that country during the Peninsular War (1808-14). (The troops also brought back from this campaign the new idea of smoking tobacco in rolls of paper - cigarettes - instead of pipes.) Dominoes was certainly popular in Spain long before it reached these shores, and spread to the Spanish colonies, especially those in South America.

It is generally acknowledged that there was another wave of Spanish influence in the late 19th century, when more sophisticated domino games, such as **Matadore**, arrived here and were taken up in London cafés and clubs. Jack Cox, who edited and added to Joseph Strutt's book in 1903, upgraded dominoes and said that it was, 'by no means a mere game of chance, and has of late received much attention'. He was referring to 'the special Spanish form of playing dominoes', which was introduced in 1879 and was, by 1902, 'in commoner use than any other form'.

Where dominoes came from originally is anybody's guess. There have been attempts to draw tenuous historic lines of connection between the ancient game of Chinese dominoes and the earliest European version apparently played in Italy, via either Marco Polo's explorations or Venetian trade routes. Chinese dominoes derived their numbering sequence from the possible throws of two dice (21 pieces) plus some duplicates. Someone, somewhere in Europe, introduced the concept of the blank suite – unknown in dice – so that the most familiar pack of dominoes today has 28 pieces, ranging from double 0 through to double 6. The individual pieces are called stones, tiles, bones or doms.

Thirty years ago, the patrons of the Bull's Head in Clipston, Northamptonshire, were baffled by a set of dominoes which the landlord had discovered in an old cigar box. There were 55 pieces in all and the numbering system ran up from double 0 to double 9. The puzzled customers appealed for any information on this giant pack, via the correspondence column in *The Morning Advertiser*. It was one of those bits of urban folklore which tend to recur, in cyclical fashion, fairly regularly in that journal – other examples being the bar stool which encourages fertility and, more recently, the pool-playing dog. The French prisoners of war at Norman Cross carved more sets of double 9s than double 6s, if the collection at Peterborough Museum is anything to go by, so both sets have a similar pedigree in this country. Nowadays though, double 9 sets seem to cluster in parts of the North West of England, in such places as Salford, Ormskirk, Bolton, Westhoughton, Accrington,

A four-handed block game using the double-six pack. Note that the blackboard offers odds and yet forbids betting.

Haslingden and Blackburn, while the double 6 pack is the norm everywhere else. Why this should be is one of the extraordinary unsolved problems of pub history and geography.

A double 12 set is made and sold in this country; I have one at home, but find that we rarely use it since it has no less than 91 pieces and is simply too cumbersome to give an interesting game. I keep hearing stories of a double 12 pub league, but have never found one – the last reported sighting was in Longton, Staffordshire.

Most pubs that play the game seriously have a domino 'corner', often identifiable by a special table with slightly ridged edges, or a large board of similar design, placed on top of the normal pub table. The ridges are there, of course, to stop the dominoes from falling on the floor during an over-enthusiastic shuffle. Occasionally, in an enthusiasts' pub, you may spot a domino clock upon the wall, with the figures one to 12 replaced by dominoes of the appropriate spottage. If you go into the pub later in the evening, or perhaps during a weekend lunchtime, you will not need such clues, since the domino 'school' will be in full swing.

The domino games played in pubs tend to be subtly different to the games described in the reference books. The games themselves tend to vary from region to region, vocabulary alters and each area has its own etiquette. The various games described here have been collected from pubs in various parts of the United Kingdom, but bear in mind that this is not the definitive list. What you really need to do is stride into the right sort of pub with an open mind, time to spare and plenty of loose change.

The Standard Game/Block Game/Run Out: Theme and Variations

This is the basic game, the foundation of all skill, knowledge and experience, and it can be played with 6, 9 or 12-spot dominoes. In many pubs, if you ask for a game of dominoes, this is the one that is usually produced. Since the overwhelming majority of pub domino games involve four players and most league matches demand that those four participants play as two sets of partners, this is the variation described here.

First of all, the players arrange themselves so that the two partners sit diagonally opposite each other. Let's assume the dominoes are double 6s, and are already out of their box and spread face-down on the table, ready for the shuffle. The shuffle is a deeply satisfying ritual. One player stirs the pack, flat-handed, in circles on the table. Each player then draws out six unseen dominoes from the pool and the game

begins. Precisely *how* it begins is a matter of local custom. Sometimes the right to play first – to have the first 'down' – goes to the player who has the double 6. With four players holding six dominoes each, there are four tiles from the original pack left face-down on the table – they are said to be 'sleeping'. If the double 6 is sleeping, the next lowest double, the 5, is the one to be played first, and so on down through the doubles. There is another way to start; as the dominoes are being shuffled, the two

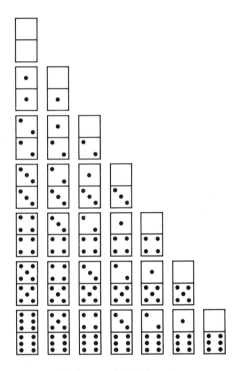

Dominoes – double-six pack

captains draw for who plays first by turning over a single tile each – the player who has the piece with the highest number of spots on it wins. Any domino can now be played to start the game and play goes round in a clockwise direction.

A minor point – with a double 6 pack you should be able to pick up your six dominoes, three in each hand, so that you can look at them and assess the situation, and then put them back, face-down on the table, in order to have a drink. (It is customary, in the better schools, to keep drinks off the domino playing area, for obvious reasons. If there isn't room on the edge of the table, there is often a shelf underneath for glasses.) This business of picking up and putting down dominoes is more tricky than it sounds and you often see novices clutching their deal in both hands throughout the game, thus going thirsty, or – even more embarrassingly – spraying dominoes in all directions in moments of white-knuckled tension. If you play with the double 9 pack, the initial deal will usually be nine pieces each – too many to cope with in a two-handed clutch. Here, the answer is to either pick them up and put them down in threes, or stand them on edge along the table so that you can see them but your opponents can't.

Once the appropriate local ceremonies and rituals have been observed, and the first player has put down the first domino, play moves to the downer's left. This player must now play a tile whose spots match one side or the other of that first domino. Play continues in this way, following the numbers on the outer ends of the steadily building line of tiles. Doubles are traditionally placed across the line of play, not lengthways.

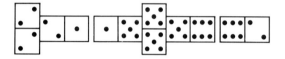

Partners Dominoes (The Block Game)
in progress

In the example illustrated above, a block game is in its early stages. First down was double 5, so double 6 must be sleeping. An attempt is being made to close up both ends with the same number; this is called 'stitching up' the ends. Although dominoes looks a relaxing game, once you are involved you will find there is not a great deal of time for reflection and, once a piece is played, it cannot be withdrawn or substituted. There is no time limit as such, but you are expected to make your move without a fuss and without wasting time.

At your turn, if you don't have a piece in your hand which will fit on either end of the line, you announce your dilemma by 'knocking', usually by rapping on the table with either your knuckle or a domino. You miss that turn and play passes on to your left; your opponents have noticed your weakness and will be plotting to stitch up the ends with numbers they now know you haven't got.

It may be that a later stage of the game will see everyone blocked and knocking, in which case both sets of partners reveal their remaining dominoes and tot up the number of spots left – the side with the least number wins. This can be enormously frustrating, since it can sometimes mean that players holding the fewest dominoes, but the highest scoring spots, can actually lose. One player, upset at losing

games this way, tried to get the rules of the double 9 game altered and his passionate plea even reached the national press. *The Guardian* reported in 1970 that the Ormskirk Domino League had defeated a motion put forward by Mr Fred Schober, that the game be decided by the number of tiles rather than spots remaining. It was a close vote – 14 to 10 – but the old spots rule prevails in Ormskirk and elsewhere.

Most games actually go on until one player has succeeded in getting rid of all his pieces. Often, house or local league rules demand that *both* partners must lose all their pieces – or 'chip out' as it is termed in some areas. If the rule is that only one player has to chip out, then his partner's remaining spots are totted up and compared with the sum total of spots held by both opponents. It is thus theoretically possible for the side which has chipped out to lose, even if the chipper-out's partner has been left holding a fistful of high-scoring pieces.

It is an education to be allowed to watch, or even join, a school of expert domino players. These people are psychologists as well as mathematicians and can usually tell you what everyone has left in their hand after only a couple of tiles have gone down. The double 9 game is not quite so easy to predict or control as the double 6 game – there are four sleeping pieces, as we have seen, in a four-handed game with a double 6 pack, but with the double 9 set play goes on over 19 sleepers.

Ten Penny Knock
There used to be a game called **Penny Knock**, which was a mild variation on the standard **block** game; inflation has now changed the name to **Ten Penny Knock**. It is played by four people who operate as individuals, not partners. During the course of play, anyone who knocks has to stump up ten pence to the player on his right who frustrated him. If the next player can't go either, he must pay up as well, to the player who put down the last piece. It is thus possible for a crafty artist to stitch up both ends, collect ten pence from each of the other three participants, and then open up the game again to his own advantage. Whoever chips out first wins and, besides collecting whatever bet was initially agreed, picks up ten pence per spot for the dominoes left in the three losers' hands. Ten Penny Knock is not a game for the faint-hearted, or for novices – you can imagine the damage that can be caused in a sharp school with a double 9 pack.

Buying-in
Another jazzed-up version of the standard game is called **Buying-in**. You need 28 people – the entire

clientele of some of the smaller taprooms – who each 'buy' one of the 28 unseen pieces in a double 6 pack of dominoes. Everyone pays the same price, which is agreed beforehand; a modest ten pence per tile would provide a pool of £2.80, a more realistic 50 pence per tile would add up to £14. Each piece is turned over and the two highest play the two lowest, leaving 24 frustrated customers with nothing to do but buy another drink and watch the game. The winning partnership cleans up the whole kitty and, in a civilised pub, would buy a round of drinks for the losers.

The Draw Game

The Draw Game is played in exactly the same way as the standard game, except that each player starts with only three, four or five pieces, depending on local custom or practice. If you are blocked, you draw one of the sleepers, and play passes on to your left. This process goes on until there are only two sleeping pieces left; these must be left untouched. If you can't go at this stage in the game, you simply miss your turn.

Blind Hughie

Blind Hughie is a game described by R.C. Bell in his book *Board and Table Games from Many Civilisations* – it was said to be popular with Fifeshire miners in the 1960s and is played with the double-6 pack. Any number from 2 to 5 may join in and each player draws five dominoes, which he lines up, still face-down, on the table in front of him. The first downer turns up the tile on the left of his collection and puts it in the middle. The player on the downer's left then turns up his own left-hand tile and, if he can match it to the first piece, he plays it in the usual way. If it won't fit on either end, he returns it – face-down – to the right-hand side of his line. Play proceeds, everyone playing from the left of his line, until someone chips out and collects spot money from his opponents. Bell mentioned a halfpenny per spot, but things must have moved on since then; I would expect ten pence per spot nowadays. If no one can get rid of all his tiles and the game grinds to a halt because everyone is blocked, the lowest hand wins and gets the difference between his spot total and his opponents'. You may feel free to join in Blind Hughie whenever it crops up, since there is, of course, no skill in the game at all and it is simply a means of gaining or losing money by sheer luck. Naturally, it is illegal.

Blind, played in some East Lancashire pubs and clubs today with a double 9 pack, is obviously a near relation of Blind Hughie. Two to five people can take part with nine dominoes being drawn and lined up by each player, who turns over and attempts to play the piece to his left. If it fits, it is played, but if it won't match either end, it is turned face-up and placed to the player's right. They have been known to pay £1 a spot hereabouts, so I am not prepared to reveal exact locations – you can lose a lot of friends that way.

Cross Games

The standard game proceeds, as we have seen, in a line which stretches from either side of the first double played; cross games can go in four directions from the first double.

Pick Up Three, sometimes called **Doubles**, was a game I first observed some 15 years ago in a lively pub called The Good Friends, in Ulverston, Cumbria. I've come across it since, with slightly different names and rules, in pubs in other parts of Britain where the beer is not so good. Four players start by drawing three tiles each from a shuffled double 6 pack – whoever holds double 6 leads. If no one has it,

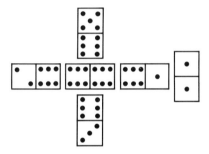

Pick Up Three (i)

the call goes out for double 5, then double 4 and so on down to the double blank. If no double is forthcoming, the game cannot begin and the pack is reshuffled and redrawn. Once a double is led, the following players may go on any of its four sides, assuming they have a piece which will match. If a player can't go, he draws a single tile from the sleeping pack. Once the first double has been covered on all four sides, no further play is possible until another double is played on one of the outer faces.

Here, double 6 has been led, the four sides of the double have been covered and someone has broken the deadlock by laying down double 1. The 5, 2 and 3-spot ends of the cross are blocked until the appropriate doubles have been played, but the end with the double 1 can now be played on. Note that there is only *one* cross, in this case centred on double 6, the first double played – when subsequent doubles are played, they are treated as ordinary dominoes, except that the end is opened up. The next illustration shows the same game several stages on.

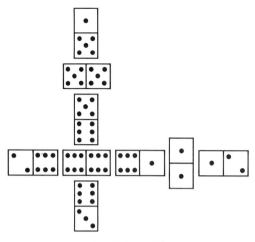

Pick Up Three (ii)

Slosh in progress

The exposed one is free for play, since the double went down some time ago. The 'northern' line has been opened up by the playing of double 5, but the west and south routes are still blocked, until the double 2 and double 3 are played. The game ends when one player has cleared all his pieces, whereupon everyone else pays him an agreed spottage fee.

This game, in a slightly different form, is known elsewhere as **Four-Ends**. In this version, if you put down the double which frees an end, only *you* can continue to play on that end. Both Pick Up Three and Four-Ends are sometimes called **Double Cross**, so some negotiation and discussion is required before you join in, just to ensure that there are no misunderstandings about who may go where and when.

Honest John is another cross game, this time played with a double 9 pack. Nine dominoes are drawn by each player and whoever has double 9 goes first. If no one holds the double 9, the lead goes to the player holding double 8 and so on. Each player can progress only along the line which leads towards himself, assuming he has a domino which will fit. If he can't go, he takes an unseen piece from the player to his left and play passes on in the usual way. Honest John sometimes goes under the odd name of **Stormy Castle**.

Another cross game is **Slosh**, although in this case local custom dictates that the pieces are played in a St Andrew's cross, rather than a St George's configuration. It was first spotted on the Lancashire/Cheshire/Derbyshire border and is played with a double 6 pack. Four players draw six tiles each, leaving four sleepers. Double 4 must be played to start the game - if the double 4 is sleeping, the pack is reshuffled and redrawn until it does emerge. Each

player in turn goes, if he is able to, along his own line only.

If anyone finds himself blocked, the player to his left can go on the blocked player's line and then also on his own, if he has the appropriate tiles. Play ends when someone chips out and he then collects the prearranged spot money from everybody else.

There are some interesting local conventions attached to this game, which I have seen nowhere else. After the initial draw of six tiles each, any player holding four doubles declares them and receives a fee - it used to be two-and-a-half pence - from the others. Anyone holding five doubles got five pence from everybody else, plus a lot of abuse. In either case, the game stopped there and then, and when all the debts were settled, the dominoes were reshuffled and redrawn.

After the first game started with the double 4 is completed, the next starting double is 5, then 6, followed by blank and 1, 2, 3, following that cycle until proceedings come to an end at closing time.

In *Board and Table Games from Many Civilisations* the same game - give or take a detail or two - is described by R.C. Bell, who had it explained to him by a landlord in Northumberland. In the far North, apparently, they call it **Ends** and play it as a two-ended line game and not as a four-sided cross.

Point Games

As discussed, the object of most domino games is to get rid of the pieces in your hand before your opponents can dispose of theirs. **Point games** form another branch of the family where the object of the exercise is to amass points during the progress of the game by conspiring to make both ends of the line add up to certain numbers, or multiples of those numbers, each time you put down a piece.

One of the earliest point games known to Europe

Eyes down at the National Dominoes Championship, 1989–90.

was called **All Fives** (or, mysteriously, **Muggins**) and was played with a double-6 pack. If three or four people played, they drew five pieces each to begin; if it was a singles match, each player took seven. Every player had to contrive to match his domino on either end of the line as usual, but also structure things so that both ends of the new line added up to five, or a multiple of five. All the points on a double counted. A point was awarded for each multiple of five, so if there was, for example, a 3 on one end and a 2 on the other, one point had been won. A double 5 and a single 5 would score 3 points. Another game, **All Threes**, followed exactly the same principles, but this time the end numbers, when added up, had to be divisible by three to score points.

For both All Fives and All Threes some clear, simple and foolproof method of registering the points as they were accumulated was needed. The cribbage board, predating dominoes by at least a hundred years in this country, was pressed into service for dominoes as well as cards and a game was 31, 61 or 121 points up, depending on how many times players decided to go up and down the board.

Eventually, some genius synthesised the two old games into a new one, **Fives and Threes** – for this game, points were scored if the end totals could be divided by five or three.

Total Spots				Points Scored
3	(3 3)		=	1
5	(5 5)		=	1
6	(6 3)		=	2
9	(9 3)		=	3
10	(10 5)		=	2
12	(12 3)		=	4
15	(15 5) + (15 3)	=	8
18	(18 3)		=	6

(Note that 15 is calculated as five 3s plus three 5s.)

No one plays all fives or all threes much, if at all, but fives and threes has become a classic pub domino game.

The match in progress, as illustrated, began with a double 6 lead (4 points), then 6-3 was played (8 points), followed by 6-2 (1 point), 2-5 (no score), 3-5 (2 points), 5-5 (8 points). This would almost certainly be considered a reckless game by experts, but it does at least illustrate the scoring system clearly.

Even if you can't score, but can follow on, you must play carefully – it may be possible in a partners game to set things up for your ally. If you cannot follow, you knock in the usual way.

You must score the *exact* number of points needed to win. If you are 3 points off game hole, it is

no use pulling a masterstroke and scoring 15, since all you will do is bust your score and go back to needing three points. Some schools inflict an even worse penalty for over-enthusiasm – your 15 points would count three to game hole and then *back* 12 points. All this can be very aggravating for a newcomer to the game, since it is possible to have a triumph snatched from your hands by thoughtless play at the very last minute. It will take several hands to score 61 or 121 points. When, during the progress of a game, a player chips out, he scores 1 point for doing so. In a partners game, both players would normally have to chip out for the point.

In 1985, a keen domino player called Keith Masters, perhaps wondering how to make ends meet, sat dreaming in the Bridge Inn, Wolverhampton Road, Walsall, and came up with the idea of the British National Dominoes Championships. He gathered together a substantial group of like-minded enthusiasts via an advertisement in *The Sun* newspaper and the event has gone from strength to strength. The first finals were held in Bloxwich and have since been at Ayr, Birmingham, Great Yarmouth and latterly, with huge success, at the Spa Royal Hall, Bridlington. There are now three events held at different times each year: a Team Singles contest, a Team Pairs competition and a Team Combination event. They attract a huge amount of entries – 810 teams for the 1991 Pairs event – whittled down by regional pub rounds to 64 teams for the final.

The chosen game for all the various permutations of the Championships is Fives and Threes, played with a double-6 pack. For their singles matches, each player draws nine tiles and the game is one leg only, 121 holes up. In partners play, each player draws six tiles and again the game is 121 points, with both partners having to clear their dominoes for the end of a hand. In all the games, there is no score for playing the last domino, unless it collects points for being a multiple of five or three.

Beware – there are harsh penalties for mistakes. If a player puts down a tile which doesn't fit at either end, he goes back 8 points on the cribbage board. The offending tile is left face-up with the sleepers and the offending player loses his turn. If a player knocks, then realises that he could have gone before the next domino is played, he goes back eight holes and cannot score on the play. All dominoes not played at the end of a hand must be turned over for scrutiny – if anyone is holding a piece that *could* have been played when he actually knocked, he loses the match there and then.

Once you go national, of course, you *have* to draw up a set of rules and regulations which everyone

The National Dominoes Championship was the brainchild of Keith Masters, in 1985.
The event now attracts hundreds of entrants.

must agree to, and that involves ruthlessly cutting through all the tangle of local differences and house rules which, for me, are part of the charm of pub games. Once the first round has been won at the Championship, the losers tend to set up impromptu games among themselves around the periphery of the continuing matchplay in the hall – we are talking serious domino addiction here. Interestingly, if you walk around the casual games, you will see that they revert back to their own local rules about how the game finishes or even how many tiles are drawn. The hall becomes a sort of living encyclopedia of varying domino practices. It is all highly entertaining and, if you haven't heard that extraordinary susurration of 64 sets of dominoes all being shuffled at the same time, you've missed a great treat.

Good Night Games

When time has been called and the last round of drinks safely ordered, it is customary in some areas to conclude an evening of dominoes by playing games which involve putting the pieces back in the box neatly and entertainingly. These games vary widely according to local custom and practice.

Often, after a hard night of Fives and Threes, all the dominoes are placed face-down on the table and each player in rotation turns over a tile at random. If it is a multiple of five or three (6-6, 6-4, 3-0, 5-4, for example) the player concerned keeps it. If it is not divisible by the magic numbers, the piece is put back in the box. Whoever gets the highest points score, totted up in the usual way, gets a small stake from the

other players and goes home with his pocket jingling with extra change. This valedictory game is sometimes known as **Boxer**.

Another of these late night exercises resembles the old card game of **Pelmanism**. The dominoes are shuffled face-down on the table. One of them is picked up and placed in the box, face-up. Now each player in turn picks up a single tile at random and turns it over for all to see. If it will match either of the ends of the domino already in the box, it is put in next to it and becomes the next object to play to. Whenever someone turns over a piece that will not match, it goes back to its original position, face-down again. The trick is to remember which numbers were where, so that when your turn comes round, you can find the one you want. I don't ever recall seeing bets or prizes on this game - it is simply a pleasant way of savouring the last pint.

There are many other games possible with a set of dominoes, but they belong to the reference books rather than the pub. If you come across **Matadore**, **Bingo Bergen**, **Sebastopol**, **Domino Pool**, **Sniff**, **Decimal**, **Colonel Cross**, **Five Up**, **Nossen** or **Seven-Toed Pete** being played in a pub, it would be most unusual, but not really surprising because an astonishing amount of experimentation goes on in some houses. If, however, you find a game being played with a double-8 pack, with the pieces progressing side-by-side instead of end-to-end, you are probably in Austria, or in the company of someone who has returned from a holiday in that country and brought the game - and the dominoes - with him.

Background

Cribbage is the British national card game – an enjoyable pastime, as impenetrable for the foreigner as cricket, the old rating system or the English tea ceremony. It is also the only card game which the government recognises and allows to be played in the British pub 'for small stakes only'. When the bill which became the 1968 gaming Act was being debated in Parliament, MPs, as anxious as ever to impress the folks back home, pressed for inclusion in the catalogue many games played regularly in their own constituencies – golden oldies such as **Whist**, **Solo**, **Bridge**, **Nap** and **Rummy**, plus regional eccentricities like **Euchre** and **All Fours**. The government spokesman, while not disagreeing with the names on the ever-growing list, said that they would allow Cribbage national recognition, but would leave local authorities to cope with local problems – an early example of devolution, or passing the buck. 'The local popularity of a game,' he said, 'is a matter which is properly within the province of the local licensing justices.'

The government's confidence in local justice has, by and large, been vindicated. The magistrates have coped quite happily with the usual roll-call of pub card games – and with some of the less usual ones too. The headaches occur when the Authorities come up against something they can't find in reference books, as illustrated beautifully in this vignette, 1971 vintage, from the Bletchley Magistrates Court.

The court had received a list for its approval which included Solo, Bridge, Nap, Pontoon, Nine Card Brag and, perhaps surprisingly, Poker-Dice. So far so good, conditional approval granted. It was then asked to give its blessing to Pink Nines, but no-one present in court knew what it was. The police solicitor said, rather plaintively, that he had been making enquiries for several days, but had found no-one who could enlighten him. In the end, after what seems to have been a period of total bewilderment, the chairman of the bench refused permission to play the game since 'it might be something we would deplore later on'. In fact, as we shall see, Pink Nines is an obscure but harmless game with a French aristocratic pedigree.

Not all publicans and punters are prepared to go through all the rigmarole with the Authorities to get approval for their taproom entertainment. A chapter on pub card games, then, should include everything you can do, legally or illegally, with a standard set of 52 playing cards – a whole encyclopedia of games – or it could be limited to just one game, Cribbage, which you can play in any pub in the land without fear of arrest. What follows is an idiosyncratic wander through the world of pub cards – a fairly straightforward account of Cribbage, notes on some of the reference book games and, finally, a few examples of pastimes which have not yet reached the reference books, or if they have, have got there heavily disguised.

The Deck of Cards

Before we come to the games, though, let's look briefly at the cards themselves, suitable objects for contemplation. Trevor Denning of the International Playing Card Society notes, in his book on Spanish playing cards that, 'Playing cards are unique . . . in their resilience to change. Nowhere else can be found examples of an imagery which the passage of centuries has left . . . so little altered in form. No detailed study of popular taste could fail to single out playing cards as artifacts of unrivalled stability.' The same could be said of British cards.

Most of today's packs of cards bear physical clues to their antiquity and colourful history – and I am not referring here to the cigarette burns, beer stains and thumbprints which decorate some of the more aged and unkempt specimens. Look carefully at the kings of clubs, hearts and diamonds – the king of clubs is the only one to hold an orb, the king of hearts is usually depicted in ermine, while the king of diamonds is usually seen in profile, holding out an imploring, empty hand. Whom do they represent? Our cards are derived from an old French design, dating from about 1480, and the heroes were people like Alexander the Great, Julius Caesar, David and Charles VII of France. French packs of cards still bear the actual names of the kings and courtiers, as well as their portraits, but we have forgotten that we are handling history when we shuffle the deck. The clothes worn by *our* court card kings are English and date from the era of Henry VII and Henry VIII, while the lappets on each side of the queens' faces and the flat caps worn by the knaves have been dated at *c.*1500–40. All the court figures are double-ended – at some stage it must have been decided that sorting out a hand of cards, when the tendency is to turn court cards the right way up, somewhat gives the game away to a sharp witted opponent.

The names of our four suits are borrowed, and in some cases Anglicised, from the 15th-century French pack. *Coeurs* (hearts) remained the same, the *pique* (pike) became a spade, the *trefle* was rechristened a club, while the *carreau* (roof tile) became a diamond. If you travel through Europe and seek out card-playing cafés and bars, you will find different packs and designs in various countries. The traditional German suits are hearts, acorns, bells and

Cards – French style. Our deck derived from an old French design.

leaves; Switzerland has shields, acorns, roses and bells, while in Spain you will find cups, swords, coins and clubs with leaves sprouting from them.

For those who feel that the introduction of playing cards into Europe is cause for celebration, David Parlett, card historian and writer *par excellence*, suggests we observe 23 March, for on that date in 1377 the city of Florence decreed that a game called *Naibbe*, which had recently been introduced into that region, should be banned – this is the very first reference we have to cards. Parlett also has a positive solution to the perennial question, 'Where did cards come from?' The answer, barring further research and discovery, would appear to be, 'from the Mamelukes of Egypt', in perhaps the 12th or 13th century. L.A. Mayer discovered an ancient, almost complete pack of Mameluke cards in the Topkapi Sarayi Museum, Istanbul, in 1939. It consisted of 52 cards divided into four suits of swords, polo-sticks, cups and coins. The Egyptian idea arrived in Italy, probably via the great trading port of Venice, then spread with truly astonishing speed through Western Europe – Florence, as we have seen, in 1377, Regensburg (1378), Constance, Brabant and Viterbo (1379), Nuremberg (1380), Marseilles (1381) and Flanders, Burgundy and Lille (1382). Each and every reference comes, of course, from the various Authorities, who tried to stem the flood by issuing decrees and ordinances banning the new game. By 1460 or thereabouts, cards were brought across the Channel and arrived in Britain.

For centuries, those in authority in England considered that while playing cards were a reasonable diversion (and a splendid way of losing money) for the aristocracy, they were much too dangerous to be allowed to fall into the eager hands of the lower orders. Almost every English monarch, therefore, legislated against cards while continuing to play at Court. In the 18th century, legislators hit upon a much more pragmatic and profitable solution to the problem – from 1765 until 1862, each pack of cards was heavily taxed, so that – in theory – only the rich could afford to play. Each pack was sealed before sale and the manufacturer had to print his name around the ace of clubs. Take a look at that card in the next pack you come across and you will see that the convention is often observed to this day, although the tax is, of course, no longer prohibitive.

Cribbage

Cribbage is supposed to have been invented by an extraordinary character called Sir John Suckling (1609–42), a poet who rates a line or two in most anthologies of English verse. He was also, according

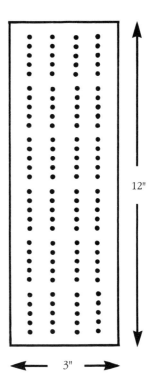

The standard crib board

to one biographer, 'the greatest gallant of his time, the greatest gamester both for bowling and cards, so that no shopkeeper would trust him for sixpence'. A later biographer noted that he had an interesting sense of priorities: 'cards and dice had an irresistible fascination for him and he is fain to admit that he prized a pair of black eyes or a lucky hit at bowls above all trophies of wit'. Suckling appears to have taken certain precautions to ensure that his card playing would be profitable: 'He sent his cards to all the gaming places in the country, which were marked with private marks of his; he got twenty thousand pounds by this way.' Sir John's remarkable career as poet, courtier, gambler, womaniser, wit, bowls player, dice roller and card sharp came to an end in 1642, when he got involved in politics, was implicated in a plot to free the Earl of Stafford from the Tower of London, fled to Paris and poisoned himself at the age of 33 – a short life, but a busy one. Modern research suggests that Suckling may have tidied up the existing rules of a game called **Noddy**, rather than have invented Cribbage from scratch, but he certainly popularised the game at Court and in fashionable circles. The first mention of the name Cribbage, according to the *Oxford English Dictionary*, goes back to 1630, when Suckling was just 21.

No pub worth its salt is without a card school in one corner.

Cribbage has a special board and a system of pegging for scoring. The board has two double and parallel lines of 30 holes in groups of five, plus two game holes. Two pegs are used for each player in singles games, or each set of partners in doubles, so there is always a leading peg and a trailing peg – this enables everyone to verify a score at a glance and ensures that there are no mistakes. In a two-handed game, you must travel up one line, then back down the parallel line, before ending up in the game hole; there are thus 61 points to the game. When four people play, they usually go up and down the board twice before finishing at 121 points up. It is worth mentioning that many cribbage boards are individually made by craftsmen and can be lovingly-polished works of art in wood or brass, while others are simple, functional and mass produced, utilising spent matches as pegs.

There is no way, other than by actually playing – preferably with tolerant, knowledgeable and patient friends over a couple of pints – that one can pick up the finer points of Cribbage. The action, which takes a long time to outline on the page, is in reality so fast and smooth, that the beginner will invariably be pondering scores and possibilities long after the opportunities have passed by. All that can be said is that the effort required to learn the game is well worthwhile and a reasonable fluency will be a passport to hours of pleasure in the pub.

The commonest version of Cribbage, to be seen in every other pub in the land, is the four-handed game, where the two partners sit diagonally opposite each other, as in Whist. There is a short, sharp flurry of ritual, almost too quick for the newcomer to follow, before the game begins; the players cut for the deal (lowest card wins, ace counts low), the dealer shuffles the cards, passing them to his right for a further cut before dealing five cards to each player, including himself. Each player looks at his cards, usually emitting appropriate noises of celebration or despair, then discards one, face-down, into the 'crib'. The crib, sometimes called the 'box', is, in effect, an extra hand which belongs to, and scores for, the dealer and his partner later in the game, so to offset this advantage the non-dealers peg three points 'for the start', at the beginning of the game. Next, the dealer passes the rest of the pack to his right for one more cut, turning up the top card of the bottom section. If this card happens to be a jack, the dealer pegs two points 'for his heels'. At this stage, the game proper – which is divided into two sections, the 'play' and the 'show' – begins.

Each player now has four cards; the player to the dealer's left begins by laying down one of his cards face-up in front of him and intoning its numerical value out loud – the ace equals 1, all face cards are 10 and the other cards are worth their pip value. The player to his left then puts down a card, calling out the sum total of the first card and his own; the next player will call the total of the preceding two cards, plus his own, and so play goes round. If anyone puts down a card which brings the total to 15, he scores 2 points, and later, the player able to call 31 pegs 2. There is a further twist to this last move – if the player whose turn it is cannot make exactly 31 because any one of his cards would take him beyond that figure, he says 'go', thus relinquishing his turn. If the next player *can* score 31, he gets his 2 points as noted. If he can play, but cannot reach 31, he scores only 1 point. At this stage, all the cards on the table are turned over, and the ceremony and the counting begin again from scratch.

However, there are other scoring complications during play: whenever someone puts down a card which is of the same numerical value as the preceding card, he scores 2 points for a pair. If the next player can play a similar card (i.e. lay out the third card of three-of-a-kind), he gets 6 points for a pair-royal. A fourth similar card, a double pair-royal (or four-of-a-kind), scores 12. Incidentally, although court cards all count as 10 during the play, they have to be individually matched to score as a pair – queen with queen, jack with jack, etc. Points can also be totted up for sequences, or 'runs', of three or more cards; these sequences do not have to follow suit and, more importantly, do not have to be played in sequential order. Thus a player may lay down a 7, which can be followed by a 5; if the next card is a 6, it counts as a three-card run and scores 3 points. If the following card is a 4 or an 8, the player responsible will peg 4 points for a run off four and so on, up to seven. The ace counts low, so ace, king, queen is *not* a run.

All the scoring during play interlocks so that, for example, after three consecutive 5s have gone down, the last player would peg 6 for a pair-royal and 2 for 15. This particular hand would sound like this, in an imaginary game:

A	'5'
B	'10 and 2 for a pair'
C	'15, 2 and 6 for a pair-royal'

If the fourth player also had a 5, it could go on:

D	'20 and 12 for a double'

The first side (A and C) would thus have got 8 points and the second pair (B and D) 14, in that particular bout of action.

When the play is ended, the show begins and all of the players one-by-one add up their scores, this time including the turn-up card, as if it was part of their hand. The dealer has, in addition to his own hand, the crib to count in as well. Now the scoring is 2 points for *every* possible arrangement of cards to total 15; 2, 6 and 12 points, as in the play, for a pair, a pair-royal or a double pair-royal. Any sequence of three or more cards pegs 1 point for each card in the sequence. (Note that A, A, 2, 3, 4, scores 8 points for *two* runs of four cards each, plus 2 points for the pair of aces.) A flush – three or more cards of the same suit – scores in the show, but not in the play. A flush of three counts 3 points, four if the turn-up card is also of the same suit. The crib only scores for a flush if all five cards, including the turn-up, are in suit – it's worth 5 points, plus a lot of abuse from the opponents, if the dealer manages it. Any hand which contains the jack of the turn-up suit pegs '1 for his knob'.

As previously recorded, the double-handed game usually goes up to 121 points; it is vital to appreciate that whichever side reaches the 121 game hole first wins the game at once – the hand does not have to be fully played out.

There are several other versions of Cribbage, but the principles remain the same; the number of cards dealt, and those put in the crib can be altered to suit the number of people playing. Some experienced veterans prefer six- or seven-card Cribbage, but these are not men to tangle with unless you really know your stuff.

Games from the reference books

Most publicans will admit, whether they have applied for official permission or not, that card games other than Cribbage are actually played on their premises, and the games most generally acknowledged are Whist, Solo and Nap. In my experience, you will often find that Rummy, Pontoon and Brag are played too, although the last two have to be handled carefully. In the 1970s, the Licensed Victuallers' Association of Stamford and District allowed seven- or nine-card brag, but insisted that it was scored on a crib board, with a maximum of ten pence per game and no kitty.

The secret, organic sub-culture of pub cards, with inexplicable fads and fancies rising and falling in some areas, while remaining totally unheard of in others, is fascinating, exhilarating – and unrecordable – because the subject is so vast and yet so changeable. There are some reference book games though, which deserve further attention and description for the dedicated and curious pub pilgrim.

All Fours

All Fours may have come to this country from France or Holland at the time of the return from exile and restoration of Charles II; it was first recorded here in 1674, in Charles Cotton's *Compleat Gamester* as, 'a game very much played in Kent'. Two hundred years or so later, it had come down in the world and was considered a low class tavern gambling game, attacked in the splendidly titled polemic *Serious Reflections on the Dangerous Tendency of the Common Practise of Card Playing, Especially the Game of All Fours*. By the 1890s, it was, according to Dr Pole's *Handbook of Games*, 'very seldom played', although it has remained in the reference books as an interesting but virtually moribund curiosity.

In the early 19th century, All Fours crossed the Atlantic and became a leading card game in the USA, until it was eventually superseded by Poker and Euchre. In America, all fours spawned other names and games – **All Fives**, **California Jack**, **French Fours**, **Shasta Sam**, **Commercial Pitch**, **Auction Pitch**, **Sell Out**, **Seven Up**, **High Low Jack** and **Old Sledge**.

The most baffling thing of all about the game, which was supposed to have died out a hundred years ago in both Britain and the USA, is that it has been played in practically every pub in Blackburn, Lancashire, in schools and leagues and knockouts, for as long as anyone there can remember. Where did it come from? Who introduced it into Blackburn? Why is it played there but nowhere else in the world? No-one knows, and the most that Blackburners can tell you about the origins of the game is that their parents and grandparents played it. That, I suppose, is as far back as collective folk memory will go – there is nothing written locally about the game. The sports desk of the local paper, *The Lancashire Evening Telegraph*, knows nothing about the game and so prints no results from the thriving league.

All Fours is a four-handed game between two sets of partners. In the Blackburn All Fours and Dominoes Sunday League, proceedings begin by cutting for 'first pitch' – i.e. who is going to play the first card. The cut in itself is unusual; the winner is the player who correctly guesses the colour – red or black - of the card exposed in the cut. Six cards are dealt to each player. The first card played ('pitched') is trumps – the right to pitch subsequently moves clockwise round the table. The object now is to win the 4 points available, 1 each for 'high, low, jack and game', which is achieved by taking the tricks (i.e. rounds of cards) containing the highest trump, the lowest trump and the jack of trumps, plus winning the 'game' point by adding up the values of the cards captured in tricks at the end of the game. (The sums for game point are ace = 4; king = 3; queen = 2; jack = 1; tens = 10.) It is thus possible to win a hand 4:0, 3:1, or draw 2:2, etc. If the jack of trumps is 'sleeping' – left in the undealt deck of cards – then there are only 3 points per hand available. You must follow suit, or use a trump, assuming that you are able to do so – failure to observe this rule can cost you 4 points. They play first to 11 points for game, totted up on a cribbage board, and a league match is decided by the best of eight games. The rules and regulations vary slightly from year to year in the Sunday League – and from league to league, for there are five Sunday leagues, mid-week brewery leagues (Matthew Brown's and Thwaites' in Blackburn), mixed leagues, men-only leagues, women-only leagues, not to mention casual games. This is, as you recall, a game which hasn't been played much anywhere else during the past century.

If ever you fancy a game of All Fours you could walk with a partner into almost any pub in Blackburn and get one; the procedure is to 'put a knock on' – i.e. take on the winning pair of an ongoing game, rather as you put coins on a pool table or take chalks for a darts game.

Here is a theory to explain the Blackburn All Fours phenomenon. At the end of the First World War, the East Lancs Regiment, full of lads from Blackburn, Burnley and Padiham, were stationed on prison guard duty in Normandy, not far from the monastery at Fécamp, which produced – and still produces – Benedictine, a sticky, sweet and potent liqueur with 27 spices. (The same regiment – sons of the fathers – liberated the same area at the end of the Second World War.) The consumption of Benedictine in Blackburn and Burnley pubs is, to this day, higher than in any other area in the UK. Bored soldiers picked up interesting foreign habits – the Duke of Wellington's men brought back the idea of cigarette smoking from the Peninsular Wars in Spain at the beginning of the 19th century – I wonder if the Blackburn men, besides discovering Benedictine, found **French Fours**, or perhaps picked up All Fours from American soldiers who arrived in France in 1917.

Euchre

The historical strands of **Euchre**, as unravelled by the author David Parlett, are marvellously complex. The game appears to derive from the Alsace region, land for years contested between France and Germany. Here it was known as *jucker*, or *juckerspiel*. In Germany, there was a similar game called *bester bube*, or *beste boeren*. These French and German pastimes are first mentioned in European literature in the early 19th century.

Euchre next appeared in America, possibly carried across the Atlantic in the luggage of German immigrants. On the other hand, John Scarne, the American card expert and author, says that it was probably introduced into America by the French in Louisiana (the French sold Louisiana to the USA in 1806 for $12 000 000 – one of the greatest real estate deals in history). An American correspondent to a journal called *The Westminster Papers*, who had clearly overdosed on Mark Twain's brand of homespun humour, described the game of 'yewker' in 1875: 'This ill-bred game ov kards is about twenty seven years old. It was first discovered by the deck hands on a Lake Erie steamboat, and handed down by them tew posterity in awl its juvenile beauty. It is generally played by four persons, and owes mutch ov its absorbingness to the fackt that you kan talk, and drink, and chaw and cheat while the game is advancing.'

David Parlett proves, conclusively I feel, although the subject is often debated, that Euchre was the game for which the extra card, later called the 'joker', was invented and incorporated into British packs in the 1880s. The name 'joker' may have come from the original Alsatian name *jucker*.

What we don't know is why, how and when the game of Euchre arrived in the west of England. To the west of Bristol it is unquestionably *the* foremost pub and club card game, and has been for many generations. It isn't mentioned in a British reference book until the 1860s, but there is a persistent story in Devon that Euchre was brought to the area by French prisoners of war who were incarcerated on Dartmoor from 1805 onwards during the Napoleonic Wars. I suppose, if a number of those prisoners came from Alsace, then one or two historical theories might begin to fit. On the other hand, there were American prisoners of war in Dartmoor from 1813–15 – sailors captured during the Anglo-American War of 1812 helped to build Princetown Parish Church, so they could conceivably have had something to do with the introduction of the game.

There is also a substantial following for Euchre around the Medway towns, in Kent. There were French prisoners of war therabouts, cooped up in hulks (decommissioned ships turned into makeshift prisons), so there is further evidence for the French connection. It seems much more likely, however, that the game was adopted by sailors from the Royal Navy, who picked it up in Plymouth and continued to play when they found themselves transferred to Chatham or Sheerness.

In Devon, the recent history of the game is much more clearly focused. In 1973, the English Euchre Association was formed in Exmouth by Fred Davey, with three main aims in view: to popularise the game, to standardise the rules and to organise a National Pairs Tournament. The Association has been remarkably successful and is now responsible for a huge range of events, including Euchre weekends at Ilfracombe, Launceston and Newquay; spring, autumn and Christmas Euchre drives; National Team Championships in May and the National Pairs Finals, usually held at Taunton in October. In 1981, the organisation changed its name to the grander-sounding British Euchre Association. The 1990 National Pairs Competition attracted almost 700 entries, representing 24 areas, including one or two far-flung colonial outposts such as Guernsey and Great Yarmouth. Although the Association's regulations are widely accepted for regional competitions, there are dozens of West Country leagues which still cling to their own rules within their own patch.

Even the B.E.A.'s rules are encouragingly flexible – the first states that 'the Euchre pack will consist of the 9s and 10s upwards and will include a 'benny' which may be the joker or the 2 of spades'. Euchre hereabouts is played with a restricted pack, plus one 'boss card', a top trump which is called the 'benny' or 'bennie'. A B.E.A.-approved pack would thus contain 25 cards; in Exeter and the Channel Islands they use 8s upwards, while in parts of Cornwall they prefer 10s upwards and a deck of 21 cards. In the south and east of Devon, the favoured top card is the 2 of spades – in the north of the county the benny is invariably the joker.

Once past these regional confusions, the basic rules of the game become clearer – it is a trick-taking game, a game where one player or pair have to contract to take a certain number of tricks while their opponents have to try to stop them. Five cards are dealt to each player; five tricks are therefore available. The trumps, from highest to lowest, run as follows: benny, jack of trumps (known as 'the right bower'), jack of the other suit of the same colour as jack of trumps ('the left bower'), ace, queen, king, 10, etc. Once the dealer has distributed the cards, usually in a group of two followed by a group of three to each player, he turns up the next card for group consideration. The player on the dealer's left can now decide on one of three calls – 'up', 'pass', or 'alone'. 'Up' means that the dealer must pick up the card, and that suit is trumps. 'Pass' literally means pass, while 'alone' means that the player concerned is going for tricks without his partner's help. (The partner's

cards are placed face-down on the table for the duration of the hand.) The suit of the turned-up card is trumps. If all three players pass and the decision comes back to the dealer, he may call 'down', which means that he literally turns the card over and returns it to the bottom of the pack, in which case the player on his left is able to call any trumps he likes. If the dealer says 'up' and picks up the card, it is the trump suit.

The aim is always to win three or more tricks out of the five – there are points for varying degrees of success. If you fail in a hand you have contracted for, you are 'euchred', which sounds most uncomfortable and means that you lose points. The British Euchre Association's rules for scoring are set out thus:

a) for a successful lone hand, for or against — 4 points
b) for a pair making a euchre — 2 points
c) for a lone hand making 3 or 4 tricks, but not 5 — 1 point
d) for a pair making all 5 tricks — 2 points
e) for a pair making 3 or 4 tricks, but not 5 — 1 point

In the British Open Pairs Competition, the match is played as the best of three legs of 21 points up, scored on a cribbage board.

Twenty Five

I was first introduced to **Twenty Five** in an Irish pub in north London many years ago and, being in less than perfect control of mind and body, I found it virtually incomprehensible. In Ireland it is, to all intents and purposes, the national card game, especially prevalent there in the period running up to Christmas, when it is played in pubs, bars, schools and village halls, often with turkeys and other seasonal fare as prizes.

Twenty Five is sometimes called **Spoil Five**, **Five Cards** or **Five Fingers** and is very close to Euchre in the sense that the object of the game is to win three or more of the five available tricks, or to stop your opponent from doing so. The trump sequence is mindbending, even if you are sober, fit, wide awake and have a degree in Higher Mathematics, although I have seen little old ladies in Roscommon, for example, who seem to have no problems at all in playing the game while carrying on conversations on other topics all through the evening.

The dealer distributes five cards to each player, in twos and threes, as in Euchre. The next card turned up after the deal decides which is trumps. The batting order of trumps always begins with 5 of trumps, followed by jack of trumps and ace of hearts. (That is not a typographical error, or a mirage brought about by a terrible thirst - the ace of hearts is *always* the third ranking trump, no matter what the trump suit is.) After that, when red suits are trumps, the sequence runs downhill with ace of diamonds, king, queen, 10, 9, 8, 7, 6, 4, 2. When hearts are trumps, the sequence below the queen is reversed, so that it goes down from 2 to 10 - the full sequence runs 5, jack, ace of hearts, ace of trumps, king, queen, 2, 3, 4, 6, 7, 8, 9, 10. There are further traps for the unwary - when red suits are not trumps, the sequence runs king, queen, jack, 10, 9, 8, 7, 6, 5, 4, 2, ace, although the ace of hearts remains the third card down in the pack, no matter what are trumps. Black suits, when not trumps, go king, queen, jack, ace, 2, 3, 4, 5, 6, 7, 8, 9, 10.

Once you have mastered these preliminary details, the game itself is fairly straightforward, the aim of each individual being to win three or more tricks. If you win three or more, you score 5 points; if you take all five available tricks, you tot up 10 points. Whoever reaches 25 points first wins the game, the stake money from all the other players, the turkey, and whatever else is on offer.

An interesting cautionary tale to round off this section on reference book games - after watching a **Nipsy** match (see p. 105) in Barnsley, I joined everyone else in the pub to discuss the match, but got distracted by a card game being played at several tables around the taproom. It was played with two packs of cards, including jokers; everyone got 15 cards each and it was clearly a type of **Rummy**, since the object of the exercise was to get rid of your cards in runs, sequences or sets of three or more cards. They told me that the game was called 'Wogga' and had been brought to the area by Hungarian refugees fleeing after the crushing of the 1956 Uprising. (The 'woggas' were the jokers.) Once I got home and started to comb through the reference books, I quickly found that 'wogga' was listed in several of them as **Kaloochi**, **Kaluki** or **Caloochi**. Scarne says that in the 1950s it was a 'favourite among women in card rooms from New York to Florida', and it is, of course, the same game I mentioned earlier in this chapter, which has been sweeping old folk's homes in Salford in the 1990s. It would need, I fear, teams of historians, sociologists, philologists and card-sharps to disentangle the story of that game's spread through the world.

Unusual Games

Although not truly comprehensive, the list that follows is, I feel, the nitty gritty of pub games research. I have played or watched these games in pubs scattered all around the country, but it takes time to gain the confidence of landlords and patrons who may not be adhering to the strict letter of the law - and there are still a lot of pubs to cover.

Pink Nines

The game which so perplexed the magistrates and police in Bletchley is a member of what is called the Stops family, i.e. games which involve playing runs of cards until the sequence is stopped, whereupon play passes on. Other examples, met within the home rather than the pub, are **Pope Joan** and **Newmarket**.

The aim of Pink Nines is to get rid of your cards in a numerical run which passes from player to player. When two or three people play, each is initially dealt 13 cards with the rest left 'behind' on the table. With four or more players, four cards are dealt off 'blind' and the rest dealt round. The first player puts down his longest run, irrespective of suit. He could, for instance, have 3, 4 and 5, but no 6; the following player must begin his sequence with 6 and go as far as he can. Ace is high and whoever plays one immediately starts a new run. The 9s of diamonds and hearts are 'wild' and can be substituted for any other card, hence the name Pink Nines. As the game draws to a close, play may be halted because no-one has the next sequential card, in which case the first player who finds himself thus blocked has the right to play any card and begin another run. The first player to get rid of all his cards clears the pool, which is a previously agreed stake from all the people involved.

David Parlett, in a fascinating passage in his *Oxford Guide to Card Games*, links Pink Nines to **Comet**, a game named after the sighting of Halley's Comet in 1682 and played in France and England until the 1750s. How and why it resurfaced in Bletchley in 1971 is one of those delightful mysteries which occur time and time again in the world of pub games.

Switch

Switch tends to be a noisy game played by younger customers in the bar and is generally frowned upon by card-school veterans because it calls for no skill at all. Many publicans don't like it either, since games of pure chance like this, if played for money, are illegal. David Parlett relates it to **Eights**, **Crazy Eights**, **Swedish Rummy**, **Rockaway**, **Crazy Jacks** and **Black Jack** - an entertaining branch of the Stops family tree by the sound of things!

Each player is dealt five cards; the next card after the deal is turned up to start the sequence. The next card may be:

   a) any card of the same suit
   b) any card of the same number - if this is played, the sequence then moves into the same suit as the new card

c) an ace, which can be played at any time, on any suit and enables the player to nominate *any* suit to follow it.

There are two further rules. If anyone puts down a jack, he can lay down with it another card of the same suit. If someone plays a 2, the next player must pick up two cards from the top of the stockpile, unless, that is, he can follow on with another 2, which means that the third player must pick up from the stock. If all the 2s are played, one after the other, the unlucky player who obviously can't follow on picks up eight cards from the stock. Anyone who can't go at any stage must pick up cards from the stock until he can.

The player left with only one card in his hand must declare 'last card' to the assembled company, so that they may consider ways of stopping him. Failure to give this warning incurs a savage penalty – the player concerned, on the verge of victory, must pick up all the stock and begin again. Once you have got rid of all the cards in your hand, you have won and can collect the stake money from all the other players.

Phat

Phat is a four-handed partners game, closely related to All Fours, but played on a league basis in and around Norwich. If you see what looks like an outsize crib board lurking in a pub in this part of the world, you are in Phat territory and looking at a Phat pegging board.

The game is basically a normal trick-taking exercise, with trumps automatically the suit of the first card played. The points system is, however, a bit more complex – anyone taking a trick containing the following trump cards scores on the pegging board as shown:

9 of trumps	=	18 points
5 of trumps	=	10 points
ace of trumps	=	4 points
king of trumps	=	3 points
queen of trumps	=	2 points
jack of trumps	=	1 point

Any other 9 or 5 of a suit other than trumps, if taken in a trick, scores 9 or 5 points.

When the hand has been played out, the partners add up the cards in their collective pile of tricks, scoring all court cards and aces as above, and 10 points for each 10. There are 80 points to be sorted out at this stage:

aces	4	(× 4)	=	16
kings	4	(× 3)	=	12
queens	4	(× 2)	=	8
jacks	4	(× 1)	=	4
10s	4	(× 10)	=	40
				80

Whichever team gets the higher proportion of this total, i.e. scores more than 40, tots up 8 points on

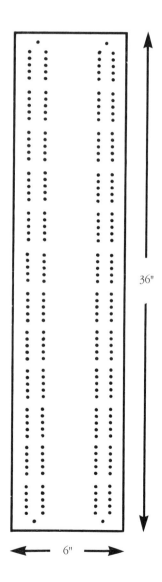

36"

6"

The Phat pegging board

the pegging board. Usually, the side which gets to 181 points on the board first are the winners.

Nine Card Don

Nine Card Don, also known as **Big Don**, **Long Don** or **Welsh Don** in various parts of the country, is another close relative of All Fours and Phat, with a few added complications. It is usually played as a four-handed partners game, with nine cards being dealt to each player. The first card pitched determines the trump suit; tricks are thereafter played for as usual. In this first stage of the game, scoring is marked on a crib board (normal size this time, with points as follows for any trick containing these trump cards):

9 of trumps	=	9 points
5 of trumps	=	19 points
ace of trumps	=	4 points
king of trumps	=	3 points
queen of trumps	=	2 points
jack of trumps	=	1 point

Any other 5-pip card, excluding the 5 of trumps, similarly scores 5 points.

When the hand has been played out, each pair skims through the tricks it has taken, just as in All Fours and Phat, counting any ace as 4, any king 3, any queen 2, any jack 1, and any 10 as 10. Whoever comes out on top in this particular burst of mathematics scores 8 points on the crib board. The cards are then reshuffled and redealt and the game goes on, peculiarly, to 91 points, once up and down the board, then up once more to the game hole.

Crash

Crash is a variant of Brag, but appears to be played only in parts of Salford and Manchester. I first saw it in the early 1970s, played in the sort of pub where strangers must tread warily and not appear too curious.

Crash often has a distinctive pegging board, with 25 holes drilled in the shape of the St Andrew's cross, although it can be played using a conventional cribbage board.

Each of the four players is dealt 13 cards, one of which each must discard before forming the remainder into four brag hands of three cards each. The four tricks, or 'points', are then played for separately, with a scoring priority running down from a prial of 3s, aces, kings, queens, jacks, 10s, etc, to run in suits, then out of suits (the highest winning), with the lowest-scoring hands being flushes, the highest card winning again. Each player starts from his own corner of the peg board and moves on one hole each time he wins a trick; the overall winner is the one who reaches the centre hole first, *unless* someone wins all four available tricks in a single hand. This is 'crash' and wins the game outright. (If scoring is

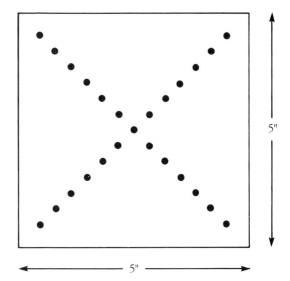

The Crash pegging board

done on a conventional cribbage board, each of the four players progresses along his own 'track' on the board and whoever is first to reach his seventh hole wins the game.)

Many pubs in Salford have a Crash board, but they are always made by a customer or a 'man round the corner'. I have never seen a commercially-manufactured board, nor come across the printed rules of the game.

Bastard

Bastard is another Salford game; David Parlett writes that it is known as **Stop the Bus** in other quarters. It is another member of the Brag family, with a similar scoring priority. Each player has three cards only and three are left in the centre of the table, face-up. At his turn, the player can either keep his hand as it is, or pick up between one and three of the centre cards, discarding the same number, face-up, if he does so. The next player, awaiting his turn, can only watch helplessly as the cards which might have suited him vanish before his eyes, and leave him silently mouthing the name of the game. The winner is the one who ends up with the strongest hand when all his manoeuvring has been completed. Bastard is a game for a taproom full of players and is often organised on a knockout basis, the top few players going on to the next round. Side-betting on the outcome of the final match can be ferocious and dangerous.

Hearts

Hearts is a not particularly subtle, but nevertheless highly enjoyable variation on the game of the same name to be found in Hoyle or any standard reference book. I discovered it in and around Ulverston almost 20 years ago. I was told that it was only played between the Lake District and the sea, and had come originally from the Isle of Man. The beer was excellent and so I believed this, but subsequent research has indicated that it is part of a vast international family including **Black Maria** from America, *Chasse-coeur* from France and *Hartenjagen* from Germany.

Back in Ulverston, each of the four players got 12 cards and, after the deal, the remaining four cards were placed face-down in the centre of the table – they constituted what was known as 'the box'. The object of the game is to avoid taking tricks with hearts in them and similarly to avoid the queen of spades. There are no trumps. Each heart you *do* end up with scores 1 unrequired point, while the dreaded black queen of spades registers 7 points. Each individual's running total is marked up on a cribbage board and with 30 points you are 'bust' and must drop out of the game. The last trick winner at the end of the hand has the dubious privilege of pick-ing up the box, if it contains any penalty cards they count against him.

In Ulverston, a game of Hearts is often begun with as many as eight players (obviously with fewer cards each). One by one, they are eliminated as they accumulate the 30 points. When there are only three players left they are dealt 16 cards each. The last pair play out the game, again with 16 cards each and the eventual winner picks up the stake deposited by all eight players at the beginning of the game.

Spoof Sevens

Spoof Sevens is a good name for a game which is usually known as **Fan Tan** in the reference books. The name Fan Tan is confusing because it also refers to a Chinese gambling game involving beans in a bowl, which has nothing to do with cards. Spoof Sevens is also known as **Dominoes**, which makes sense (see next paragraph), or **Parliament**, which does not.

The full pack of 52 cards is dealt out to the four players, who have all contributed an initial stake to

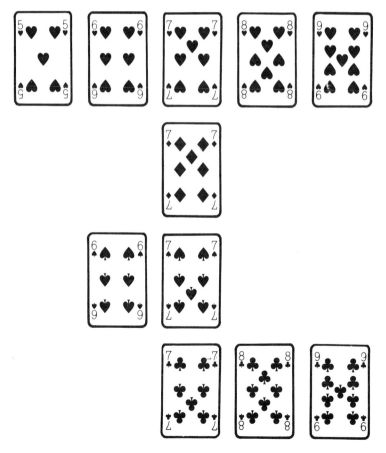

Spoof Sevens

the pool or kitty. The player on the dealer's left leads and must play a 7; if he hasn't got one he pays a contribution equal to his first stake in the pool and the next player takes the lead. Once a 7 is down, the only cards that can be played are the 6 or the 8 of the same suit, or another 7. The 6 or 8 is laid to the left or right respectively of the first 7; the next 7 played is placed above or below the first one (see diagram). The aim is to follow on, one card at a time, in sequence and suit, as in dominoes proper. Eventually, a pattern begins to build up.

If you have any card that can be played, you must play it. If at any stage you cannot follow on, you pay a further contribution into the pool. The winner is the first player to off-load all his cards – he collects the original stake money plus all the penalty cash deposits which have built up during the game.

Racing Aces

When you are young and foolish and attempting to make a name for yourself as an amateur drinker and gamester in the seedier parts of town, you tend to get involved in some highly entertaining but idiotic games. **Racing Aces** is a classic of the genre. The four aces are laid out in a horizontal line, face-up, then six cards are dealt out by the banker from the top of the pack in a vertical line to the right of the aces.

The banker now turns over the rest of the cards in the pack, one by one, and the aces move up a place each time a card of their suit is turned up. Whichever ace moves past the sixth position first wins the game. The spice of the game, indeed the whole point of Racing Aces, is the money riding on the result. As soon as the initial, preparatory, ten card layout is set out (see diagram), the players literally put money on the ace they fancy. The banker offers odds, before the game or the betting begins, based on the vertical line of cards. If, as in the example shown, several cards of one suit (diamonds, in this case) appear, then the odds on the ace of that suit will be high. Since no clubs at all appear on this particular race line, then they are all, bar the ace, in the pack and likely to be turned up. Therefore, the odds offered on the ace of clubs will be low. Someone like Scarne, the American gambling guru, could probably reel off the odds and decide what to do – we mere mortals simply place money on a card and hope for the best. Racing Aces can be very exciting in its later stages, when the currency-laden aces are poised only a place or two from home and the results hinge on the turn of one or two cards.

Indian Poker

Generally speaking, you have to be moderately drunk and in tolerant, friendly company to play **Indian Poker**. Each player is dealt a single card, which he does not look at, but places high in the centre of his forehead like a Red Indian's feather, holding it in place with one finger in such a way that all the other players can see what it is. Everyone bets on his own card – which, of course, he can't see – on the perceived strengths or weaknesses of everyone else's cards, which he can see. As the more sane and sensible participants drop out, convinced that the evening is getting out of hand and that they are foreheading a low card, the survivors bet again, adding to the original stakes. Eventually, either closing time intervenes and the highest card wins, or the game boils down to two players and one of them gives in. The winner, naturally, takes all. I don't recall ever seeing the end of a game of Indian Poker; my recollection is that hysteria sets in and people fall over, thus negating the event, or that the landlord, wives or girlfriends put a stop to things.

Three-of-a-kind

Three-of-a-kind is the only repeatable name among many given to what is essentially a drinkers', rather than a card players', pastime. The full pack is dealt out, face-up, one at a time, in rotation, to each player. When the first jack turns up, the player holding it orders a drink; when the second jack arrives, the player with it pays for the drink; when the third jack is dealt, the player who gets it has to down the drink. There are interesting possibilities for the contents of the drink – I've seen some thoroughly unpleasant combinations, such as the juice from a jar of cockles mixed with Angostura bitters and a dash of Pernod, for instance. Culbertson, another American card guru, goes one better and calls the game **Four-of-a-kind**. His version is even sillier, since he adds a kitty, contributed to by all players. The pool is won by the last player left on his feet.

Background

Some accounts of the early history of **Skittles** claim that it originated in 3rd- or 4th-century Germany, when monks and priests encouraged their peasant flocks to set up clubs, or *kegels*, and throw stones at them. The *kegel*, normally a weapon carried for self-defence, had come to represent a sin or temptation and the successful casting of a stone, which knocked over the club, swept aside the bad thought, word, or deed. It's an interesting religious concept – skill at skittles brings absolution. As the years passed and the game developed, religious life must have become even more confusing for the German peasantry – by the 13th century some German towns were using three pins, clubs or *kegels*, while in others the number went up to as many as 17. Skittles is still known as *Kegelen* in Germany and the Low Countries and still has a huge following, although nowadays they tend to throw or bowl in a more orthodox and less spiritual way, at nine pins.

For clues to the existence, variety and popularity of Skittles in medieval England, we are again indebted to the Authorities, who compiled lists of amusements in order to condemn them and place them beyond the reach of the lower orders. Edward III outlawed **Kayles** (**Cayles** or **Keiles**), which presumably derived its name from the French *Quilles*. This was originally a game where players threw sticks, batons or cudgels at a line of pins which could vary in number from six to eight. Interestingly, in France they still play a game called *Les Six Quilles*, which involves throwing a *rondin* – a little log – at six pins, with the object of leaving one standing. Later medieval English lists included, or rather excluded, **Cloish**, or **Closh**, which involved throwing a ball, rather than a baton or log, at nine skittles, and **Loggats**, which replaced wooden pins and missiles with examples made from animal bones.

Benjamin Strutt catalogues several different games of Skittles apparently popular in Britain at the beginning of the 19th century, including **Ninepins, Skittles, Dutch Pins, Four Corners** and **Half Bowl.** We shall come across modern versions of these games in due course, but it is perhaps worth pointing out one curiosity, which Strutt describes as the 'double exertion' of bowling and tipping, in both Skittles and Dutch Pins. After throwing one or two balls from an agreed distance, the player was allowed to approach the skittles and 'tip' down as many as he could with a ball aimed from point blank range. Dutch painters of the 17th and 18th centuries often illustrated this – a bowler standing almost on top of the skittles or pins – but it seems to have been a feature of the game which didn't catch on for long in

Britain and it is certainly not known now. However, in France, in the Garonne Valley, they play a game called *Grands Quilles*, where the player slings two heavy balls at the skittles from a long distance, then one from close range. The centre, or 'king' pin, counts 9 points, the others count 1 each, and the game is 31 points up. It would seem then, that certain conventions in European skittles were perhaps adopted, but soon discarded, when the game arrived in Britain.

Thomas Hughes had it right, I think, when he wrote in 1857, in his novel *Tom Brown's Schooldays* that, 'Life isn't all beer and skittles; but beer and skittles, or something better of the same sort, must form a good part of every Englishman's education.' An exploration of the huge variety of skittles games played in the British Isles today would indeed be a very broad education and would call for a multiplicity of skills. Once you have grasped the essentials of West Country Skittles and have some idea of its infinite variations, you must start all over again with **Old English**, or **London Skittles**, which is quite a different game. Move to the Midlands and your problems begin all over again as you struggle to cope with two subtly different versions of **Long Alley**. Oxfordshire's **Aunt Sally** will take a summer season or two to sort out, and then there are the challenges of at least three quite distinct games of **Table Skittles – Devil Among the Tailors, Hood, Northants** or **Leicester Skittles** and **Daddlums**. Then, of course, there's **Ten Pin Bowling**, which comes, as a pub game, in various shapes and sizes, as well as a string of oddities, including **Rolly**, Half Bowl and others. It would require a lifetime's research to produce the masterwork on Skittles; in the meantime, this chapter serves as the briefest of introductions to a fascinating and complex subject.

West Country Skittles

West Country Skittles is a convenient blanket term for what is without question the most popular and prolific member of the whole Skittles family. Travel west and you will come across alleys in Berkshire and Oxfordshire; as you move into Gloucestershire, Wiltshire and Hampshire, you will find them thicker on the ground; as you go deep into Somerset, Dorset and Devon, there are literally hundreds of venues for the game.

The main principle of the sport remains the same wherever you are – you roll, or throw, three balls at nine skittles and knock down as many of them as you can – but the rules, customs and terminology change subtly but significantly from county to county, from village to village and even from pub to pub. I shall take one example of a league, and its conventions, and divert from it from time to time.

The Cirencester and District Skittle League, whose member teams come from pubs and clubs within a 15-mile radius of the town, had, in 1991, 84 teams competing in six divisions, with two up, two down promotion and relegation at the end of each season. With nine players to a team, plus reserves, that means that roughly a thousand people were involved in league play, Monday through to Friday, from the end of August to early May – and Cirencester is quite a small place.

The playing surface of the alleys in the league varies from pub to pub; sometimes it is concrete, sometimes wood. However, the pitch, from the throwing or bowling line to the front pin, is always 24ft long and up to 6ft wide. Over the West Country as a whole, the pitch may vary from 24 to 45ft in length – not all of them are flat and true; sometimes the surface is cambered, by accident, wear or design, which adds considerably to a player's problems.

There are no strict regulations in Cirencester about the size of the balls used. George Brazier, the league's secretary, says that they vary from 'tennis ball to cannonball size', and can be made of wood, composition material or hard rubber. A team buying a new set of balls will try to get something they think they will be able to manage better than anyone else – gamesmanship is an accepted part of West Country Skittles and home ground and equipment advantage is a fact of life. In some Eldridge Pope pubs in Dorset, the three balls used per throw are different sizes and weights and must be rolled in the traditionally correct order, smallest and lightest first. In Bath, they use hard rubber balls which must be 4½in in diameter at the beginning of the season. The Bath game, incidentally, has established an eastern colony with the emergence of the Dover and District Skittles Association.

Cirencester's nine pins, each 10in high, are set in the familiar diamond shape; the lower half of the front pin is painted white, while the two quarter pins facing the striker have a 1½in white band around the middle. In Cardiff, which is an exuberant and busy skittling city, they put single bands of white tape around the front quarter pins (the 'left copper' and the 'right copper') and a double band around the front pin. All skittles were traditionally made of wood and most of them still are, but experiments are taking place and it is possible to find plastic or polycarbonate skittles. Some sets will have eight skittles the same size and one, the 'king' pin, slightly taller; the king pin is often in the centre of the pack, but sometimes at the front. In Devon, you may come

across an old ten-pin skittle alley – there's a splendid and thriving example at the King's Arms in Stockland, where there are six teams flourishing.

The basic scoring system in West Country Skittles is more or less uniform – each player has three throws, or bowls, and his score is simply the total number of skittles knocked down. If he flattens the frame with his first or second ball, then all nine pins are set up again for him to complete his turn. Thus, in theory – and sometimes in practice – it is possible to score 27 points with a three ball turn, if the first, second and third throws are 'stickers', or 'floorers'.

The number of players in a league team match varies from place to place; in Cirencester there are nine members in a team and three players from each team 'bowl out' alternately. There are six legs to a match. The Bath League has eight players in each team and all eight bowl out one after the other – 'It gets them all in the pub at the same time', I was told. The first team to win five legs wins the game. Cardiff teams consist of 12 players; they play best of five 'rolls' – 'legs' to everyone else, except in the ten-pin alleys in Devon, where the six-a-side teams play the best of eight 'hands'.

Some areas play a highly skilled version of the game called **Nomination Skittles** – here you have to nominate which pin you are going to aim at first. This is why front and quarter pins are marked – it makes it easier to confirm that a nominated pin was indeed the one struck first. If you miss the nominated pin, your score doesn't count, although any skittles you knock over stay down, leaving you less to hit for the rest of your turn. In Cirencester, they have a Nomination Cup for star players who have emerged as their team's best scorer; in the final, each player has six throws, just 18 balls, to do his stuff. Bath has a Nomination League, but in Cardiff, I am told, they regard Nomination Skittles as a gambling game sometimes played to settle which player has the strongest nerve and the most accurate arm.

One of the team trophies contested in Cirencester is the Corners Cup – this is the variation of the game listed by Benjamin Strutt as Four Corners and the object then, as now, was to set up and then demolish just the four corner pins – front, back and two sides – in the least number of throws. Some experts have been known to knock down all four with one shot.

League Skittles is a winter activity; in the summer, when the game is not taken quite so seriously, all sorts of frolics can be organised by individual pubs or groups. Teams can be all ladies, all gents, or mixed and of almost any size, depending on demand. On the other hand, it is not unknown for a landlord to shut down the alley except for private bookings, or to turn it into a family room or extension to the restaurant to cope with tourists.

Long Alley

In 1572, Dr John Jones, a physician of Buxton in Derbyshire, sought to drum up trade and published a book called *The Benefit of the Ancient Bathes of Buckstones*. Besides recommending the water, Dr Jones encouraged his patients to take up 'bowling in allayes, the weather convenient, and the bowles fitte to such a game, as eyther in playne or longe allayes, or in suche as have crankes with half bowles, which is the fyner and gentler exercise'. He could have been writing exclusively about bowls, of course, but it is often unclear in such cases whether bowling really meant skittling and Timothy Finn, in his book *Pub Games of England*, has pointed out that this may be the first printed reference to the Skittles game called **Long Alley.**

I first came across Long Alley in Leicestershire some 20 years ago, when it was played in dozens of pubs, particularly between and around Market Harborough and Leicester. The alleys were either separate, enclosed buildings across the pub yards, or long huts, open on one side. As the name suggests, the outstanding feature of the game is its long pitch, which can be anything from 33 to 36ft from throwing line to front pin. In this part of the world, the missile is not a ball, but a 3 or 4lb capsule-shaped log, which is thrown, with one bounce, at a frame of nine pins. The pins are bigger than the ones found in the West Country – they are about 14in high, club-shaped and often metal-collared at the base. There is a king pin, with an extra wooden bobble on top of the usual club, which gives it a 2in advantage over the rest of the pins.

Alleys can have different surfaces – some are uniformly smooth concrete or asphalt, others are roughly cobbled or planked to within a couple or yards of the front pin and evened out with railway sleepers or slate thereafter. Since the log, or 'cheeses' as they are more often called, are thrown rather than rolled, and have to bounce only once before they hit the pins, it doesn't really matter what the surface of the first 25ft of the alley is like.

The odd shape of the cheese means that Long Alley in Leicestershire is quite different to other Skittles games. As a newcomer, you will find that your first throws, no matter how accurate, will bounce in frustrating and apparently unpredictable ways. The locals, on the other hand, can use the impact of cheese on pitch to deliberately angle shots at awkward patterns of skittles with dazzling skill.

A little further north from Leicestershire, in between the cities of Derby and Nottingham, Long Alley changes in small but significant detail. In Ilkeston, in Derbyshire, an immensely rewarding place for the pub pilgrim, they throw – not logs – but rough applewood balls from a distance of 27ft. The throw is from the 'chuck-hole', or 'chock-hole', which is a footprint – in new alleys, it's trodden into the concrete before it has set, in older venues it is simply worn in the stone over many years by a million right feet.

A yard in front of the forward pin is the 'tin'; nowadays this is an oblong sheet of thin steel, but in the old days it was a tin advertising poster, 'rescued' from a wall or shop front. You have to throw the ball so that it bounces beyond the tin before it hits the front skittle; if it falls short and hits the tin, everyone will hear the clatter of the foul throw – if you miss the front pin your score doesn't count either. I saw a young player in a league match miss the front pin with his first shot, which nevertheless demolished three pins to the left and one at the back; on his second throw he missed the front pin again and knocked down three pins to the right; with his last throw he hit the front pin and the one left standing behind it. Although he had knocked down all the skittles with the regulatory three balls, he had only scored two points. Throwing at this distance, and concentrating on the legitimate area of bounce beyond the tin, it is very easy to throw three balls which actually pass between the pins without knocking down any at all – at The Beacon pub, which is a fanatically keen Long Alley venue in Ilkeston, they have a toy duck on a child's trolley, which has to be dragged up and down the alley by the hapless victim of this misfortune, to the cheers and jeers of the assembled company.

Ilkeston's Winter League has five players per team – they play best of three legs for a match. In the summer, the pubs with outdoor alleys join in and there are ten players to a team.

This version of Long Alley, played with balls rather than cheeses, and using the tin, is widespread, with only minute differences in the rules, in this part of Derbyshire and Nottinghamshire. I suppose the reason so little seems to be known about it outside its home patch is that this area of the East Midlands is not as popular a tourist area as the West Country. The origins and history of both the ball and the cheese game remain elusive. Long Alley has a rumbustious, unsophisticated, medieval feel to it, but as far as I know, no-one has investigated the matter thoroughly and what comment there has been remains largely guesswork. Contemporary players

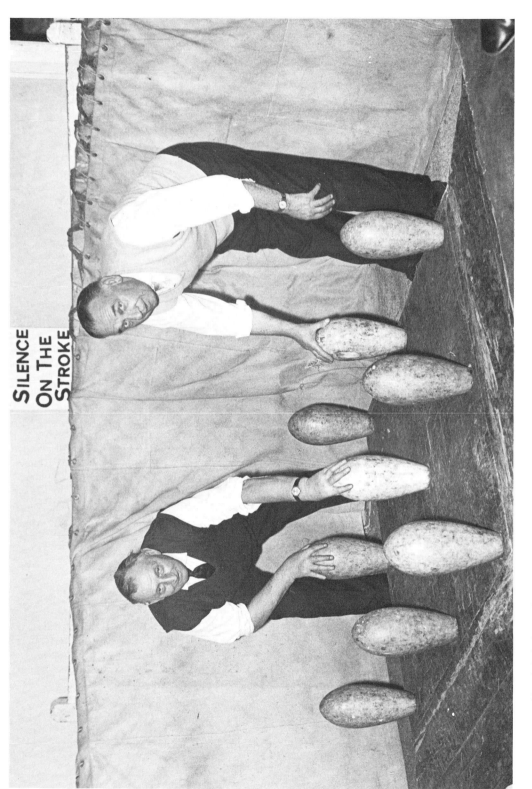

Old English Skittles at The Freemasons Arms, Hampstead, North London – one of only three places in Britain where the game can still be played.

are content to point out that their grandparents played before them, and to leave it at that. I was very pleased to see, in the Ilkeston League, that some of the equipment was brand new, supplied by local craftsmen. There are new alleys each season, too, they told me, so the future of the game seems bright. I for one, can't think of a better way of spending a Sunday lunchtime . . . someone should organise coach parties to Ilkeston so that the rest of the world can learn what beer and Skittles is all about.

Old English Skittles

Old English Skittles, also known as **London Skittles**, is now only played at three locations, all of them, appropriately enough, in London. This is the game described so affectionately and brilliantly by the late A.P. Herbert in his novel *The Water Gypsies*. The chapter entitled 'The Christmas Cup' is as good an account of a pub game as you are likely to find anywhere – unlike so many middle class writers on pubs and pub games, Herbert really knew his stuff, played the games he wrote about and actually liked pubs and pub people.

In Herbert's early playing days, the 1920s, there were between 20 and 30 alleys in the London area, including his local, the Black Lion at Hammersmith. This version of Skittles had moved into the capital many years before, from its original home in Hampshire where, Herbert used to tell people, it had first been played in the New Forest in the 14th century, using bones of deer as pins. Whether this was a piece of artistic licence linking Old English Skittles with **Loggats**, or whether he had actually come across some evidence, we may never know. Guy Tunnicliffe, the Secretary of the Hampstead Skittles Club, which operates in the basement of the Freemasons Arms on Downshire Hill, leans towards another theory, that the game was brought to this country by Europeans, probably the Dutch, who originally played a similar sport on the decks of their ships. All the old pubs and clubs which used to play the game were on, or near, the Thames, which suggests that the river may have been the game's route into the capital. The club at the Freemasons opened for business in 1888, as the Hampstead Lawn Billiards, Quoits and Skittles Club.

From the records, we know that Old English Skittles was codified in 1900 by the Amateur Skittles Association, so it remains the only game in this section for which national rules and regulations exist. In the 1920s, when he first started to play, Herbert said that many players 'regarded Skittles as the real thing and rather looked down on the game of ninepins'.

The scale of the game seems majestic and monu-mental, although the throw is actually shorter than in Long Alley or West Country Skittles. The Freemasons' alley, or 'run', is 21ft long and sunk perhaps 4in deep in the floor. The frame upon which the skittles stand is hornbeam boarding, slightly raised from the floor. Each pin stands on a circular brass plate and the plates are laid out in the usual diamond pattern. The tubby hornbeam pins are 14½in high, 3in across at base and top but a stately 6½in diameter across the belly – they weigh 9lbs each.

In the old days, the players used to employ 'stickers-up' – men who would reset the tumbled skittles all night for sixpence and a pint or two. These old boys really must have earned their money and beer – after only twenty minutes or so of voluntary sticking-up, you can feel muscles beginning to strain with the effort of bending over and lifting heavy pins. Someone at the club once calculated that a sticker-up would lift nearly 2 tons worth of hornbeam in the course of a long evening of Skittles.

It is the missile, the 'cheese', which gave the London game its unique flavour and character – the cheese is a discus-shaped piece of lignum vitae and can vary from 8½ to 12in in diameter and can weigh anything from 4 to 6lbs. A journalist, writing about the game in the 1950s, described the cheese aptly as being 'as big as a frying pan, thick as a telephone directory'. A.P. Herbert described the game as 'Homeric' – and you can see why, since the throw looks more like an Olympic discus attempt than a mere game of Skittles. 'Owing to the robust nature of the game', says the membership card of the Freemasons, 'members are advised that they play at their own risk.'

The aim of the game is, of course, to knock down as many pins as possible in the fewest throws, but the system of scoring is extraordinary. Instead of totalling the number of tumbled pins, you count the number of throws it takes to knock down the full frame of nine skittles, rather as a golfer scores the number of strokes needed to hole the ball. You are only allowed four throws for a turn, frame or 'chalk'; if any pins are left standing after four throws it is kindly assumed that the fifth cheese would have completed the job. Thus the worst score you can have for a chalk is 5 – the best is 1, which occurs if a player knocks over all nine skittles with his first cheese – a 'floorer'. If, at any stage in the chalk, only one pin is left, that too is assumed to be gone by the next throw and the score is adjusted accordingly. Therefore, if you knock down eight pins with your first throw, you are given a score of 2 without having to throw again. In a singles match, or in most league matches, the game goes to the player who first gets

The cheese, seen here in mid-flight, is 'as wide as a frying-pan and as thick as a telephone directory'. Its size and shape are peculiar to Old English Skittles.

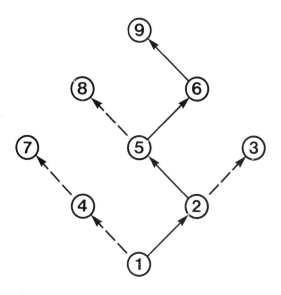

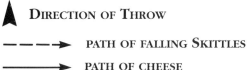

▲ DIRECTION OF THROW

− − − → PATH OF FALLING SKITTLES

────→ PATH OF CHEESE

A 'floorer'

to seven winning chalks. There are six players to a team these days, for most league matches.

When a new player joins a Skittles club, he or she is officially classed as a novice and the long but friendly process of initiation, tuition and encouragement begins. The skills of Old English Skittles are not easily acquired, since the mere act of pitching the ponderous cheeses calls for considerable physical

effort and a good sense of balance and direction. Tradition and experience have proved that there is a correct way of doing things – to score a floorer, the cheese should hit the leading pin at a precise spot high on its right shoulder. Thereafter, the cheese follows a predetermined destructive path to the back of the frame, while the other skittles are 'bundled up' by tumbling pins. The diagram (left) shows precisely what should happen, with the solid line indicating the cheese's route and the dotted line showing how the pins fold up.

To meet with full critical approval, the cheese should come to rest neatly, just over the far corner of the frame – there is, after all, a right and a wrong way of doing things. All the foregoing applies to a right-handed player, left-handers should start by hitting the front pin high up on the left shoulder . . . you could, on the other hand, throw a 'bolter', where the cheese goes straight through the pins without knocking any of them over – a shot which is greeted with a mixture of disbelief and sympathy.

The beginner is shown diagrams and given the names of broken frames – the patterns of skittles left after one or two throws. Each broken frame is a problem with a precise solution, and in most cases a single cheese, correctly thrown, will do the trick. There is even a special competition, the Broken Frames Championship, which offers points for the satisfactory resolution of pre-set patterns – the more difficult the geometry, the more points are allocated.

The shelves behind the bar at the Freemasons groan under an extraordinary array of brightly polished cups, shields and trophies – the Page Cup, the Course Cup, the Novices Championship, the Pairs Championship, the Broken Frames Champion-

Novices 2 points

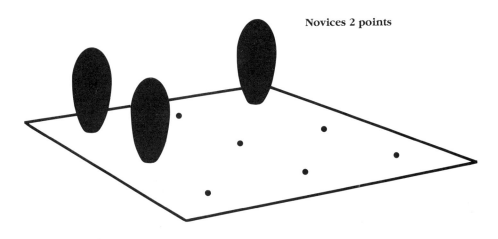

Knock on with closed cheese

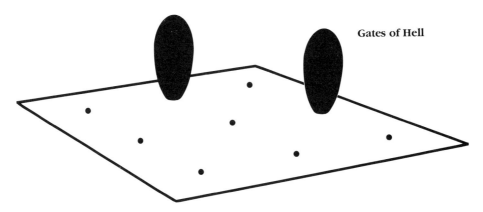

Gates of Hell

*Knock on with a closed cheese high on the outside
of either pin.*

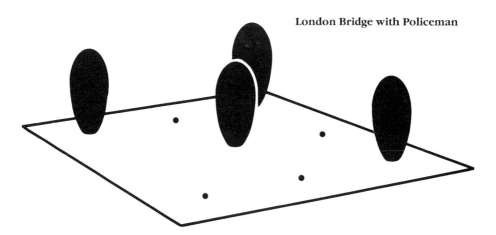

London Bridge with Policeman

Impossible in one shot.

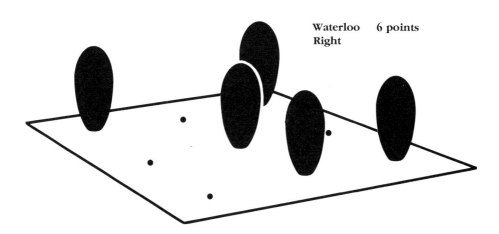

**Waterloo   6 points
Right**

ship, the Floorer Cup, the Eight Pin Plate and the St Dunstan's Shield – but one can't help feeling anxious about the game's future. The River Fleet runs underneath the Freemasons' and in 1980, after a severe Hampstead monsoon, the cellar was flooded badly, leaving the club's historical records pulped and cheeses and skittles bobbing around in the water. The alley and game were not put back into playing order until 1987, thanks to the efforts of the club members. It could easily happen again. There are only two other alleys left – one at the Duke of Devonshire in Balham and the other at the National Westminster Bank Recreation Club in Norbury. The three clubs compete for the St Dunstan's Shield, but otherwise tend to keep themselves to themselves.

There is talk that Fullers brewery might be persuaded to build an alley somewhere within their London territory. If that was to happen, it might be the first sign that a truly magnificent game is on its way back.

Table Skittles

Occasionally, you may come across a very old **Table Skittles**, or **Bar Skittles** set, fettled up lovingly by a local craftsman – a joiner, carpenter or cabinet-maker – for his local pub and renovated through the years. The Plough, at Blundeston in Suffolk – reputed to be the same pub from which Charles Dickens' famous character, the carrier Barkis, set off in the novel *David Copperfield* – used to have a beautiful table, made by the local undertaker 140 years ago. The ball, chain and pins had been replaced several times, but the rest of the table remained much as it was when it was first made, when Dickens himself

The equipment used for the game Devil among the Tailors. The serious league players call the game Table Skittles, or simply Skittles.

was still alive. The Plough has Victorian evenings and Dickens days - and they still play the Table Skittles game enthusiastically, although the original table was taken away by a former landlord a few years ago.

Table Skittles, also sometimes known as Devil among the Tailors, has a wooden ball tethered by a light chain to a swivel on top of a pole; the ball is swung clockwise around the outside of the pole so that as it returns towards the thrower, it ploughs through nine small skittles set up in the conventional diamond pattern on a pedestal within the baize-lined box. Each player has three throws to a turn, rather like darts, and scores points equivalent to how many pins he knocks down. The pins are re-set after a floorer, so the maximum score from three balls is 27. At The Plough, a game is 'up the board and back', which means 121 points.

The game is known as an old bar or café game in other European countries. In the Flemish part of Belgium and in northern Germany it is known as *Tafelkegelen*, while in Finisterre, in Brittany, they call it *Le Birinic*. Both Germany and France have, or have had, giant outdoor versions, so it is an open and interesting question which came first - was it an outdoor game which was miniaturised and brought indoors, or was it an indoor game which was scaled up and taken outdoors for the summer?

John Jacques and Son Ltd, who became famous for their introduction and commercialisation of several traditional games, including Croquet and Happy Families, have, for a long time, supplied Table Skittles sets but they used to acknowledge traditional regional differences and make slightly different sets for the various areas they supplied. The skittles and ball used in the Staffordshire leagues were, for example, slightly larger and heavier than those preferred in Wales, while the West Country type was different again. Now, sadly, the company makes just one heavy-duty league model and claims to have no knowledge of the niceties of regional variations.

There are Table Skittles sets of varying sizes in play in pubs the length and breadth of Great Britain, but pending further discoveries, I think Staffordshire is the place of pilgrimage for the serious seeker of the truth - there are leagues in places such as Leek, Macclesfield, Longton, Burslem, Stoke, Newcastle-under-Lyme, Ipstones and Cheadle.

The standard Table Skittles game is 101 up - exactly out, or 'deadhole to count', as the locals would have it. Each player has three throws per turn and matters are further complicated by the additional rule - in some schools - that the front pin must be struck first, before anything else can count - the same rule adhered to in Long Alley. The throw must

be from the bottom end of the table and should go clockwise round the pole; the front pin in Table Skittles is, of course, where the back pin is in ordinary skittles. Those new to the game sometimes try to throw straight at the pins, without circumnavigating the pole, or stand halfway along the table and shoot straight across at the skittles - this is the equivalent of filing the pieces of a jigsaw puzzle to make them fit and is quite contrary to the spirit (and the rules) of the game. In some Staffordshire leagues, the tables have a brass rail along the left-hand edge, running up to the pole, to make sure that the cross-shot cannot be played.

In The Potteries, Staffordshire, some interesting variations on the standard game can be found. There is **Twenty-one**, where the front pin must go down first and the frame is set up again after each *single* throw. The object of the game is to score exactly 21, or as near to it as possible; you can 'stick' if your nerve fails when you have scored, for example, 19 and doubt your ability to knock out just two pins from the full frame of nine. If you go over 21, you are 'bust' and out of the game - just as you would be if you played the card game of pontoon.

Round the Board involves knocking down a single pin each time you throw. You *must* actually fell a pin with each throw - 'fresh air shots' are not allowed. The frame is set up again when you have demolished it pin-by-pin, and your final score is simply the total of single pins you hit. The skilled players can score well over 100 going round the board and since there is usually money riding on the result, it is not recommended for beginners.

In the **Card Game**, each player is dealt five cards and must discard them by scoring their equivalent on the skittles board as follows:

1 (ace to 5)	1 shot allowed
6 to 8	2 shots allowed
9 to 10	
jack (11)	
queen (12)	3 shots allowed
king (13)	

Some advanced thinkers believe that the five cards should be dealt blind, then turned up and disposed of one at a time; others allow the players to turn over their entire hand, study it and work out the best way of eliminating it. Luck can play a part here, since you might go for your queen but instead get rid of your jack by missing one pin. Whichever way you play, the winner is the one who disposes of all his cards first.

In the **Dominoes Game**, Fives and Threes translates easily to the skittles board; the result of your three throws must be divisible by 5 or 3 to score, and 15 skittles down (after a floorer and a re-set) would tot up 8 points $(5 \times 3) + (3 \times 5)$. They go to 16 or 21 points up for game, scored on a cribbage board.

Hood Skittles

The lineage of **Hood Skittles** is quite clear – it is a miniaturised and domesticated version of Old English Skittles. Someone, somewhere, brought the original game out of the cellar or shed and onto a table in the corner of the taproom.

The skittles involved are the same shape as those used in the London game, but are much smaller – only 5in tall. They are set out in the familiar diamond pattern. The missiles are called cheeses, or sometimes balls, and they are very much like small Dutch cheeses, 3in across, 1½in thick, flat on top and bottom and rounded on the rim – they fit comfortably in the hand. The throw is 7 or 8ft, the same sort of distance as a darts throw. The table, or 'board' as it is often referred to, is more like an outsize armchair, with a flat seat which holds the pins, thickly padded arms and a frame stretched around it at the back, with a net, cloth, or hood to stop flying cheeses and pins from causing too much damage.

Hood Skittles is one of those pastimes perfectly familiar to pub goers within its own territory, but almost completely unknown outside it. If you were to draw a circle on a map, say 25 miles in radius from the centre of Northampton, you would have encompassed the majority of the pubs and clubs which play, although there are leagues in Luton, the southernmost boundary of events, and isolated tables in Birmingham up in the North.

The naming of the game presents something of a problem. I have called it Hood Skittles, as did games historian Timothy Finn, because of the characteristic hood, or goalposts-with-nets arrangement at the back of the chair. The awkward fact is that no-one who plays the game knows it under that name – they simply call it Skittles, or Table Skittles. Recent editors of *The Good Beer Guide*, listing East Midlands pubs blessed with good beer *and* this form of skittles, have taken to calling it **Northants Skittles**, and the Boat Inn at Stoke Bruerne, where I first played over 30 years ago, has a notice over the table proudly announcing 'Northamptonshire Skittles; Please Throw Underarm'. This seems a bit unfair on Bedfordshire, where there are town and country leagues, and Leicestershire, where they use slimmer pins, framed closer together, and call the game **Leicester Skittles**. Hood Skittles it shall be, to avoid any further confusion.

There are dozens of leagues, but it is difficult to single out what you might call the 'standard' league game. In the South Northants Winter League, they play seven singles matches to decide a game; each player is given five 'lives', which are chalked up on the board as five short vertical lines – exactly as you would for a game of Killer in Darts. Each of those lives is decided by a three-cheese contest, scored in the usual way, with pins being reset for a floorer (all skittles falling to the first throw) or a 'stack' (all skittles down after the second throw). If you lose, a 'life' is crossed out; five lives thus obliterated and you have lost that singles contest. In some areas, if both players down the same number of pins and a life is tied, they use the 'on-off', 'first and third' or 'up and down' method to resolve the issue – the first player throws again and chalks up the sum of his first and total throw. Thus, if he knocks over six skittles with his first throw and 12 with all three cheeses, he scores 6–12 and his opponent must top both scores, with two lives at stake instead of one, to beat him.

In the Dunton Bassett League, which has no less than six divisions of country pubs across south Leicestershire, they play eight to a team and all eight players bowl out to set their opponents a target for a leg, and the match is the best of seven legs. They don't bother doing anything complicated to resolve a tied leg, but simply award each side half a point.

There are eight players to a team in the Welford League as well. They all bowl out, but tied legs are replayed there and then. The game is the first to seven legs, so proceedings can go on for hours.

There are micro-climates of opinion on all sorts of issues as you travel from league to league. In south Northants, they use yellow plastic skittles and cheeses for practice, but insist that serious league play must involve only wooden pins; across the Dunton Bassett League the rule is exactly the opposite – the plastic pins and cheeses are the ones approved for league matches. All leagues allow the use of bounce-off-the-side cushions – an essential skill in the game – to get rid of some patterns of pins such as 'London Bridge'. However, some areas will, and some areas will not, let you get away with a 'back hit', where the cheese rebounds off the rubber or net at the back of the chair.

Once the league match is over, there are other exercises to be seen and enjoyed – games for money, or pints, and virtuoso trick shots to impress the onlooker. **Killer** is very much like its equivalent darts game – the first player throws left-handed, to set a score to be aimed at; player two must top that score or lose a life; player three must better player two's score and so on. Any number can play and each participant usually has three or five lives. The last player left in scoops the pot – usually ten pence from everyone. Killer is an enjoyable introduction to Hood Skittles for the stranger wandering into the territory, since there is an element of luck involved and if you lose, you don't let anybody down.

A more 'serious' bit of relaxation is the game known as **Nines** and there are two versions of this. In the first of these, players simply throw nine cheeses at the pins and whoever gets the highest total score picks up the stake money.

The other game of Nines is a bit more sophisticated – you have three throws to a turn and aim to knock down exactly nine pins each time. You are given five turns and record your score in a box:

	1	2	3	4	5
A	9	9	8	7	7
B	9	9	9	6	7
C	9	8	7	8	8

The twist to the tale is that when you write down your score you are allowed to put it in any of the five boxes, the aim being to score the highest 'across the board' – player B has won the game illustrated by scoring 99, 967. So, if you get a 9, you put it in the left-hand box; if you score poorly, you put it in the right-hand box.

Dominoes is another of those examples of cross-fertilisation so common in pub games. Here, in the skittles version, you give yourself a point for every total divisible by 5 or 3 that you score with the usual three throws – all nine skittles down would score 3 points, for example. The game is 11 points up. In the stricter schools, you must always throw all three cheeses each turn – you are not allowed 'fresh air shots'. So, for example, if you have scored 6 with your first two throws and would actually be content to 'stick' there for 2 points, you must throw your last cheese and go for nine pins and 3 points. The real problems occur at the end of the game when you only need, say, 1 point (i.e. three pins) for victory. You must go 'exactly out', which means that you must pick out one pin with each cheese.

Thirty-one Up is the self-explanatory title for a game which is rarely played nowadays. You proceed in the usual way, with three throws to a turn, and you must score 31 points to win, totted up along a cribbage board. Again, the story has a sticky ending: you must go out *exactly* on 31 and all your cheeses must be thrown and must score.

The Long Nine is not a game but a piece of magic – all nine pins are lined up touching one another, the end of the line facing the thrower so that, in effect, he sees only one pin. The trick is to throw a cheese and remove the middle pin, without disturbing the others. It is possible and I have seen it done. The other trick shot, though, I have to report as theory rather than observed fact. A cheese rests flat in the middle of the board, with a skittle standing on top of it. An expert can throw another cheese, knock the base cheese from under the skittle, but leave the skittle standing. It seems a bit like the pulling-the-cloth-off-the-table-without-disturbing-the-crockery trick – one wouldn't like to try it for fear of looking stupid and only a professional magician could get away with it.

Most of the tables were made by a firm called W.T. Black's (Woodworkers) in Northampton and, although the firm ceased trading years ago, their handiwork can still be seen in pubs all over the region. Most of their tables are numbered chronologically according to their construction and collectors have spotted over 200 of them. About ten years ago, Colin Swinfen, a joiner in South Kilworth, Leicester, started building new tables, based on the old Black's Northamptonshire pattern and, although it is not a full time job, he gets enough new orders to give him a couple of months work a year. And, of course, old tables can be refurbished – a cheaper process than buying a new one, which will cost somewhere in the region of £500. A set of skittles, which usually comes as a box of ten, will set you back about £80. It's nice to see new equipment being produced; 15 years ago it looked as if the supply had dried up and Hood Skittles might have been heading for an inexorable decline. Now the game is booming and there are even tales of sets being installed in private homes and brand new leisure centres.

There is very little to be said about the history of the game, although everyone is sure it has been around for a long time. There is a persistent claim that the thickly-padded arms on the tables were actually originated by W.T. Black's great-grandfather, which would take it back to the early 19th century. Eventually, someone in the area will get down to a serious study of the game and we will know more. In the meantime, the best course of action is to get yourself to the East Midlands and enjoy the game – in my estimation, one of the nation's top ten pub attractions.

The only Daddlums table still in play is this one – at The Vigo Inn, in Fairseat, Kent.

Daddlums

Many years ago, the Gun Inn at Dedham, on the road between Colchester and Ipswich, used to display an ancient trophy in one of the bars, which was inscribed 'Ye Olde Dedham Pewter Pot for Daddlums and Darts, 1760'. Anything inscribed 'Ye Olde' is likely to be fake, but if the Gun Inn's trophy was genuine, then it is the earliest non-literary evidence for either version of the game that I have come across. Daddlums is a form of Table Skittles peculiar to the south east of England and now, sadly, on the verge of extinction.

Until very recently, The Swingate pub at Guston, in Kent, used to have a Daddlums table and indeed advertised the fact in *The Good Beer Guide,* stressing that if anyone wanted to use the table, they should telephone in advance to book it, which suggests that there was some considerable demand. The Swingate has changed hands and the new owner now says cheerfully that he's never heard of Daddlums and doesn't really want any games at all in his pub. The landlord giveth, and the landlord taketh away . . .

Mrs Ashwell, at The Vigo Inn, Fairseat, Sevenoaks, in Kent, on the other hand, is very proud of the Daddlums table in her pub and has recently had it carefully refurbished. The table, at first glance, looks a bit like a Hood Skittles board, except that it is much longer and narrower and the pins are smaller, being only 3in high. The cheeses are tiny, too, and look for all the world like biscuit-sized miniatures of the cheeses used in Old English Skittles. When you play the game, however, it soon becomes apparent that it requires a technique of its own - the rebounding from the sides ploy, so useful in Hood Skittles will simply not work here because the retaining walls on the Daddlums table are too close together and too thinly padded, and the cheeses are too light to bounce convincingly. Although all the artifacts are smaller than those used in Hood Skittles, the throwing distance is longer, for the diamond of pins stands at the far end of the 5½ft long table and the throwing line is another 9 feet from the front edge of the table. Mrs Ashwell says that under the old rules of the game, you had to throw from a line 14ft from the leading edge of the table, which explains why old records of the game register comparatively low scores - very few floorers in the good old days, apparently.

The technique then, as now, is to throw the cheese so that it lands safely on the table and slides flat towards the pins. I've never seen anyone try to throw the Daddlums cheese directly at the pins, as one does in Old English Skittles, although I suppose it could be done.

In theory, any of the games with bigger skittles could be transferred to the Daddlums table; in practice, one of the popular games in Nines. Here, you have nine consecutive throws and knock over as many pins as you can. If you clear the board at any time, the pins are reset, but what seems to happen more often is that you tumble eight pins in a few throws, then spend the rest of your time, and cheeses, trying to get rid of one solitary skittle which defies demolition. The game is usually played to the best of five legs.

The main doubles game is reminiscent of one of the variations of Hood Skittles - five lives are chalked up and won or lost by the totalled scores of the participating partners, who throw three cheeses each. The 'tie-breaker' in this version is a one-cheese contest between one player from each side.

Daddlums tables were never mass manufactured and never standardised, so even when there were a few of them around in Kent and Suffolk, no two were exactly alike. After the Second World War, the game was all but killed off by another game which *had* been recently codified and standardised - darts - especially the game played on the London Treble dartboard. A former landlady at The Vigo Inn, some 20 years ago, put it like this, 'A little fellow from the East End of London came round in an Austin 7 with a boot full of dartboards in about 1947 or 1948, and that was that.'

Patrons of the pub continue to play Daddlums enthusiastically and, with Mrs Ashwell in charge, there is no need to worry about the game's immediate future there. They play in splendid isolation, and Mrs Ashwell knows of no other pub in Kent which has a table and could supply a challenge. The long-term outlook is bleak, unless - as in the old days - a local craftsman can be persuaded to build tables.

Ten Pin Bowling

The Dutch took their game of **Ninepins** to America in the 17th century. The game became popular, but attracted to its rinks and alleys a crowd of undesirables - gamblers, drunks, pimps and criminals - so that during the 18th century, local authorities started to clamp down. Skittles players got round the prohibitive legislation, which was clumsily aimed at *Nine* Pin Bowling, by adding a tenth pin and changing the traditional diamond pattern to a triangle - hence **Ten Pin Bowling**.

At the end of the 19th century, the National Bowling Association and the American Bowling Congress, among other controlling bodies, drew up rules and codes of conduct which ensured the games expansion and respectability. This clarified procedure over fallen pins – they were to be removed after every bowl – and ruled that balls falling into the side gutters of the lanes were 'dead'.

After that, technology took over. Immaculate 60 ft lanes were developed, together with balanced bowls, automatic pin spotters, ball return units, and digital score read-outs.

In the 1960s, Ten Pin Bowling invaded Britain as a pre-packaged, unified and efficiently-organised pastime. Bowling alleys sprang up in major cities; some of them had as many as 36 lanes, not to mention resident coaches, or tutors, nurseries for the kids and built-in bars and refreshment centres. Then something went wrong and the boom collapsed as suddenly as it had erupted. By the 1980s, only a handful of alleys remained, patronised by a hardcore of dogged adherents. Around the time of writing, there has been a surge of interest with new complexes springing up in town suburbs.

All this has little or nothing to do with the pub, except for the survival of **Ten Pin Skittles** in a few Devon pubs, as already noted, and the occasional appearance of miniature Ten Pin Bowling alleys in pubs.

Half-bowl (Rolly)

Many people I speak to – and practically all journalists and radio or television interviewers I meet – assume that pub games are dying out. As I hope this book will prove, the story is a lot more complicated than that – very few games actually die out, although they sometimes retreat into near anonymity and obscurity. Usually, though, someone, somewhere, is still playing. Take the fascinating and convoluted story of **Half-bowl**, or **Rolly**, for example . . .

During the course of exhaustive winnowing through past-bound volumes of the publicans' newspaper, *The Morning Advertiser*, I came across a maddeningly brief and incomplete piece about a game called Rolly, written in the early 1950s. The report referred to 'four skittles and a half-moon shaped ball' being preserved in the flag-floored kitchen of the Chequers Inn at Dereham, Norfolk, and went on to claim, somewhat bewilderingly, that 'this was the game which inspired bar billiards'.

Much later, as I probed deeper into games history and mystery, I found that Strutt had written about what must have been the same game, or a very close relative, in 1800 in *The Sports and Pastimes of the People of England*. It was an uncharacteristically clear report, worth quoting at length: 'Half-bowl is one of the 'new imagine' games prohibited in 1477 in favour of archery and received its denomination from being played with one half of a sphere of wood.

Half-bowl is practised to this day in Hertfordshire, where it is commonly called rolly-polly; and it is best performed upon the floor of a room, especially if it be smooth and level. There are fifteen small pins of conical form required for this pastime; twelve of which are placed at equal distances upon the circumference of a circle of about 2½ ft in diameter; one of the three remaining pins occupies the centre; and the other two are placed without the circle at the back part of it, and parallel with the bowling place, but so as to be in a line with the middle pin; forming a row of five pins, including two of those upon the circumference.

In playing this game, the bowl, when delivered, must pass above the pins, and round the end pin, without the circle, before it beats any of them down; if not, the cast is forfeited; and, owing to the great bias of the bowl, this task is not readily performed by such as have not made themselves perfect by practice. The middle pin is distinguished by four balls at the top; and, if thrown down, is reckoned for four towards the game; the intermediate pin upon the circle, in the row of five, has three balls, and is reckoned for three; the first pin without the circle has two balls and is counted for two; and the value of all the others singly is but one. Thirty-one chalks complete the game; which he who obtains first is the conqueror. It this number be exceeded, it is a matter of no consequence; the game is equally won.'

I still cannot for the life of me see what all this has to do with **Bar Billiards**, except for the comparatively minor point that the far pin, or skittle, must be rounded like a lighthouse, and not knocked over, before you can register a score. In Bar Billiards, of course, you lose your score if you knock down a pin, but otherwise there seems no connection at all between the game banned in Britain in 1477 and the game brought to this country from Belgium in 1933.

It was, however, in Belgium that I came across Half-bowl again, in 1990. An organisation called the Flemish Folksport Council, based in Leuven, south of Brussels, has had the splendid idea of putting together a series of 'Folksport Routes', which are essentially pub or bar game trails, to be followed on foot, by bicycle or car. Several of these 'Folksport' leaflets mention bars, cafés or restaurants which play a game they call *Pierbol*. There are table versions and floor versions of the game, but the general rules remain the same – a hemispherical wooden bowl is trundled around a circle of ten, or in some cases 13 skittles and must round the far pin – 'the fool' – before knocking down any scoring pin. They've been playing *Pierbol* in Kortrijk (Courtrai) and in the north-eastern part of East Flanders, since at least

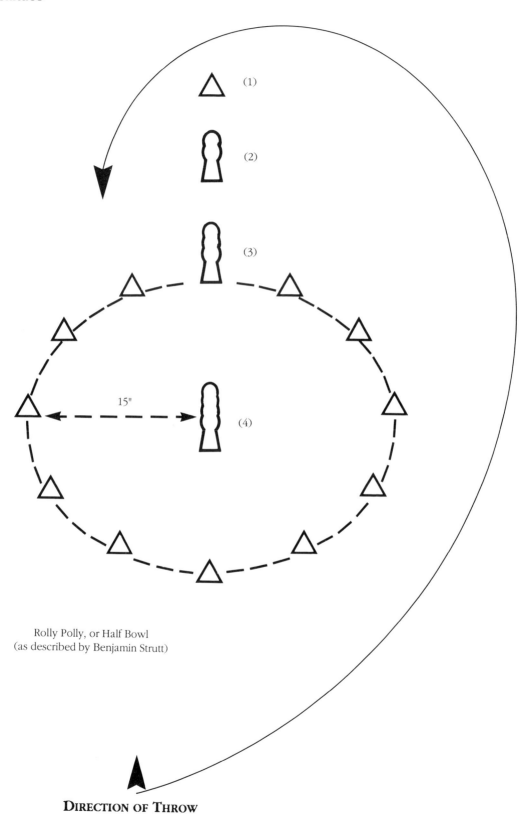

(1)

(2)

(3)

15"

(4)

Rolly Polly, or Half Bowl
(as described by Benjamin Strutt)

DIRECTION OF THROW

1900 and the researchers in Leuven reckon that it can be traced back to 17th-century France, where it was known, curiously, as 'the game of Siam'. They still play a game called *Media Bola* in parts of Spain, too, and it sounds very much like the pastime that Strutt observed so carefully in 1800, in Hertfordshire. Half-bowl did make a brief, eccentric come-back in Britain, too. Back in 1957, again according to the assiduous historians of Leuven, there was an organisation calling itself The Foolish Bowling Association, which practised a variant of the game at Littleborough, Lancashire – and Littleborough is just four miles from where I live! It's funny how this business of pub games takes you round in circles . . . Regrettably, no trace of The Foolish Bowling Association remains in Littleborough.

A final thought – Half-bowl is not the inspiration behind Bar Billiards, but it may well have naturally led on to Devil Among the Tailors, or Bar Skittles – the game with the ball on the chain. Both are skittles games and both involve the ball going around the rest of the pins before it knocks anything down. The table version of *Pierbol*, which they play in the Café Kaatspell, in Hamme, south of Antwerp, has nine skittles set out, not in a circle but in the conventional nine-pin diamond pattern, plus one extra pin around which you have to steer your half-ball – it looks for all the world like the game played in Leek, Staffordshire, but without the pole and chain.

Aunt Sally

Aunt Sally was, for most people, one of those cathartic fairground games, where men could viciously throw balls at a wooden female face on a stand, and win a prize by smashing clay pipes in the figure's ears or mouth. By and large, the coconut shy seems to have taken its place, although the phrase itself lingers on, like 'king pin' and 'bear garden', often used but rarely thought about in its original context.

In Oxfordshire, however, centred on the city and stretching into many of the neighbouring towns, villages and hamlets, Aunt Sally is the name given to a vigorous and burgeoning outdoor pub game, which – when it bothers with origins at all – claims a fairground ancestry. It may well have a much more fascinating background than that.

Unless you actually come across a match in progress, it is remarkably easy to pass a pleasant summer's evening in one of the participating pubs without realising that the game is there. There is a true story, which tells of a new landlord from outside of the county, taking over an Oxfordshire pub in winter and not realising that he had any Aunt Sally commitments until two teams turned up on his doorstep one Wednesday evening in May, expecting to play.

In the typical garden or yard of an Aunt Sally pub, there is a narrow 10 yard concrete pitch, which often goes unnoticed, or is mistaken for a path. At the end of this stands a hollow metal post, 2½ft high and often wrapped round with rubber inner tubes. (Local supplies of the latter are not too hard to come by – after all, Oxford is famous for car factories as well as dreaming spires.) Behind the post, a tightly-stretched triptych of canvas, some modest flood-lighting, and perhaps a tell-tale blackboard for chalking up the score, complete the fixed scenery.

When a game is imminent, the stage is swiftly and subtly rearranged and brought to life. The chairs and tables, previously spread at random in the garden, are grouped in lines along the pitch for thirsty supporters. An official arrives with a swan's neck swivel and the 6-in doll, or skittle, which looks a bit like an outsize champagne cork, painted white. The swivel is inserted in the top of the hollow post and the doll is perched on its tiny platform, 2½ft from the ground. These essential items are usually kept in the pub, to save them from souvenir hunters.

Most teams bring their own sticks, six 18- × 2-in ash batons to a set, rounded at each end, like truncheons but without a grip or taper. They are carried, very professionally, in long, narrow canvas bags, and polished lovingly with talcum powder, or burnished with fine sandpaper, so that they slip smoothly out of the hand on the throw. (No-hoper teams tend to arrive with all their sticks bundled into a milk crate.) The length of the throw is 10 yards, from a raised wooden strip called the 'hocking'.

The object of Aunt Sally, simply stated, is to knock the doll off the swivel by throwing a stick at it – it could be described as a form of Skittles in reverse with the skittles thrown at the 'cheese'. Although there are many ways of throwing the stick, the wooden doll *must* be struck cleanly (see p. 73) – if the stick strikes the swivel or the post first, the so-called 'blob shot' does not count. This can be confusing for the beginner, since the swivel often twists round on its pin, with a metallic rattle, after a good shot. The trick is to listen for the initial impact of wood on wood or, if still in doubt, to watch the 'sticker up', provided by each team. He crouches by the post, like a fielder at silly mid-on, and judges each shot, swiftly returning the doll to its place if it is knocked off.

Eight players throw consecutively for a team in a normal league match and each player throws six consecutive sticks. Thus, in a single leg, or 'horse', it's possible for a team to throw down 48 dolls – in fact, no side has ever scored more than 39 in one leg, which gives some idea of the level of difficulty and skill involved. A match consists of the best of three horses, and a team winning all three scores 3 points in the league.

There are tales of legendary skills, such as those of the player who was reputed to stand a lighted candle on the doll. With his first stick, it was said, he put out the candle's flame, with his second he knocked off the candle, and with his third he scored a clean hit on the doll. What he did for an encore is not recorded. Then there are the players who consistently score highly. They are called 'sixer-men' for obvious reasons, and they are very few and far between. In all the games I have seen, a six score was greeted with wild applause and a symphony of car horns and rattled beer mugs, while a 'blob' - no score - received muttered sympathy rather than derision.

During the summer season, the *Oxford Mail* devotes a page of news each Wednesday to the progress of the Glemorangie Aunt Sally leagues, teams and individual stars; all 'sixers' are dutifully recorded, as are all 'blobbers'. There are write-ups on some of the key matches, and the results of all the matches, from the premier league to section 24, are given in detail .

The Glenmorangie Oxford and District Aunt Sally Association is the largest of the local leagues, and the fact that it has no less than 24 divisions, with ten teams in each section, shows that the game enjoys tremendous support. There is promotion and relegation, and some of the teams in the first division are so good they have to be handicapped. Television viewing in that part of Oxfordshire must take a terrible battering in the summer, which can't be a bad thing.

Aunt Sally is actually expanding; in 1957, the Oxford and District League had 120 teams on its books and at the last count, in 1990, they had 235 teams in their 24 divisions. The game is now also played beyond its home patch and you will come across pitches in neighbouring Gloucestershire, Berkshire, Warwickshire and Buckinghamshire. The secret of the game's success is, I feel, that it is one of those pastimes which can be enjoyed at any level, from the keen-as-mustard, practise-every-night approach in the premier divisions, to the casual, throw-with-one-hand-in-the-pocket attitude in the lower depths.

The latest development has seen the emergence of the first Aunt Sally World Championships, organised by the Abingdon Lions and Morland's Brewery on August Bank Holiday Monday, with 128 teams (of 4 players) playing on 12 lanes. It's one of those events where the serious teams will have their eye firmly on the £500 first prize, while the others will perhaps find consolation - and fun - going for the prizes on offer for the Funniest Dressed Team, or the Best Dressed National Team (i.e. Scottish, English, Irish, French, German, Spanish).

The Oxford League began just before the Second World War, and indeed the magazine *Picture Post* carried a picture of the unsuccessful candidate in the famous 1938 pre-war by-election cradling sticks in an attempt to cajole votes. The landlord of a pub in Garsington claims that the equipment was discovered (which must mean *re*discovered) in the loft of Garsington Hall in the 1920s. Mr E.F. Whitbread, the one time secretary of the Oxford Association, read in a book that people at the Henley Regatta, in 1863, were throwing stunted bludgeons at an Aunt Sally. In his book *Under the Parish Lantern* the now-famous country writer, Fred Archer, noted that, at a fête in his beloved Cotswolds, someone had an idea 'that might be different, we would throw rick pegs at coconuts instead of the usual balls; this proved quite successful, the coconuts falling more by luck than judgement.' None of which proves much, except to reinforce the local theory that the pub game was adopted originally from country fairs.

It is possible, of course, to go further back than this, and the essential clue here, besides the basic simplicity of the game, is the club, stick, baton or cudgel used as the missile. This could take it back to the game of **Kayles**, or **Kails**, of course - but there is a more interesting theory.

Strutt describes 'the barbarous and wicked diversion' of throwing at cocks, which was formerly very popular among the young. A cock was tied by one leg to a small stake in the ground, and these 'marksmen' paid for the privilege of throwing 'cok-steles', or clubs, at the unfortunate bird. If the bird's leg was broken, it was supported on sticks to prolong the 'enjoyment'. Whoever killed the bird took it home for the pot. 'Magistrates have put a stop to it', says Strutt. 'It is nearly, if not entirely, discontinued in every part of the kingdom.'

The sequel is worth quoting in full, since it provides some sort of a link with this pastime and Aunt Sally. 'Upon the abolition of this inhuman custom, the place of the living birds was supplied by toys made in the form of cocks, with large and heavy stands of lead, at which the boys, on paying some very trifling sum, were permitted to throw as heretofore.'

Strutt goes on to say that the new pastime never became popular and was soon discontinued. Perhaps he didn't keep his eye on the Oxfordshire fairgrounds and pubs of the 19th century. He was, after all, wrong about dominoes.

Aunt Sally, the hugely-popular Oxfordshire Skittles game. Here, the doll has just been sent flying by a successful throw.

In 1936, as part of the National Playing Fields Association programme, playgroup leaders were trained in the art of Skittles.

There are games in Europe and beyond which bear a passing resemblance to Aunt Sally – *Pagschieten* in Belgium and Holland, *Jeu de Billon* in France and *Jukskei* in South Africa – but the Oxfordshire game has a character and identity entirely its own.

Irish Skittles

Many Irish games were invented or revived and codified in the late 19th century by the Gaelic Athletic Association, as part of a nationalist policy of conscious cultural and political repudiation of all things English – Gaelic football and hurling are classic examples from the catalogue. I'm not sure where or whether **Irish Skittles** stands in that pantheon of protest, but it is an unusual, complex and fascinating game and deserves more attention. It would export well, too.

At the annual All Ireland Skittles Championships, they play with five pins, standing within a 5ft diameter circle, chalked or painted on the ground. Each player throws four batons, one by one, from a 33⅓ft mark and must not just knock the pins over, but hit them clear of the circle in order to score. The batons look very much like Aunt Sally sticks – smooth rounded 'logs' of wood, about 10 to 12in long and of 3-in diameter. The pins are quite different to anything seen in Britain, being some 4in tall, 3in in diameter at the base, tapering to 2in across the top.

Each pin has a different value – the centre one scores 10 points, the pin closest to the thrower counts 1, while the pin directly behind the centre is worth 4. The left pin is good for 2 points, the right 3. Interestingly, there is a 'tin' on the floor, 3⅓ft from the front pin, which has the same name and fulfils the same purpose as the tin in Long Alley in Leicestershire, Derbyshire and Nottinghamshire – the missile must bounce beyond the tin and in front of the pins to be valid.

A classic display of skill would clear the three in-line pins scoring 1, 10 and 4 with the first baton; the second and third batons would clear left and right pins respectively; all five pins would then be reset for the fourth baton and a genius would take out the centre line of pins again – a total score of 34 points from the four throws.

In Northern Ireland, the 'big ring' game is played, as far as I know, only in Rostrevor. There is a similar but scaled-down version of the game played in a flourishing three-division pub and club league in South Down, with five small pins in a 2ft circle and smaller batons. The scoring here is 1, 5 and 2 for the pins 'in line', with 3 points for the left-hand pin and 4 for the right. Again, the pins must be clear of the circle to score at all. The game is 41 points, to be scored exactly and there are five players to a team, each of whom play a singles match against an opponent. Tuesday evening is the time to catch a match – the season runs from May to August.

Billiards. (From 'School of Recreation,' 1710.)

An early form of billiards shown in a print of 1710. The French added a third ball and got rid of the hoops; the British followed suit, but fitted their tables with pockets.

Background

Charles Cotton's book, *The Compleat Gamester* (1674), has already provided an early reference to the card game of All Fours; his favourite game of all was not cards but **Billiards,** an occupation he was driven to celebrate in dire verse:

'Billiards from Spain at first deriv'd its name
Both an ingenious and cleanly game
One Gamester leads (the Table green as grass)
And each like Warriors, try to gain the Pass
But in the contest ere the Pass be won
Hazards are many into which they run.'

There is great confusion about the origins of the game. A little later, beyond the epic verse quoted, Cotton himself contradicts the Spanish claim and says, 'Billiards had its first original from Italy and for the excellency of the Recreation is much approved of and plaid by most Nations in Europe and especially in England.' Subsequent French historians said that the game was invented by the English, while English historians have attributed it to the French, all of which is in the fine old tradition of modesty and *politesse* between the two countries, rather like the English calling a condom a French letter, while the French know it as a *capot d'Anglais*.

The object of 17th-century Billiards was to propel an ivory or wooden ball by means of a mace or cue, from the near end of the table, through a movable wooden hoop (i.e. the 'port' or 'pass' at the far end), then work back again to the 'king', which was a wooden pin - the final trick was to bring the ball to rest as near as possible to the king without knocking it over. The opponent aimed to carry out the same complex manoeuvre and points were scored by 'winning and losing hazards'. A 'winning hazard' meant that you drove your opponent's ball through the hoop, while a 'losing hazard' involved going through the hoop off your opponent's ball. Cotton described the game as 'five (points) by daylight and three by candlelight'. If a player toppled the king, he had to start all over again. If a player was a 'fornicator', which meant that he had passed by accident through the back of the hoop instead of the front, he had to 'pass twice through the forepart' before he could continue. The holes, which on the more expensive tables had string, or even silk, pockets to stop the balls crashing to the floor, were obstacles, rather like bunkers in golf. It all sounds a bit more like **Bar Billiards** than anything else, although there are echoes of **Croquet** in there as well.

Benjamin Strutt speculated that Billiards had at one time been an outdoor game, played on the ground - he was almost certainly right - although no-one knows exactly when the translation occurred. Norman Clare, now retired as chairman of the Padmore-Thurston Group of Billiard Table Manufacturers, devoted a great deal of time and thought to the history of the game and came up with two fascinating pieces of pictorial evidence. One is a woodcut from the year 1480, showing shepherds playing a game involving a hoop, a king post, balls and implements to propel them, on a gravel pitch surrounded by a low wickerwork fence. The other is an engraving of 1694 which depicts Louis XIV of France engaging one of his courtiers in what is clearly the same game but indoors and raised to table height.

The outdoor game is examined in more detail elsewhere (see p. 159 for an account of **Mell**, or **Lawn Billiards**); we now follow the intriguing trails which lead through Billiards to **Snooker**, Bar Billiards, **Bagatelle** and **Pool**. They are all cue games and, as Cotton pointed out, they are played on a 'table green as grass'. **Bar Football**, because it is played on a table, is tucked into the end of this section.

Billiards

In the second half of the 18th century, a cultural chasm opened up between Britain and the rest of Europe as far as Billiards was concerned. In France, Spain and Portugal, the hoop and the king were dispensed with - and so were the pockets, or 'hazards'. A red ball, the 'carambole', was added to the two whites and a game evolved based entirely on 'cannons' - cue balls hit so that they struck both the red and the opponent's white. This was the game that Mozart knew and loved and, it was said, derived musical inspiration from. To this day, British holidaymakers come back from Europe, or former European colonies, baffled by the bizarre game that they've seen played with enormous enthusiasm in corner cafés - 'billiards without pockets' - which is known variously as **Carrom Billiards**, **Carambole** or **Carambola**, and **Three Cushion Billiards**.

The hoop and the king disappeared from the British billiard table too, but the pockets, now numbering six (one at each corner and one in the centre of each long side) became not obstacles, but objects of the game. The French idea of the third ball, the red, was adopted and gradually the British game evolved, with points scored not just for cannons, but for going in off white or red and potting white or red. This was the version of Billiards carried to those parts of the world under British power or influence, while the French and Spanish empires went pocketless.

Hustlers were about at the very early stage of the game's development, especially around tables in London taverns and coffee houses. In 1796, Sir John Fielding, Chief Magistrate at Bow Street, warned against 'sharpers', as they were known: 'If one finds you in the least inclination to Cards, Dice, the Billiard Table, Bowling Green or any other form of gambling, you are morally sure to be taken in, for this sort of gentry are adepts in all the arts of knavery and trickery . . . avoid him as a pest.' On the other hand, Queen Victoria, as a young princess, was an early devotee and records a game – with evident enjoyment – in her diary in 1832, when she was only 13 years old. A table was delivered to Windsor Castle soon after her coronation in 1837 and another to Buckingham Palace in 1840. This set the seal of approval on the game and the nobility and gentry took it up with even greater enthusiasm – no aristocratic home was complete without its billiard room.

During Queen Victoria's reign, the equipment needed for the game improved dramatically. Wooden beds, list cushions and coarse baize gave way to slate beds, vulcanised rubber cushions and fine, smooth cloth. Specialist manufacturers, like John Thurston, plied their trade using wool from Hungary, South Germany and the Balkans, rubber from Malaysia, timber from Britain and South America and slate from North Wales. Cues were pointed, tipped and chalked, while it was estimated that 12 000 elephants were slaughtered in a single year to provide sufficient billiard balls for Britain – only four balls could be carved from a single tusk. Fortunately, a substitute was found – in 1868, John Wesley Hyatt and Peter Kinnear developed a ball made of cellulose nitrate, camphor and finely ground animal bones. However, it had a tendency to explode if struck too forcibly, and was eventually replaced by various sorts of plastic.

The Billiards Association was formed in 1885 and laid down definitive rules for all the games then played on billiard tables in Britain; it was a long and interesting list and included games with extra balls added to the original three. It seems that you could play not just Billiards, but **Life Pool**, **Black Pool**, **Russian pool** (or **Slosh**), **Mug's Pool**, **Pyramids**, **Cork Pool**, **Coronation Cork Pool Billiards**, **Skill Pool** and **Shell Out**. At their meeting held on 11 December 1900, the Billiards Association decided it was time to add another game to their collection. It was called Snooker.

Snooker

There are no mysteries about the origins of Snooker; its history is very well documented, and it was an inspired amalgam of at least three earlier games – Pyramids, Black Pool and Life Pool.

Pyramids was played with 15 red balls, set up in a triangle at the far end of the table, and a single white cue ball. You set out to pot more of the reds than your opponent and won money on the difference between your total and his. Black Pool added a black ball to Pyramids and you had to pot the black after you potted a red. For Life Pool, each player had his own coloured ball and was allowed three 'lives' – he lost a life each time his own ball was potted by an opponent. There were different sets of Life Pool balls, depending on how many people wanted to play; the largest set, for 12 players, consisted of white, red, spot yellow, spot green and spot brown. Some of these games, sometimes under different names, are still played occasionally – usually for money – by hustlers in quiet pubs and clubs. Joe Davis played Black Pool, which he called **Pink Pool**, gambling with Derbyshire miners in the 1920s. Alex Higgins played Life Pool, to make a few pounds, in a club called The Jampot, in Belfast, in the 1960s.

A precise history of Snooker was outlined by the late Sir Compton Mackenzie, who interviewed the inventor of the name, Colonel Sir Neville Chamberlain, just before the Second World War, when that gentleman was in his 80s. The game apparently emerged in Jubblepore, India, in the monsoon season of 1875: 'It befell during the Rains that Sir Neville, then a young subaltern in the Devonshire Regiment, anxious to vary the game of Black Pool which was being played every long wet afternoon on the Mess billiard table, suggested putting down another coloured ball, to which others of different values were gradually added.'

The name of the game emerged when a player missed an easy shot and Sir Neville called out, 'Why, you're a regular snooker!' The sobriquet was considered appropriate since, at that time, it was used to describe first year army cadets at Woolwich. Sir Neville neatly sidestepped a thumping by consoling the player, saying that they were all 'snookers' at this new game.

Early descriptions of the new game are confused and confusing, since different colours were placed on different spots and awarded different values – until 1882, when an officers' committee meeting at Ootacamund, in the Nilgiri Hills in southern India, set out the rules upon which everyone finally agreed, and which are recognised to this day. There is a plaque in the 'Ooty Club' in Ootacamund to commemorate this historic achievement.

Another character now enters the story – John

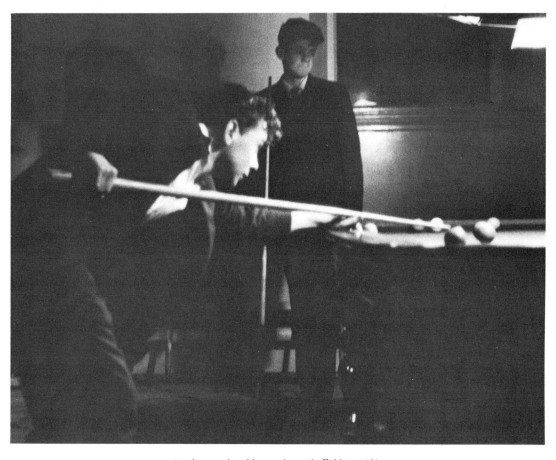

Snooker, as played by youths in Sheffield, in 1963.

Roberts, a professional Billiards player and British champion, undertook an exhibition tour of India, paid for by an assortment of Indian princes. Billiard tables were hauled about that vast country on the backs of elephants so that Roberts could display his skills. From one of his patrons, the Maharaja of Cooch Behar, Roberts picked up the rules of the new game of Snooker – the Maharaja having got them from the Ooty Club. When he got back to Britain, in 1885, Roberts spread the word.

However, it took a long time for Snooker to gain general approval and even longer for it to overhaul Billiards in popularity. Norman Clare points out that, in the mid-1930s, a billiard hall with 15 tables would require 15 sets of billiard balls and only three or four sets of snooker balls. After the Second World War, the situation was completely reversed and there would be 15 sets of snooker balls and only five or six sets of billiard balls required.

Many billiard halls and billiard rooms in pubs closed down in the 1950s, killed off, it was said, by the growing popularity of television. Ironically, when television went into colour it proved to be the kiss of life for Snooker. Philip Lewis, a BBC producer in Birmingham, developed the game for the small screen; the first transmission of *Pot Black* was on 23 July 1969. There were teething troubles – in the early days the studio had to be filled with cleaners and barmaids to provide a 'studio audience'. Lighting was a problem because strong lights dried out the cloth on the tables, making the balls run faster, and light reflected off the balls, causing players to misjudge angle and distance. On one occasion, new formica strips along the top of the cushions melted in the heat, burning the players' hands. On other occasions, light bulbs exploded and rain came in through the roof and fell on a table in play. The legends multiplied, but gradually the game became more popular with viewers, culminating in 1985 with a final between Steve Davis and Dennis Taylor, which was watched by 18.5 million people, 45 per cent of the viewing population.

Nowadays, it is so familiar and so popular here that it is sometimes difficult to grasp that Snooker is almost as peculiarly idiosyncratic and insular as **cricket** - it is a relatively obscure cue game played in Britain but in very few other places with any great enthusiasm. Pool is far more popular in America and Australia, and Carom Billiards is more favoured in Europe. When Steve Davis lost that epic television final on the last ball to Dennis Taylor in 1985, his manager Barry Hearn took him off to Brazil to play the local version of snooker against Rui Chapeau, the Brazilian champion. **Brazilian Snooker**, one of the many South American cue games, is played on an 8-ft table with a single red. The game was televised and watched by 40 million viewers - more than twice the number for *Pot Black*.

As we have seen, there were many games played on a billiard table with various numbers and combinations of colours. One of my favourites, apparently played on the battleship HMS *Nelson* in the late 1920s, consisted of seven officers, each holding a colour on the appropriate spot, during rough seas. On the command 'Let go!' the balls were freed and the first one to roll into a hole won money for its minder from all the other players.

It might be difficult to reproduce the conditions for the *Nelson* game on dry land, but there is another easy gambling game you can play - see who can pick up the most snooker balls in one hand from the centre of the table, without using the side cushions for help. Five is the average achievement, but George Hunt from Barnsley, South Yorkshire, holds the record, which is nine.

For the normal game of Snooker, there are 22 balls on the table to begin with - the white cue ball, 15 red balls worth 1 point each when potted, yellow (2), green (3), brown (4), blue (5), pink (6) and black (7). Joe Davis invented a new game in 1959, which he called **Snooker Plus** - he added two more balls - orange (8) and purple (10), thus bringing up the maximum score possible on a single break from 147 to 210. However, even he couldn't score a maximum and the game seems to have vanished, although you will sometimes find snooker sets which include an otherwise inexplicable orange and purple.

A full-size billiard and snooker table takes up a great deal of room and more and more you will find that such room has been converted into more profitable space in pubs - concert rooms, discos or restaurants hold many paying customers, whereas the old billiard room kept only half a dozen ticking over. Given the circumstances, I am surprised that so many pubs *do* still have full-size snooker tables.

In Accrington, Darwen and the surrounding area in East Lancashire, they have snooker leagues in pubs and clubs using three-quarter or even half-size tables and it is from this territory that I have picked up a couple more games which are sometimes played to provide some variation and relaxation from the rigours of normal league play.

Crash is a game for six players, each of whom draws from a hat a slip of paper upon which is written a colour - yellow, green, brown, blue, pink or black. You keep your own colour a secret. The table is set up in the usual way, as if for snooker. The first player cues off and must cannon off a red and the yellow - until this is achieved, by one player or another, the next stage of the game cannot begin. After that, the object is to pot a red, and your own colour, which wins the game. If you pot a colour other than your own, which you are entitled to do in order to confuse everyone, it is simply re-spotted. Crash, as you will have gathered, is a game of bluff and counter-bluff, as well as skill, related to Life Pool, but with some affinity with another old game, **Savile Snooker**.

The day after I had been introduced to the mysteries of Crash in Barnoldswick, Lancashire, I happened to be reading a splendid book called *Snookered* by Donald Trelford, the editor of *The Observer*, in which he described with relish the rules of a game included in the ancient annual frolics between the Savile and Garrick Clubs in London. In Savile Snooker you have to pot 15 reds without touching a colour - the penalty for hitting a colour is an undisclosed cash sum. If the yellow is involved in a 'foul' stroke, it is the custom of the assembled clubsters to call out 'bollocks!' It was Philip Lewis, the BBC producer who re-invented snooker for the small screen, who pointed out that green cloth games had always been popular with the upper and lower classes - only the middle classes despise them.

Golf is a game for four to six players, using only the cue ball and six colours, spotted in their usual places. You draw your colour from a hat (no secrets this time) and you have to pot it into each of the six pockets, starting at nearside left and working round clockwise to nearside right. Each time you pot your ball it is re-spotted on its original patch. If you miss, the turn simply passes to the next player - if you are snookered, or pot someone else's ball by mistake, you go back one 'hole', or pocket.

Bar Billiards

A form of Billiards known as *Billard Russe* (Russian Billiards) was played in Belgian bars and cafés in the late 1920s, and soon spread to similar establishments in northern France. It may have developed

Billiards – back in the good old days.

from a Flemish game called *Schuiftafel*, still to be seen in bars and cafés in northern Belgium, which involves striking flat wooden discs with a cue up a wooden table and into holes protected by pegs or skittles. On the other hand, there were odd versions of Billiards, involving skittles on the table, in Germany, Holland and Britain, at the end of the 19th century. And why was the game called Russian Billiards? Does that label give a clue to the game's origins or does it simply reflect a certain suicidal element in the play? All we know is that there were problems with the coin-operated timing mechanism on the original Belgian tables, which were solved in 1933 by a French firm, Dennis Frères, and Belgian tables with French timing clocks began to spread all over Europe.

David Gill, an English businessman, came across *Billard Russe* while on a walking holiday along the Belgian-French border in the early 1930s. He was much taken with the game's charms, came back to Britain and entered into an agreement with Jelks of London, a billiard table manufacturer, to make a British version of the Belgian table. It was said that the new tables, which were substantially built and slate-bedded,

were an improvement, technically and aesthetically, on the original design. Gill called his import **Bar Billiards**, a clever name with associa-tions with both the pub and the baffle-bar, which drops to stop play when time has run out. Other British firms took up the game as well – one of them, Sam's Atlas, working out of Hoddesdon, Hertfordshire, brought the game from Belgium at about the same time. Other firms simply copied Gill's initiative but had to think of another name for the game. 'Russian Billiards' and 'Russian Bagatelle' were considered, but dismissed as commercially unwise in the anti-Russian climate in Britain, in the 1930s. 'Skittle Billiards' and 'Snookerette' were two of the new flags of convenience which emerged.

The first pub to take one of Gill's tables was The Rose and Crown at Elham, near Canterbury, in Kent, in December 1933. You had to pay 6d (two-and-a-

A bar billiards table. The game was introduced from Belgium in the 1930s and remains popular in the south of Britain.

half pence) to play, which sounds trivial until you know that a pint of bitter at the time cost 4d (one-and-a-third pence). The game caught on quickly, in spite of being expensive at a difficult economic time. The first Bar Billiard League in Britain was organised in Oxford, in 1936, and a year later there were leagues in Reading, Canterbury and High Wycombe. Nowadays, the All-England Bar Billiards Association controls the game across 18 counties, mostly in the South, where league play is strongest and tables thickest on the ground. In the rest of the country, the game is comparatively rare, but by no means unusual. The Association lays down clear rules for the game, but elsewhere – outside their ter-ritory – there are interesting variations in, for example, the number of skittles used and the way they are set out on the table. There are different types of skittles, or pins, too – some are mushroom-shaped, others are pegs with stout wire cross-pieces through their heads, but in both cases the design is intended merely to stop the skittles falling down the holes and blocking the sink, as it were.

An Association-approved bar billiards table has nine holes sunk into its surface, each marked with its score value ranging from 10 to 200. There are three pins – two white ones either side of the 100 hole and a red (or black) in front of the 200. (If the pins, or skittles, are not on the table, then they are probably in safe-keeping behind the bar and available on request.) All you need now is suitable change for the slot machine. The cost of a game, expensive to begin with in 1933 (at 6d), was pegged at that price until the 1960s, but has now gone up to 50p, or in some cases £1. Economists might argue that a game of Bar Billiards has always been index-linked to the price of a pint.

The coin, or token, releases one red and seven white balls and the clock can be adjusted to offer any game time from five to 20 minutes, but a League-approved clock should give between 15½ and 19 minutes' play. To begin a game, the red ball is spotted before the red pin, then one white ball placed within the D on the baulk line and fired off. You must can-non off the red on this first shot, and subsequently hit either the red, if it is available, or a white in play before going in off or potting a ball to score. Once a ball is holed, it disappears and rolls back towards you under the table, to re-emerge in a compartment of the tray at the near end of the table. The hole is num-bered, as is the return compartment, so it is a simple matter to keep track of your shot score. The accumu-lated total is tracked on a snooker-type scoreboard at the head of the table.

The red counts double the score of whichever hole it goes down. In most areas it is then used as the next cue ball; in some places, it is re-spotted and fired at with another white. If you get to that stage of accumulated incompetence which leaves *all* the balls in play on the table, then the nearest ball to the baulk line is pulled back and used as the cue ball. If a ball leaves the table, or rebounds back from play and comes to rest between the baulk line and the near cushion, the current break is lost.

The pins are hazards, far more dangerous than bunkers to a golfer – if you tumble one of the white ones, you lose your current break and play reverts to your opponent. If the red (sometimes the black)

skittle goes down, you lose your entire game score and have to start again from zero – exactly the same principle as with the kingpost or pin back in the early Billiards of Charles Cotton's day.

Eventually, your time will run out, the clock will stop whirring and the baffle-bar will fall, so that balls which are potted will no longer return to the ball tray. Play continues, using the nearest ball to the baulk line as cue ball. When there is only one ball left, the last flourish of the game takes place. The ball is placed on the spot on the baulk line and must be struck in such a way that it rebounds off the side cushion and sinks gently into the 200 hole. The red pin looms menacingly over this hole, so there is a fair chance that you will knock it over instead of potting the ball, and thus lose the entire game on the last shot of all.

Bar Billiards can be a game of astronomical scores. In league play, I am reliably informed, individ-ual scores of 12 000 are not considered unusual. In fact, the current highest break in league play is the astounding 28 530, clocked up by Keith Sheard, in 19 minutes and five seconds, at the Crown and Thistle, Headington, Oxford, in July 1984. A deter-mined team of five players also got themselves into *The Guinness Book of Records* by scoring 1 754 733 in 24 hours at The Shipwright's Arms, Chatham, Kent, in May 1990.

Some experts, finding the normal game too easy, have invented a fiendish set of additional rules which render the game all but impossible for mere mortals. Only nominated scores are counted – if a break exceeds or fails to reach the nomination it is not allowed. A call of '200 plus', however, is awarded all points over and above 200. If the cue ball goes in off red, it counts double. The final 'new' rule is the real killer – all nominated calls must be for shots directed at holes closely guarded by pins. 'All this means,' said the inventors, when they revealed their new game in a magazine called *Games and Puzzles,* in 1973, 'is that instead of continual pots and in-offs, shots off the cushion and in off cannons become equally impor-tant and much more fascinating aspects of the game.'

To watch truly dazzling Bar Billiards, you should try to see a big match organised by the Association. There is an All-England Pairs Championship in Eastbourne in March, spread over three days at the Lansdowne Hotel. The singles confrontations – one contest for men, the other for women – are held in the recreation rooms of the Atomic Energy Establish-ment at Harwell in June – the same venue hosts the Inter-county Championships in September. Eric Hill, the secretary of the All-England Bar Billiards Associ-ation, reckons that the All-England Championships, organised by the Wokingham League at the Crest Hotel, High Wycombe, in May is 'the big one', although some might argue that the British Isles Open Championship, held each November in Jersey, is the event to win, if only because the competition is tough and the prize is a holiday for two in an exotic location.

Players from the Channel Islands and the mainland are prone to good-humouredly rubbishing each others' talents because a simple difference in rules divides their game and ensures that home-table advantage reigns almost supreme. The Channel Islanders always fire from the spot in the centre of the baulk line, while the English players are allowed to operate from anywhere along the straight side of the D along the baulk line, once a game is in progress. Civil wars have been fought for less, but Bar Billiards is a friendly game and the mainlanders flock to Jersey for the November Championship and the islanders invade the mainland to take part in other big contests. There is also an annual International match – a Jersey 'select' versus England mixed team event, played in February, alternate years home and away. Jersey select from 354 registered players, England from 9000, but the islanders still tend to win at home. The oldest fixture in the calendar is the Inter-Island contest between Jersey and Guernsey, which has been going on at the end of their league season each May, home and away, for 35 years.

The popularity of any pub game tends to rise and fall with the fads of fashion. Although Bar Billiards is still a reasonably common sight in pubs all over the country, I get the impression that it is on a slow downward curve. This may come as a surprise to places like Oxford, High Wycombe, or Jersey, where the game flourishes as ever, but elsewhere it has been replaced by the 'new' game of Pool. In some places, the landlord has calculated that a dining table, with paying customers, will turn over more money and more profit than splitting a bar billiards table's take with the rental company. Twenty years ago, High Wycombe had five divisions, each with 16 teams; now it has three divisions with 14 teams in its league. One renter told me that, in the 1970s, there were 120 tables within five miles of the clock tower in the centre of Oxford, now there are between 40 and 50. On the other hand, Bar Billiards is far too good a game to disappear, and there are companies renovating and selling old tables successfully, so the nostalgia factor is already at work.

Bagatelle

Very little is known about the origins of **Bagatelle**, but in Britain, from about 1775 to 1850, it was cer-

tainly as popular and widespread as Billiards. John Thurston, who was so influential in the development of Billiards, advertised himself for many years as a 'maker of Billiard and Bagatelle Tables and Billiard Furniture'. His sales journals have been preserved and they show that between 1818 and 1845 the firm was busy putting Bagatelle, as well as Billiards, into London pubs. Sadly, no-one plays Bagatelle any more in London – all Thurston's tables have vanished, as have most of the pubs he supplied.

In 1845, Bagatelle was popular enough to be restricted; Section 13 of the Gaming Act of that year forbade 'play on a public billiard table, or bagatelle table, from 1 am to 8 am, and on Sundays, Christmas Day and Good Friday'.

When I first started seriously looking into the repertoire of pub games, it seemed to me that Bagatelle was a dinosaur, an historical shadow, a game which had enjoyed a long burst of popularity, but had then been overtaken and overwhelmed, Darwinian fashion, by fitter beasts like Billiards, Snooker and Pool.

In Chester, in the early 1970s, I discovered quite by accident a group of people who still played Bagatelle and appeared to be wholly unaware that they were supposed to be extinct. They had a league, involving some 30 pubs in two divisions, and they pointed out that they were by no means alone – there were similar organisations involving pubs and clubs, in the nearby towns of Queensferry, Flint and St Helens. The Chester and District Bagatelle League is still going strong and is still organised into two divisions, although a few tables have vanished in the last 20 years. Since that first discovery, I've found that the game is played not just in the North West, but in a dozen pubs in Bristol, a few venues in Walsall, and a league of 40 pubs and clubs in Coventry . . . I'm reminded of the story of the field harvest mouse which, until ten years ago, scientists had assumed to be all but extinct – then a researcher conducted a thorough exploration of a few fields and found that, far from being extinct, the creature was living in its thousands in perfectly happy obscurity.

Confusion often arises between Bagatelle proper, which is played on long narrow tables, and what I choose to call **Children's Bagatelle**, which is played with marbles on a 2ft-long wooden board, studded with patterns made out of small nails. This latter pastime has a long history too, and eventually evolved into **Pinball** and **Pachisi**, a Japanese gambling game, but all that is another story entirely. I mention it only because at least one pub in the current *Good Beer Guide* advertises Bagatelle amongst its attractions, but this refers to the kids' game.

A match-play bagatelle table can be anything from

The Boys Billiard Championship, 1954, in progress at Burroughs & Watts Hall, Soho Square, London.

6 to 10ft long, 2 to 3ft wide and 2ft 6in from the floor. It is semi-circular at the far end, and cushioned and clothed like a conventional billiard or snooker table. Instead of holes, or pockets, it has nine numbered wooden cups sunk into the cloth at the far end of the table; the 9 cup is in the centre, circled by numbers 1 to 8. Some tables, in particular the ones in Coventry and Bristol, have two stringed pockets as well, three-quarters of the way up, one on each side. I've seen working drawings for a table manufactured by Gillows and Taylor of London in 1771 and, apart from a set of rather delicate fluted legs, it looks much the same as a modern one.

There are several games which can be played on a bagatelle table. In the Chester and District League the game is as follows: a black ball is spotted in front of the cups and a player has eight cue balls to strike up the table, one after the other. The black *must* be hit before anything else can happen; if it goes into a cup, it scores double, if it remains on the table, it remains the primary target ball. The technique seems to be to get the black into one of the high-scoring cups as soon as possible – the longer it rolls around the table, the more difficult it is to hit, as it gets hidden behind the other whites. If the player doesn't hit the black first, then his errant cue ball is simply removed from the table by the referee and doesn't score. Once the black is down, any ball will do as a target, but the player must cannon off another ball to score – the only exception to this occurs if eight of the nine holes are already filled and therefore he has only one cue ball left. In this fairly unusual situation, he can cannon off the side cushion to score.

Bagatelle table

This sequence of eight balls is called a 'stick' and in a league match, each player fires off two sticks, then his opposite number from the other team does the same. When all eight members of both teams have done their dual stick stuff, the totals are added up and whichever team has the highest aggregate of points wins the match. The maximum to be scored on a stick is 54 points – the black in 9, counting 18 points, and one ball in each of the other cups, scoring $1 + 2 + 3 + 4 + 5 + 6 + 7 + 8$. You could also score 0, of course, and that's really quite easy – you fire off all eight balls, hit the black each time, but fail to cup anything at all. They call this a 'green field', or a 'Tom Jones'. A good team will register the occasional maximum and each player will average 40 or more points per stick.

The game played in the Coventry Mitchell & Butlers Bagatelle League is markedly different to the Chester League game – and it strikes me as being much more difficult. Coventry tables are large – most of them are 10ft long – and they have the two string pockets as previously described. Play is with two red and seven white balls; the reds are spotted, 6in up from the breakline, touching the cushion, one on each side of the table. They function as the black does in the Chester game, in that you must hit a red before you can score, and you must keep on hitting a red first until they are both potted or cupped. The additional rule is the killer – you must also nominate the pocket or cup you are going for. If you miss a red, you forfeit 5 points and if you slide into an un-nominated pocket or cup, you forfeit that score to your opponent. The reds count double the score indicated on the cup and a red in a pocket counts 20 points, while a pocketed white registers 10. The game is 121 points up.

There are about 40 bagatelle tables in the city, most of them in clubs but a few in pubs. The Club and Institute Union (C.I.U.) League operates on Mondays, the Coventry M & B League on Tuesdays and some teams play in both, so they have a busy time from October to April, which is the usual run of the league season. There are other events in the summer, notably the Mitchell & Butlers World Cup, which happens every two years and in 1991, was stretched across a series of weekends from the end of May to the end of July. The bagatelle world, as you might imagine, is a small one, and the competing teams are England A and B, Scotland, Wales, Ireland and a polyglot group calling themselves the Rest of the World. The Barras Hotel in Coventry is the venue and M & B go to town, supplying the teams with banners, rosettes, T-shirts and, of course, trophies.

Wherever it is found, Bagatelle is played on old tables. Peter Clare, the present managing director of Thurstons in Liverpool, can remember only one new table being built in the 22 years he's been working in the family business. Because they are so old, the tables have invariably developed individual characteristics and home-table advantage can be very strong – I saw a top-of-the-league team in Chester humbled by a mediocre outfit because the players found that all the angles they were trying to calculate simply did not apply to this 'foreign' table, which was wider and slower than their own. In the Coventry League, tables have to be inspected and registered before the season begins and, after that, cannot be repaired, or even repositioned, without further inspection. A little bit of hustling creeps in from time to time – Mr Simpson, the secretary of the Coventry League, says that in the past they've found teams up to all sorts of tricks to make a home table practically unplayable by visitors – slipping a twopence piece under one of the legs, for example, can produce some interesting effects.

Tactics in Bagatelle are difficult to describe and can only be learned through experience. The novice will find that many balls tend to perform wholly ineffective tight skidding turns round the semi-circular cushion at the top of the table, or tend to bounce over or flip drunkenly round the shallow wooden cups instead of settling snugly into them. At least one of the secrets of the game would seem to be to take things slowly and gently.

There are a few other games which can be played on a bagatelle table. In **Sans Egal**, one player takes four red balls and one four whites. The black is spotted as for Bagatelle (Chester version) and again scores double. The players take alternate single shots from the break line and each scores for all his own balls cupped by himself or his opponent, plus the black if he holes that. Whoever scores the most points in a 'hand' of eight balls cues off the next time. The game is a previously agreed 21 or 31 points up. Hoyle adds a further complication, that each player must strike the black until it is cupped – failure to do this results in a 5 point deduction from his score.

The **Cannon Game** is played with only three balls – red, white and black. Black is spotted as usual. The non-striker's ball goes up amongst the cups and varying local rules place it either between the 9 and 1, or between the 5 and 9. The striker, cueing off from the break line, attempts a cannon off the black and his opponent's ball, scoring 2 points if he succeeds and the appropriate score for cupping any balls after the cannon. He continues to play for as long as he can cannon, replacing the cupped balls on their original spots. Once the cannon is missed, play passes to his opponent, who cues off his own ball from the break line. The game score is fixed beforehand by the players involved – it can be anything from 11 to 31, depending on how long they choose to play.

Mississippi – an extremely popular game in late 18th-century Britain – introduces a new piece of equipment, a bridge, pierced with nine numbered arches, which is slotted across the width of the table between the striker and the cups. Each player cues off a ball and whoever gets through the highest scoring arch begins the game and plays all nine balls successively. Each ball must be cannoned off a side cushion, then it scores according to the arch it passes through, plus the cup in which it comes to rest. Players are not supposed to go through the same arch twice.

Trou Madame is played under much the same rules as Mississippi, except that the balls may be driven straight through the arches, without cannoning off a cushion first. In another variation on this simple theme, the arches score for the striker, the cups against him. Trou Madame was formerly known as **Small Trunks** and is referred to as such in Burton's *Anatomy of Melancholy*, published in 1621. It is still played by children in Belgium, who put the numbered arch on the ground and flick marbles at it.

It is generally assumed that Bagatelle must have originated in France, if only because of the name, although the French call it *Billard Anglais* and the Germans know it as *Tivoli*, according to Thurston's multilingual catalogue. I'm fascinated by the similarities between Bagatelle and Bar Billiards (the latter was known as *Billard Russe* in France and Belgium, you will recall). Bagatelle came first, but I suspect that Bar Billiards must have been developed from it – both games have nine cups, or holes, within the surface of the table, both involve cannoning off red, or black, before a score is allowed, and both are cue games played from one end of a long narrow table. More work here, I feel, for an historian with a lifetime to spare.

Pool

At the end of the 19th century, as the Billiards Association was codifying cue games in Britain, the National Billiard Council was working to the same end in North America. Among the games they sorted out, Pool was to become the best known. There were many different Pool games, involving up to 15 numbered balls and a cue ball and, to add to transatlantic misunderstanding, they all went under the generic name of Pocket Billiards. Pool tables came in various sizes, but for serious competitions the 9ft by 4½ft became the norm, a table that British billiard and snooker players would regard as 'three-quarter size', since their competition tables were and are 12ft by 6ft.

Pool North American style obviously developed from the various Pool games – **Pyramids**, **Black Pool** and the rest – known in Britain (and India) in the 1880s, but became much more important and widespread throughout the United States and Canada. It was known in Britain only as part of the action in a host of American films – when *The Hustler*, a Robert Rossen movie starring Paul Newman as Fast Eddie Felson, came out in 1961, there was not a single pool table in a British pub. The Pool revolution here began in the late 1960s and early 70s, pushed through by several shrewd entrepreneurs. By the time the sequel to *The Hustler*, a film called *The Color of Money*, was released in 1986, the British Association of Pool Table Operatives reckoned that there were 45 000 tables in pubs and clubs in the UK. The transformation has been truly astounding. A game which was completely unknown some 20 years ago has now become the most familiar pastime in the British pub. In fact, the only comparison would be the swamping of pubs by trebles dartboards in the 20 years following the Second World War.

There is confusion as to who brought Pool to Britain, and which route it followed into the country. I've heard several theories advanced, with tables being brought in from Malta, Italy, France and Australia. In the early days, there was certainly a profusion of different tables – the first type I ever saw, being used in the Manchester and District Pool League in 1973, was made by a French company, René Pierre. It was 6ft long and had ring pockets, like a bar billiards table. The cue ball was 1⅞in in diameter, while the object balls were larger, at 2¹⁄₁₀. Rex Williams, the famous British billiards and snooker player, introduced René Pierre tables into Britain a year or so before that. He had seen coin-operated tables used in Australia, where he had gone to give demonstration matches, and thought that the game might catch on in Britain. Ansell's Brewery was persuaded to run a pilot scheme in half a dozen of their Midlands pubs. It was immediately successful and Mitchell & Butlers then became interested and started putting tables in their pubs, too.

At roughly the same time, or perhaps even before Rex Williams was enjoying his initial successes in the Midlands, Neil Hawke, the former Australian Test bowler, was involved in northern England in the distribution of a different table, called a 'Poolomatic'. It was also 6ft long, but had purple and orange balls of

1⅞in in diameter, plus a 2in cue ball, imported from Australia.

Another pool pioneer name put forward is that of Ron Hulme, then operations manager for a large leisure group, who saw Pool being played in Italy and introduced the game into Scotland, in the early 1970s.

Some television coverage may have helped the process along, although Pool has never reached a sizable television audience in Britain. In January 1973, the then American Pool champion, Steve 'The Doc' Mizerack, visited London and beat John Spencer, the English Snooker champion, at both Pool and Snooker. Prior to that, Pool had been added to the Olympiad of pub games encompassed by a Yorkshire Television series called *The Indoor League*.

The British Association of Pool Table Operators (B.A.P.T.O.) was formed in 1975 and in 1979 players organised the English Pool Association. It was then that both groups agreed to resolve the confusion about table and ball size – the standard table for competition games is now 7ft long, with a 1⅞in cue ball and 2in playing balls, although you will still see all sorts and sizes of tables pushed into convenient spaces in pubs. There are very few American tables

over here, so hardly anyone has much experience on the 9ft table.

The 15 object balls in Pool are individually numbered. Numbers 1 to 8 are solid colours, while 9 to 15 are striped. Sometimes, matters are simplified by having seven yellow balls, seven red, plus the black. When the balls are potted, they rumble mysteriously along channels underneath and on each side of the table, usually coming to rest where they can be seen clearly reflected against internal mirrors, through perspex or glass screens. They can only be released for play by a coin-operated machine – some of these have a knob which must be pulled out to release the balls. It is a useful tip to make sure that all 15 balls are actually free – I have seen otherwise solid and respectable citizens driven to apoplectic fury because they have released the knob too soon and found a ball or two still trapped in store. When play begins, the object balls, once potted, stay down for the duration; thus the smaller cue ball is not barred and will return to you along its own private underground track if it is inadvertently sunk. This barring of the object balls is important since it limits the number of variant games possible on a British pub table.

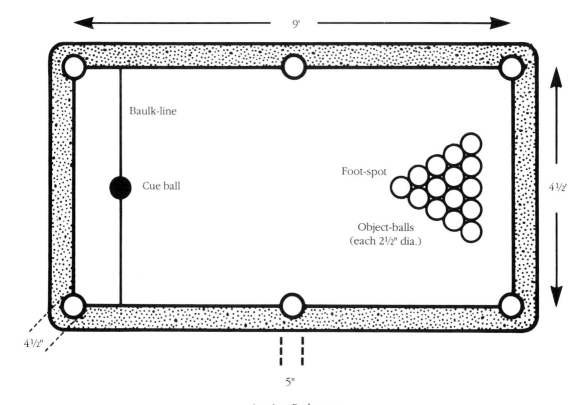

American Pool set-up

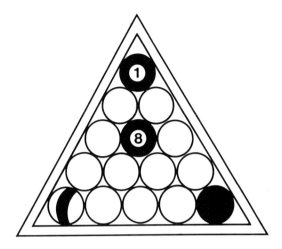

Rack-up for Eight Ball

In Britain, the overwhelmingly popular Pool game is **Eight Ball**, where the object balls are racked up so that the black ball, the vital number 8, is tucked securely in the centre of the third row - actually at the precise intersection of imaginary lines crossing the table from the centre to the top corner pocket. A striped ball is placed at one rear corner of the triangle, a solid colour goes at the other end - apart from that, stripes and solids can be mixed up anywhere in the triangle. The object of the game is to pot your numerical sequence, either solid coloured balls 1-7 or stripes 9-15, in any order, then sink the 8 ball black.

The game usually starts with the toss of a coin to decide who takes the break shot. The winner places the cue ball anywhere in the D on the baulk line and fires away at the object balls. He must crack the object balls firmly enough to pocket one of them, or at the very least get two of them to hit the cushion. If he *does* pocket one, then whichever sequence it belongs to, 1-8, 9-15, stripes or solids, becomes his target - he must pot the rest of them and then get the black down before his opponent can get his numbers and the black pocketed. If he pots the black before he has pocketed his seven-ball sequence of stripes or colours, he loses the game there and then - the same dire penalty applies if he shoots the black off the table, or goes in off black. Eight Ball in Britain is a much simpler game than Eight Ball in America, where you must call - or nominate - the object ball you are trying to hit and the pocket you are aiming for.

The general rules of British Eight Ball are similar to those of Billiards or Snooker. Players go alternately, a break coming to an end when anyone fails to pot a required object ball. There are a number of foul strokes which, if perpetrated, give an extra shot to your opponent. These include going in off any ball except black; failing to hit any other ball with the cue ball; 'jumping' the cue ball over another ball; and playing with both feet off the floor.

Eight Ball can be enjoyed by almost any combination of players, but is usually a singles match, or a series of singles matches added up to make a team event. The most venerable English contest is the National Team Trophy, first won in 1977 by the seven-man team from the Jolly Carter pub in Manchester. The first British Individual Championship was won by Dave Dolman in 1981, the first Ladies' Championship by Hazel Dabrowski in 1984 and the first Three-Man Event by the Royal Oak, Leigh, Lancashire, in 1985. All these events are contested annually in an orgy of Pool organised by B.A.P.T.O. at the Tower Ballroom, Blackpool, over a long weekend in November - you have to fight your way through various area and regional rounds to qualify.

When a host of expert Pool players are gathered together, they tend to amuse themselves by playing other variations of the game for money. **Speed Pool**, for example, simply demands that you pot all 15 balls in any order and in any pockets, as quickly as possible, against a stopwatch controlled by a sober and reliable referee. Everyone pays an entrance fee and the player registering the fastest time wins all the money.

In **Killer**, each competitor is allowed three 'lives'. The first player breaks off and is allowed one more shot; he aims to pot as many balls as possible until he misses one. His score is 1 point for each ball potted. The second player has to take up from where the first left off and must better that score, or lose one of his lives. When only one ball is left, the whole set is racked up again. Play passes round the assembled company like this until, one by one, players tot up three lost lives and drop out. The winner is, of course, the survivor of the marathon, who still has a life or two left, but has seen all his opponents fall by the wayside.

The game Paul Newman, aka Fast Eddie Felson, played in the film *The Hustler* was **Straight Pool**, also known as **14.1 Continuous**. A version of this is also played behind the scenes at county matches and major championships in Britain, when players are not involved in the official Eight Ball games. The object is to pot 14 of the 15 object balls, one after the other and in any order, leaving just one ball in play. If you succeed in doing this, the 14 balls are racked up again and the break continues until you fail to pot a ball. Your opponent then starts with the situation as you have left it. One point is scored for each pot. In the British variation of the game, each player pays £1 to enter and his name and score are chalked up on a blackboard, remaining there until it is bettered by someone else. The balls are racked up anew for each player. Thus, at any stage in the play it is possible to wander into the room and see at a glance who is winning and what the current winning score is; there is no limit to the number of times a player can go. Proceedings come to an end at an agreed time, usually before the finals of the major Eight Ball contest, and whoever has registered the highest score collects everyone else's £1 entry fee.

Rack-up for Nine Ball

The Color of Money followed the fortunes of not-quite-so Fast Eddie Felson 25 years on, and by this time the main game was no longer Straight Pool, but **Nine Ball Pool**. There have been considerable efforts to introduce Nine Ball Pool into Britain's pubs and clubs, since it can be played quite easily on any size of coin-operated table. It is also the game played in Europe, especially in those countries such as Germany and Sweden, which take American Pool very seriously, so there is some merit in the argument that top players should get experience of Nine Ball Pool before they venture into representative matches in Europe. However, there has been considerable reluctance to play Nine Ball Pool in pubs in Britain, I think quite simply because people feel that, with only nine instead of 15 object balls in play, they are not getting their money's worth.

For Nine Ball Pool, the balls, numbered 1–9, are racked up in a diamond shape, with number 1 on the point of the diamond facing the baulk line and number 9 in the centre of the pack. The rest of the object balls, numbers 2–8, can be mixed up anywhere in the diamond. The object of the game is to pocket the 9 –

but you must always hit the lowest-numbered ball on the table first. The player breaking off must hit the number 1 ball first, then pocket a ball or make two balls reach a cushion, otherwise a foul shot is called and the balls are re-racked for his opponent to start the game. In theory, you can win from the break, assuming that you hit number 1 first and pot number 9, but this rarely happens.

Billiard tables, whether of American or British design, have invariably been rectangular, but there have always been maverick manufacturers who have come up with something different. Monsieur Mingaud, the Frenchman who is credited with the invention of the leather tip on the billiard cue in the early 19th century, mentions a triangular table in his writings, although no plan or drawing of such an oddity survives. Thurston's produced an octagonal table in 1910; it was 10ft × 6ft and had two sides much longer than the others. The pockets were set in the centre of each straight section. Orme & Sons of Manchester marketed a 10ft-long oval table between 1903 and 1912. However, neither of these styles attracted customers and both were commercial failures. Undaunted by this, several modern manufacturers have come up with octagonal, hexagonal and circular pool tables and they seem to have had more success. One hexagonal design, called 'Rotapool', has some claims to practicality; the whole table can be rotated, so that cue play can always take place from the same spot, which means that pubs which haven't got space for a conventional pool table can put one in a cramped corner. I'm sure it's all good fun, but I bet you wouldn't get Fast Eddie Felson to play on one of those things.

Table Football

Football is indisputably an English invention, a transformation of medieval mayhem in the streets into a codified, institutionalised spectator sport for Saturday afternoons, followed – in some places – by traditional mayhem in the streets. It is curious, therefore, that the pub version of the game, **Table Football**, was developed not in Britain, but on the Continent and imported here approximately 50 years ago.

Rumour has it that the game originated in Germany, France or Italy, sometime between the First and Second World Wars. I remember seeing what was referred to as **Continental Football** in some pubs in Britain in the 1950s – and being thrashed in the early '60s by steel-wristed Frenchmen and Spaniards abroad, where the game seemed much more popular and was taken more seriously in bars and cafés.

In the mid-1970s, there was a flurry of activity in British colleges and universities, with table football championships organised by the Leeds firm which made Brighouse tables. Then, in 1978, the Americans arrived, in the shape of Tournament Soccer tables from Seattle. American champion players came over and, for ten pence a game, you could take on the likes of Doug Furry, Jim Wiswell, Jim Zellick, Larry Solk or Vicki Chalgren. If you beat them over the best of three games, you won £50. Tournament Soccer lost very little money during the course of the promotional exercise – and sold, it was said, almost 2000 tables in the U.K. within the year.

The British National Championships were set up with the first finals being held in Birmingham in 1978 – the winners went on to have a crack at the World Championships in Minneapolis. There were 7000 entries in the U.S.A., the first prize was $30 000 and it was all televised. Back home, the British Table Soccer Association (B.T.S.A.) was formed and produced a bi-monthly newsletter, with news, match reports and regularly revised national rankings. This buzz of interest and activity continued for three or four years.

Then, in the early '80s, Tournament Soccer lost popularity in the U.S.A., the British promotional effort petered out and, in 1982, B.T.S.A. was disbanded. There is now no national organisation and no local, regional or national championships, although there are still, of course, many pubs and clubs with tables and many enthusiastic individual players. There are European Championships, nowadays played in Germany on Loewen Automen tables, and there are still American and World Championships, usually on Tornado or Dynamo tables, but British players have no means of qualifying for these events, other than turning up and requesting a game.

During the course of a pub pilgrimage in search of Table Football, then, you may come across Brighouse or Vitalite tables from Britain, Loewen Automen tables from Germany, Garlando tables from Italy, René Pierre tables from France, or Tournament Soccer, Tornado or Dynamo tables from the U.S.A. – among others.

All the tables look pretty much the same to the untutored eye. The table contains two teams of 11 'men', rigid plastic or wooden figures, fixed on rods. The rods can be pushed – by spring-protected handles – backwards or forwards across the pitch, and can be twisted or spun round to give kicking power to the men. The two teams are skewered on eight rods, interspersed to give each side a 1:2:5:3 formation, from the goalkeeper forwards; the game can be played as a singles event, with each contestant controlling four rods, or as a doubles, with each pair in charge of two. The fixed position of the rods is cleverly devised to give exciting action – near to each goal, the keeper and two full-backs compete with a single line of three strikers. In mid-field, five men from each side struggle for supremacy. The coin-operated machine should provide nine balls.

In the days when there was a British National Championship, a game was won by whoever scored five goals first and the match was the best of five games. (The French, by the way, have remained interestingly out of step with the rest of the world, and René Pierre tables are built on a 1:2:4:4 configuration, which means that players are practically unbeatable on their own patch, but presumably must find it difficult to cope elsewhere.)

I play the game of Table Football with cheerful, slow and clumsy incompetence, so it doesn't make much difference to me what sort of table I come across, but connoisseurs say that the American and German tables are the best, with the fastest, smoothest action, and 'players' with rounded, rather than square feet, which means that the ball can be spun as it is kicked. Vitalite tables are approved of too, since they are supposed to be like the original Tournament Soccer models.

Table Football is a pastime which divides pub games enthusiasts into distinct and sometimes warring camps – there are those who will travel miles to a pub with a table and others who will flee the house when a machine is installed. If you are playing the game, your concentration and commitment are total. There is simply no time for reflection or sociability, and it is perfectly natural, when tension is released by a goal, to let rip with a triumphant yell. There are few rewards, however, for the other inhabitants of the room. The players, stooped and frantic over the table, block the view of spectators. The football terrace enthusiasm of the players and constant racket of the control rods inhibits conversation and there is always the danger, if the table does not have a plate glass top, that the ball will fly up out of the field of play and cause personal injury, or plummet into someone's pint. Table Football, then, is a healthy and vigorous addition to the pub game repertoire, but is perhaps best confined to a room of its own.

It is also a young person's game, since it calls for very fast reflexes, iron wrists and an eye keen enough to follow the ball which sometimes moves with astonishing speed. When 'table-football wrist' sets in (rather like housemaid's knee or tennis elbow) the time has come to take up dominoes and make way for the younger generation.

Evidence that cricket has always been linked with the pub.

Background

After the pub, the mechanical lawn mower must be one of Britain's more enduring contributions to civilisation. Edwin Budding took out his patent on the machine in 1830, Ransomes of Ipswich began commercial manufacture a couple of years later and by the 1850s, 30 and 40in models, pulled by horses wearing special leather 'boots', were keeping the turf in order.

Consider what happened in the 50 years after that – in a phenomenal flurry of creative energy, the Victorians reassembled and codified a list of rough and ready peasant games, and one or two cumbersome aristocratic pastimes, into the catalogue of sports we all know and occasionally love. All depended on carefully tended and uniformly cut grass.

At a meeting in The Freemasons Arms, Queen Street, London, in 1863, **rugby** and **football** parted company over the issues of 'pushing, hacking, tripping and shinning'. The first FA Cup Match took place on grass at The Oval in 1872; the first Football League season was 1888/89. In 1871, the rules for Rugby Union were drawn up at the Pall Mall Restaurant, London; in 1895, at a pub in Huddersfield, 21 northern clubs broke away to form the Rugby League. **Cricket** goes back a little earlier, but the modern game was shaped in this extraordinary period – over-arm bowling was first approved in 1864 and proved less dangerous than was thought, although prudent batsmen took to wearing 'unmanly' pads.

The County Championship began in 1873 and the first test match in England was played in 1880. (The earliest cricket test of all was between the U.S.A. and Canada, 30 years earlier.) The first coherent set of rules for **Lawn Bowls** was drawn up in Scotland in 1848/49. The most prestigious handicap contests in **Crown Green Bowling**, the Talbot and the Waterloo, began in 1873 and 1907 respectively. **Croquet** arrived from Ireland – with a misty history in France and Italy – in the 1850s. In 1870, the first championships were held at the All England Croquet Club in Wimbledon. In 1877, one lawn was set aside at the club for the new, improved game of **tennis** and, by 1882, the word 'croquet' had been dropped and Wimbledon became the All England Tennis Club.

It was all quite breathtaking – all the more so, since at the same time, the grass sports cult was exported worldwide. And, as we shall see, the pub connection in this green grass revolution was strong. **Bowls**, although a green grass game, deserves and gets a chapter to itself (see p. 109).

Cricket

César de Saussure, a Swiss gentleman visiting Britain, observed his first game of cricket in 1728. He noted that 'everyone plays it, the common people and also men of rank'. Beyond that, he thought the pastime far too complicated to understand or explain. 'They go into a large field', he said, 'and knock a small ball about with a piece of wood.' At least de Saussure could claim that he was a foreigner; our own Dr Johnson seemed equally bewildered by the noble game, and defined it in his dictionary as 'a sport in which the contenders drive a ball with sticks in opposition to each other'.

The origins of cricket are obscure. The French encyclopaedia, *Larousse*, says, somewhat disdainfully, that cricket is merely a modification of a game called, in France, *crosse* or *criquet*. British sources prefer to think that it was a shepherds' game in south-eastern England, where the downland sheep kept the grass conveniently short, long before the advent of the lawn mower. The term 'wicket' may have come from the shepherds' target – the wicket gate of the sheepfold. Early cricket bats were curved and could have been developed from a shepherd's crook; early in the 17th century there is a reference to the 'crooked staff wherewith boys play at cricket'.

As always, I prefer the historical evidence offered by the pub – there are 20 pubs in Hampshire called The Cricketers or The Cricketers Arms, and 27 in neighbouring Surrey. The geographical case rests.

The game had fringe benefits in its early days; the wealthy were able to gamble and everyone had an excuse to drink. The Authorities decided, in 1748, that cricket was 'a very manly game, not bad in itself, but only in the ill-use made of it by betting more than ten pounds on it, but that is bad and against the law'. No-one took much notice. On 12 August 1749, a cricket match was advertised in *The Ipswich Journal*, 'to be played between Eleven Men from Manningree, Mistely and Brightlingsea, and Eleven Men of Colchester; to meet at George Johnson's, the Sign of the Fencers in Tenant's Lane, Colchester. Wickets to be pitched at One o-clock, and play for Eleven Guineas, at Colchester aforesaid; where all Gentleman Cricketers and others, will meet with a hearty Welcome, from their humble servant, George Johnson'.

An early centre of the game was Hambledon, in Hampshire, where, in the latter half of the 18th century, the village team at Broad Halfpenny Down took on all comers, including '22 of England' and, more often than not, beat them. The Bat and Ball Inn, still standing by the site of the old ground, was once the headquarters of the cricket club. The Hambledon

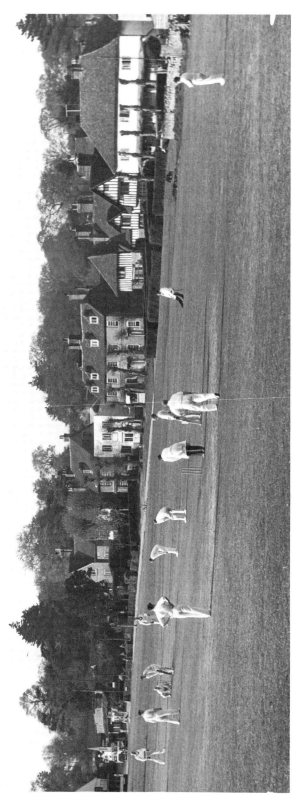

Think of England and you think of cricket on a village green – with a village pub nearby.

team was organised and run by wealthy patrons, but the best players were local craftsmen and farmers. One of the great all-rounders was John Nyren, the landlord's son, who remembered, in his old age, the halcyon Hambledon days of the 1770s: 'The ale too! – not the modern horror under the same name, that drives as many men melancholy mad as the hypocrites do; – not the beastlinesss of these days, that will make a fellow's inside like a shaking bog – and as rotten; but barleycorn, such as would put the souls of three butchers into one weaver.' He had something to say about cricket, as well as beer, and wrote one of the first coaching manuals.

Gradually, some of the rougher details of the game were ironed out – the curved bat was swapped for the straight, the stumps became three instead of two, the home side's right to pitch the wickets in the place that suited them was curtailed, and the fieldsmen were no longer allowed to stop or catch the ball in their top hats.

There were some interesting possibilities for development, which were not followed up. One such example comes from *The Kentish Gazette* for 29 April 1794: 'Cricketing on horseback – A singular game of cricket will be played on Tuesday 6th of May in Linstead Park between the Gentlemen of the Hill and the Gentlemen of the Dale, for a guinea a man. The whole to be performed on horseback. To begin at nine o'clock and to be played out. A good ordinary in the ground by John Hogben.'

The rules of the game had been drawn up, excluding horses, some 20 years before when a group of gentlemen gathered at The Star and Garter, in Pall Mall, London, and sorted things out over a drink.

Thomas Lord, one of the key figures in the early history of cricket, literally moved his pitch from site to site in London, before settling on the now famous ground – Lord's – at St John's Wood. He was always keen to provide a pub close to his pitch and was the lessee of a house called The Allsop Arms. There was a small mishap there in 1814: 'A shocking incident occurred on Thursday at New Lord's Fields. The landlady of the house had occasion to use a small quantity of gunpowder . . . and it went off with a great explosion.' The landlady, the ground and the game survived and Lord's has been a pleasant place to watch the game and enjoy a drink ever since.

Lord's is, of course, one of the grander (and more expensive) places to combine those two summer pleasures. Connoisseurs of Englishness might prefer village cricket and the village pub – and there are plenty of places where both can be enjoyed. The Poplars, at Wingfield, Wiltshire, has its own ground and its own team playing on Sunday afternoons and

Wednesday evenings from May to September. The Haycock Hotel, by the River Nene at Wansford, Cambridgeshire, has a pitch too, classically framed by water and willow trees. The Wansford-in-England Cricket Club perform most summer weekends.

At The Harrow, West Ilsley, Berkshire, you can seat yourself strategically outside the pub and enjoy the village pond to your left and the village green, with cricket three times a week in summer, to your right. The aptly named Cricketers, at Redbourne, Hertfordshire, has the local team on view from mid-April onwards. From the front garden of The Beehive, in White Waltham, Berkshire, you can see the cricket across the road; in the back garden there is a Pétanque pitch (boules for hire) and **Aunt Sally**, imported from the landlord's previous pub in the Cotswolds. There's a pretty cricket pitch, lined with trees in the approved fashion, outside The Two Brewers, Chipperfield Common, Hertfordshire – they claim this was the first British location for a televised cricket match and have pictures in the clubhouse to prove it. The Michelin guidebooks have a phrase – 'worth a detour' – it applies to all these pubs, and many more where two of Britain's best institutions, cricket and the pub, compliment each other so beautifully.

Bat and Trap

There are records of an ancient form of **Bat and Trap** being played at Ye Olde Beverlie Inn, in Canterbury, as far back as 1570. The pub overlooks a green where some of the very earliest 18th-century cricket matches took place, which all goes to show that the two games have been played more or less side by side for centuries; it also knocks on the head the theory that one game developed from the other. In fact, both cricket and Bat and Trap probably grew independently from some earlier amusement, perhaps **Club Ball**, or a medieval form of **Stoolball**. Nowadays, they also play **rounders** on the green outside Ye Olde Beverlie, so a foreign folklorist, if he stayed there long enough, could view three traditional, eccentric English games and go home very confused indeed.

The largest Bat and Trap league is that covering Canterbury and District, where they have over 60 teams operating across six divisions. There are two smaller, but no less lively, leagues covering the Medway Towns – the Courage and Dickens leagues – and another couple of organisations, one in Ash, the other around Ashford, in Kent. Bat and Trap then, is very much a Kentish phenomenon; it is extremely popular in that county, but completely unknown anywhere else in Britain.

The trap is a simple device for launching a ball into the air so that the batsman can give it a good clout. A Canterbury-and-District-approved trap is an oblong wooden box, between 22 and 24in long, 5in wide and 5in high. Set into the top of the box, there is a narrow piece of wood, spoon-shaped at one end and pivoted in the middle like a miniature see-saw – it is called the 'striker'. A 2¼in, hard rubber ball is placed on the spoon bowl, then the batsman taps the other end of the striker smartly with his bat, so that the ball goes up into the air. There aren't any rules that tell you exactly how to do this, so different players adopt quite different techniques. Some stand at the side of the trap and work one-handed, holding the bat as a tennis player might hold his racquet; others adopt what looks like a more cautious approach and stand directly behind the trap, dropping the bat, two-handed, onto the striker, then shovelling the ball clumsily but effectively down the pitch.

There are rules governing the maximum dimension of the bat – its striking face should be oval-shaped, not more than 8in long and no more than 5½in across at its widest part. This leaves a fair amount of latitude for local craftsmen, who have turned out all sorts of bats over the years, some looking like old-fashioned canoe paddles, others like distorted table tennis bats, and yet more metal-bound monsters looking like offensive weapons.

The pitch in front of the batsman is 21 yards long and at the far end of it are two stout, white-painted posts, 7ft high, set 13ft 6in apart. White lines, or white tapes, mark the side boundaries of the pitch. It is the batsman's job to get the ball off the trap and into the air, then hit it straight down the pitch so that it passes between the posts at the far end. The fielding side stand in a line between and just behind the posts. If the ball travels to them without bouncing and one of them catches it, then the batsman is out. This is a fairly rare occurrence, much debated in league pubs after a match. What usually happens is that the batsman's hit is good, the ball rolls between the posts, and one of the fielders simply stops it with his foot. Now the bowling ritual begins.

The trap has an extension on the front, which holds a 5in-square wicket, or flap, hinged at the bottom, painted white with a black circle on it. A bowler from the fielding side throws, hurls or trundles the ball under-arm down the pitch, aiming to hit and flatten the wicket. The line between the posts acts as a bowler's crease and the bowler must have one foot behind the line when the ball leaves his hand. Over-enthusiastic bowlers have been known to fall flat on their faces in an effort to get more pace over less distance – leaving just one toe hooked over the line.

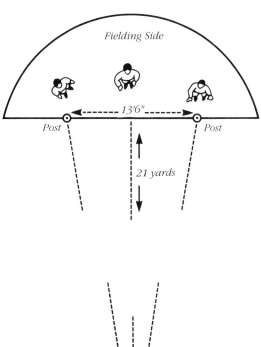

Bat and Trap

The condition of the grass pitch is obviously important – the rules require that 'the grass should be cut to an acceptable length'. It is not easy at the best of times to roll a ball along the ground for 21 yards and hit a target which is only 5in across – if the grass is long, unkempt or sodden, bowling becomes a matter of luck rather than skill. Home players, of course, know their own pitch and all its irregularities. The away team usually has some practice, before the match begins, to try and find the line which is hollow- and bump-free.

The batsman is not allowed to defend his wicket when bowling takes place, but must stand well back, affecting a nonchalant stance, and watch what happens. If the ball hits the flap and the wicket goes down, he is out and the next player on his side comes in to bat. If the bowler misses the target, then the batsman has scored a 'run' without actually moving, and the whole ceremony begins again – the batsman

The Kentish game of Bat and Trap – the bowling team are at work here.

strikes the ball off the trap and the next player on the fielding side has to try to bowl him out.

Progress is recorded, run by run, wicket by wicket, on a special score pad. 'CO' stands for 'Caught Out', 'BO' means 'Bowled Out'. The other way a batsman can get himself dismissed is by 'KO' which is 'Knocked Out' - this applies if he fails to hit the ball off the trap, or hits it so that it goes out of bounds, or doesn't reach the posts and cross the line. The most spectacular 'KO' occurs if the batsman hits the ball so high and so hard that it passes more than 7ft above the line between the posts.

In the old days, they used to have ten to a team in the Canterbury bat and trap league; nowadays they have eight. When all eight batsmen have got themselves out in one way or another, the roles are reversed and the fielding side comes in for their turn at the trap. Whichever team has scored the most runs when everyone has batted wins that part of the game, which is called an 'innings'. A league match is decided on the best of three innings.

There are all sorts of combinations at work for all sorts of cups and trophies, during the summer months from May to September, in Kent. There are men's, women's and mixed teams, four-a-side matches, plus doubles and singles tournaments. In July and August, you can often catch all day Bat and Trap festivals, orgies of activity, usually for charity. Aficionados will tell you that the most exciting and keenly-fought contests are the final stages of the Skam or Henry Court Knockout Challenge Cups. Truth to tell, I've derived most enjoyment from more amiable mid-league, mid-table matches where the folk are out for a decent game, but want a few beers and a few laughs among pleasant company. If you are lucky with your time, location and match and the weather is kind - then it can all be quite idyllic - a brick-walled backyard rather like an open-air room, bathed in sunshine; the clack and thwack of bat, trap and ball; roses and runner beans climbing and blooming; swallows swooping across a clear, blue sky; entertaining banter from the teams and supporters, and good beer. It's really quite easy to get carried away . . .

Bat and Trap players in Kent claim that their game is ancient, although the present Canterbury League was formed in 1922. Frank Atkinson wrote the definitive account of the history of Bat and Trap (and **Knur and Spell**) in *Folk Life*, back in 1966. He found a reference to **Trap-ball**, an ancestor of the Kentish game, in an early 15th-century French manuscript. *The Oxford Dictionary* comes up with the first English reference in 1591 - not far off the claims of Ye Old Beverlie Inn. Over at the Cambridge and County Folk Museum (not present day Bat and Trap territory), there's a commercially-produced Victorian boxed set, dating from the 1860s, with tackle and rules today's players would understand. My hunch is that Bat and Trap was another of those toys, evolved from a traditional children's game, which the pub took over in earnest sometime in the second half of the 19th century.

Stoolball

Stoolball was an ancestor of both Bat and Trap and cricket. Tradition has it that while shepherds were throwing at wicket gates, milkmaids were idling away their evenings by setting their three-legged stools on edge and throwing stones at them. Another theory has it that the stool was actually the bat, but no-one actually knows.

In 1671, John Aubrey described a more sophisticated version of the game, with some detail, in his *Natural History of Wiltshire*: 'It is peculiar to North Wiltshire, North Gloucestershire and a little part of Somerset near Bath. They smite a ball stuffed very hard with quills and covered with soale leather, with a staffe commonly made of withy, about three and a half feet long . . . A stobball ball is of about four inches in diameter and as hard as a stone.'

Aubrey's view of the geographical reach of the game was unnecessarily limited - it was certainly played, in the 17th century, in Lancashire, Bedfordshire, Wales and Sussex, and probably in other places as well. Oliver Heywood, a travelling preacher noted for his crowd-pulling sermons, was more than a little miffed, on Easter Sunday 1681, to see that the young blades of Halifax, Yorkshire, had not turned up for his performance, having better things to do: 'There was hundreds of people at Clark brig, in the churchyard, on the green and all along the town . . . playing at Stool-ball and other recreations, without any control.'

The game seems to have petered out, then flickered briefly in a revival in Sussex during Victorian times, as a genteel contest on the lawns of country houses. They called it **Juts**.

Modern Stoolball is credited to Major Grantham of Balneath Manor, Sussex. In 1916, he developed a new version of the older games, primarily to provide physiotherapy and a not-too-demanding sport for convalescing soldiers. It soon outgrew these somewhat sombre beginnings. The Stoolball Association as formed in 1924 and three years later was flourishing in Sussex, with over 1000 clubs in membership. The game is still hugely popular in its home county, although it hasn't strayed much, if at all, over the boundaries.

Stoolball has more than a passing resemblance to cricket. It's an 11-a-side game and the wickets are 1ft square boards, hoisted on poles, each structure being 4ft 8in high and 16 yards apart (although the bowling creases are only 10 yards from each wicket). The regulation ball is solid, and covered in leather; the rounded bat, about 7½in across at its widest part, has a short, sturdy, spliced handle and is flat at the front, bevelled at the back. Runs are made, but the batsman touches the wickets rather than the crease. A century, oddly, is a score of 50 runs and is considered a special feat – often a tiny commemorative plaque will be fixed to the back of the centurian's bat, to mark the event.

There are eight balls to an over, and the ball must be bowled underarm and must reach the batsman on the full toss; if it falls below the mark painted on the first 24in of the wicket pole, it is deemed a 'no-ball', with a one-run penalty against the bowling side. Most league matches are of 18 overs or so for each side.

No-one wears gloves or pads for this game, so players sometimes take home an interesting collection of bruises. On summer evenings and weekends you will see teams, sometimes women, sometimes just men, often mixed – competing in dozens of league and cup tournaments. The Eastbourne Area Mixed League, for example, has nine divisions, with promotion and relegation hotly contested each season. The game is such fun – I can't think why it hasn't travelled.

Baseball

It didn't occur to me until late in life that there was something odd in the fact that Derby County played football at a place called the Baseball Ground. Towards the end of the 19th century, Francis Ley, a local industrialist, laid out the ground and built the Baseball Hotel in the hope and belief that **baseball** would become Britain's national summer game. Apparently, the game was brought to this country by a couple of touring American professional teams and caught the public interest, being played largely by teams from the football clubs of the day. Derby and Preston North End, were early winners of the league championships then organised. Baseball reached its peak of popularity during the inter-war years and, incredibly, American record books show that an England team was the first winner of a worldwide amateur championship, organised in 1938. The last game of baseball at the Baseball Ground was in July 1944, when a team of Derby County soccer players took on a U.S. Air Force squad. The pub sign still depicts a striker about to make a hit, but the inside of the pub is now a minor shrine to the Rams, the Derby County football team.

There are those who argue that baseball was a game exported to America from Britain, not the other way about. Strutt describes a children's game of the late 18th century called **Tipcat**, in which a player had to strike the wooden missile, then run round a series of bases, guarded by fielders. If he completed a circuit of the bases without being caught out or in effect 'stumped' by one of the base guards, he scored a run. In Wales, especially around Cardiff and Newport, they play a game called **Welsh Baseball**, which they reckon predates the American sport, although the Welsh Baseball Union was not formed until 1905, almost 40 years after the first American organisation, the National Association of Professional Baseball Players.

Welsh Baseball is reminiscent of the American game but is played by teams of 11, rather than nine, who use a sort of cricket bat with a flat face, and dress more like soccer players – they turn out in shorts, shirts and trainers, with no protective 'armour'. They clout the ball as far as they can and, having done that successfully, scamper round four bases in a square called a 'diamond', to achieve a run.

There are about 60 teams operating in eight leagues, mainly in Newport and Cardiff, and they come from factories, old boys' associations, clubs – and of course from pubs. The Gower or The Tavistock pubs in Cardiff would be good places to gather information, although the games themselves are played almost invariably on specially prepared pitches in local authority parks; the season runs from mid-May until the end of August. There are four ladies' leagues in the area and, until the education cutbacks of the 1980s, Welsh baseball was a popular schools' game.

Besides the ups and downs of league play, there are cup competitions and representative matches – Gwent versus Glamorgan, for instance, and – most astonishingly of all – an annual Wales versus England international match, the English team emerging from six or seven clubs in the Liverpool area.

Football

Soccer, rugby league, rugby union, and even **Australian rules** and **American football** were all legitimised and codified in the 19th century, but shared common roots in earlier medieval pastimes which were infinitely bloodier, noisier, more dangerous to life, limb and property – and much more difficult to control. The game of football, through the streets and fields, with unlimited numbers on either side and no rules to speak of, was first noted at

Chester in 1533. The theory then was that the pastime had originally stemmed from an incident some 700 years before, when a group of Saxons had kicked around the severed head of a Dane by way of ritual celebration of a victory in battle. Then again, it could have been some ancient fertility ritual, or a symbolic battle between the forces of good and evil, or a signal of the passing of the seasons . . .

Whatever the reason, there were, up until the middle of the 19th century, at least 50 towns which had their own version of the game usually, but not always, played on Shrove Tuesday. The Authorities, predictably, were not at all happy - witness this order from the court-leet of football-mad Manchester in 1608: 'Whereas theire hath bene heretofore greate disorder in our towne of Manchester, and the Inhabitants thereof greatelye wronged and charged with makinge and amendinge of their glasse windowes broken yearelye and spoyled by a company of lewde and disordered persons usinge that unlawfull exercise of playing with the ffootebale in ye streets of the said towne, breakinge many mens windows and glass at their plesures, and other great inormyties. Therefore Wee of this Jurye doe order that no maner of persons hereafter shall playe or use the ffootebale in any street within the said town of Manchester.'

Some things never change. The main football activity in Manchester these days is confined to Maine Road and Old Trafford, City and United respectively, but certain elements from among their supporters, the Kippax Street Boot Boys and a few unreconstructed Stretford Enders, have been known to behave like a 'company of lewde and disordered persons' in the streets of the city after a football match.

If the rules of street football were a little vague, team selection was usually precise - often the rivals came from different parishes, such as those of St Michael and St Paul, in Alnwick, Northumberland, or the 'Uppies' and the 'Downies' of Workington, who were respectively colliers and steelworkers versus sailors and dockers - quite a match that must have been. In Scone, Perthshire, the bachelors used to play against the married men, while at Musselburgh, near Edinburgh, it was the unmarried women versus the matrons (the matrons, it was said, never lost).

There were conflicting views on the merits of the game. A French tourist of 1719 wrote that, 'In Winter, footballs is a useful and charming exercise; it is a Leather Ball as big as one's head, Fill'd with Wind: this is kicked about from one to t'other in the Streets, by him that can a get at it, and that is all the Art of it.'

In July 1765, a forthcoming attraction was proclaimed in *The Northampton Mercury*: 'This is to give NOTICE to all Gentlemen Gamesters and Well Wishers of the cause now in Hand, that there will be a Football Play in the Fields of Haddon aforesaid, on Thursday the 1st day of August, for a prize of considerable Value; and another good Prize to be play'd for on Friday the 2nd. All Gentlemen Players are desired to appear at any of the Publick-Houses in Haddon aforesaid each Day between the Hours of Ten and Twelve in the Forenoon, where they will be joyfully received, kindly entertained etc.'

However, things didn't turn out too well and the next issue of *The Mercury* explained why: 'We hear from West Haddon, in this County, that on Thursday and Friday last a great Number of People being assembled there, in order to play a Foot-Ball Match, soon after meeting formed themselves into a tumultuous Mob, and pulled up and burnt the Fences designed for the Inclosure of that Field, and did other considerable damage.'

Eventually, the Authorities decided that football must go and, one by one, the towns and villages concerned found that their annual punch-up transferred from the streets to the playing fields. Some didn't give up without a fight. At Derby, in 1846, the Authorities, having decided to stamp out the game, found that some miscreants had thrown a ball and fought for it down the river. A detachment of police tried to intercept, but were overpowered and someone threw a brick at the mayor. The culprit was caught but then rescued 'by considerable violence being offered to his captor'. The Riot Act was read and, led by a county magistrate, a posse of dragoons, specials and regular police set off to give chase to the ball. There was a tussle at Normanton, but eventually the Authorities won - there were no more matches in Derby.

Astonishingly, a fair selection of these games survived and are played to this day. Get yourself into the right pub on the right day and you can see football as it used to be - raw, untamed, and chaotic. It can be very entertaining.

At Atherstone, on the Warwickshire–Leicestershire border, on Shrove Tuesday, the ball is thrown from an upper window of The Three Tuns pub at 3pm. The game ends at 5pm and whoever holds the ball then is the winner. The ball itself is filled with water, although an amendment to the rules allows it to be deflated half an hour before the full-time whistle goes. In 1979, the police took half an hour to disentangle and disperse the scrum.

The traditional Royal Shrovetide Football at Ashbourne, in Derbyshire, was first noted in the late

17th century – the 1682 fixture was called off because of severe frost. The last attempt to stamp out the game was in 1891, when the town was swamped by police from all the surrounding districts. A Mrs Woolley was persuaded by enthusiasts to carry the ball under her voluminous skirts, past the police cordons and into the market place. There, from an overhanging window, the ball was thrown and the match began. Many of the players were arrested, prosecuted and fined, but the money to pay the fines was raised by public subscription and the game has gone on ever since. In 1928, the then Prince of Wales was persuaded to throw the ball to begin the match, hence the inclusion of 'Royal' in its title.

If you go into The Green Man or Blackamoor's Head in Ashbourne, you will see, hanging up behind the bar, a collection of brightly-painted and inscribed footballs. These are mementoes of the Shrovetide game, for each time a goal is scored, the scorer is presented with the ball, which – after the match – is repainted with coats of arms, inscribed and treasured forever. The pub is the nerve centre of the game, so many of the winners donate their trophy to the house, where they can keep an eye on it.

The actual game begins at 2 pm each Shrove Tuesday and Ash Wednesday, after an official lunch at The Green Man. The ball is thrown up at Shawcroft Meadow, where the Henmore Brook, which divides the town, is piped underground. All the locals born north of the Henmore play for the 'Up'ards', while those born to the south turn out for the 'Down'ards'. The goals, one the wheel of a disused water-mill, the other a concrete post marking the site of another water-wheel, are three miles apart. A great deal of the action takes place where the Henmore comes out of its pipe, near the centre of the town. Here, you will see huge, wet, muddy scrums, called 'hugs', which often go on for hours. Once play eventually breaks away into the fields, it is tricky to follow and you have to rely on briefings, often incoherent, when the match has finished. If a goal is scored before 5 pm, another ball is thrown up; in 1890 and 1967, a record three goals in a day were scored. In 1956, it is recorded, one player somehow got the ball into his car and drove to the Clifton wheel to score a goal and, in 1965, a 13-year-old boy scored, the youngest player ever to do so. Everyone seems to enjoy themselves immensely, except perhaps the shopkeepers, who have to keep their premises locked and boarded up, and the passing motorists, who are diverted miles around the outskirts of the town. The connoisseurs of the game now say that the Shrove Tuesday match is 'for the tourists' and the Ash Wednesday game 'for the town'.

The football at Hallaton, in Leicestershire, is intertwined with the remnants of another murky, ancient folk custom – the hare hunt, and the whole event goes under the splendid title of the Hallaton Bottle Kicking and Hare Pie Scramble, on Easter Monday. The 'balls', for the game are actually small iron-hooped wooden barrels called 'bottles'; there are three of them. The match begins at 2.15pm, after complicated manoeuvres in the morning, involving the blessing and distribution of a hare pie at church, the decorating of the bottles with red, white and blue ribbons, brass-band-led processions from The Royal Oak to the church gates and on to The Butter Cross in the market square, and from The Fox Inn to Hare Pie Bank, where the rest of the pie is strewn about and scrambled for before the actual game begins. It's a field day for folklorists as well as footballers.

The teams are Hallaton (numbers unspecified) versus the neighbouring village of Medbourne (and friends). The goals are a small stream at one end of Hare Pie Bank and a gap in the hedge at the other, and the game kicks off after a bottle has been thrown in the air three times. It's the best of three; if one side or the other scores two consecutive goals, they don't bother to contest the third. The winners go back to The Butter Cross and celebrate by drinking beer from the bottles, balls or barrels, perching on and around the monument.

This celebratory day was first recorded in 1770, although it had been going on long before that. In 1790, a new parson, full of zeal for reform, tried to stop it, and to divert funds to a more respectable cause. A chalked message informed him that 'No Pie = No Parson and a Job for the Glazier'. The game went on.

The Isle of Axholme, on the borders of Yorkshire, Lincolnshire and Nottinghamshire, is the venue for a medieval throwback called the Haxey Hood Game. Here, the proceedings are even more steeped in mystery, tradition and ceremony, but the actual game, once they get down to it, is straightforward and rough. The story goes that the game commemorates a gift of land in the 13th century, by a Lady Mowbray to a group of 12 villagers who saved her hood when it blew off as she was on her way to church. The present local vicar thinks it probably goes back even further than this, to dark, evil, pagan fertility rituals involving animal and human sacrifice.

On the 6th January, Old Christmas Day, (or the previous day, if the 6th is a Sunday), an 'apparition' calling himself 'King Boggan' arrives, with his attendants, at the Church Green. The full committee comprises the King, 12 'Boggans' and the 'Fool', all wearing strange costumes. The King has a long red hunting coat, riding breeches and boots and a hat decorated with artificial flowers. He carries a long staff with willow twigs bound around it and tufted on top. The standard Boggans wear red jerseys and jeans, while the fool has multi-coloured patched trousers, a red jerkin and a green skull cap with badges and a feather on it – his face is blackened.

The Fool opens the ceremony perched on a mounting block outside the church, making the traditional speech which explains some of the history of the game and the rules. He always ends by saying, 'Hoose agen hoose, toune agen toune. If thou meets a man hook 'im down. But don't 'urt 'im.' As he speaks, the Boggans set fire to damp straw at the foot of the block. They call this 'smoking the Fool'. It is at this point that onlookers tend to shiver – and not just from the cold.

Next, everyone troops off to the top of Haxey Hill. King Boggan places himself in the centre of a 100-yard circle of his Boggans and throws a 'hood' (a rolled up piece of sacking) in the air. The younger, apprentice players scramble for it and whoever gets it must try to evade the Boggan guardians and reach one of the local pubs. If he succeeds, his reward is 50 pence. (Time marches on; when I first saw the Hood Game, the prize was 5p.) Twelve hoods are fought for like this, then the thirteenth, which is a much stouter affair of stitched-up leather, is thrown up. This time, everyone joins in a huge scrum, called a 'sway'; the object of the exercise is to get the hood to your home pub.

There used to be three pubs involved – The King's Arms and The Duke William at Haxey, and The Carpenters' Arms, at Westwoodside. It went down to two when the landlord of The Duke William decided his carpets were more valuable than the tradition. The Duke changed hands and rejoined the tradition in 1990, after an 11-year absence, together with a brand new recruit, The Loco Wine Bar, in Haxey.

It often takes hours and is always dark before the sway reaches one of its goals, and the huge, sweating, swearing melee has been known to roll through walls and over parked cars and root crops. One year, I saw a film crew there; they lit up the scrum with half a dozen maroons on the end of long poles. The fireworks spluttered and sparked, and threw a flickering orange and red glow over the sway as it blundered hither and thither across the cold, dark, empty fields like a steaming slow-motion dinosaur.

Eventually, the hood is forced across the threshold of one of the pubs, the game is over and everyone takes a drink or two. The hood stays hanging behind the bar of the victorious house until the next year.

After a shaky year or two, the future of the Haxey game seems assured; the King and his Boggans now have the financial support of the Transport and General Workers Union, no less.

The connection between the pub and the *modern* game of football is strong; there are as many pubs named after football as there are those honouring cricket. I am especially fond of The Rover's Return, in Blackburn, Lancashire, which has nothing to do with Britain's favourite TV soap opera, *Coronation Street*, but was named in the 1970s, when Blackburn Rovers were relegated from the first division of the Football League. (They're still struggling to get back upstairs.) The Happy Wanderers, not far away, in Bolton, was so-named when Bolton Wanderers won the FA Cup in the late 1950s. The King's Head in Denton, Greater Manchester, used to have a sign up with a picture of Denis Law, the famous penalty-area predator, who played for both Manchester United and Manchester City. The Lion of Vienna, near Bolton, is named after Nat Lofthouse, the former Wanderers and England centre-forward, who acquired the title after a particularly torrid game against Austria, in 1952. Then there are the pubs named after the teams – The Gunners, The Hammers, The Trotters, The Magpies, The Saints, The Robins, The Spurs, The Sky Blues . . .

Every British league club has at least one local – an unofficial HQ for the diehard terrace supporters, where members of the board, opposition fans – not to mention angels – fear to tread. In the larger cities they tend to be somewhat spartan places with tough publicans and barmen, who are not too keen on selling bottles to take out. There's one more connection – there are a substantial number of pubs whose regulars fondly imagine that they can consume vast quantities of beer through the week and emulate their Saturday heroes in Sunday leagues. They form pub teams, join the leagues and, although there tends to be a high incidence of half-time sickness on the touchline, they win lots of trophies. Check the display of cups and trophies on the shelves behind your local bar – they are just as likely to be for soccer as for darts, dominoes, pool, or any other games mentioned in this book.

Knur and Spell and Allied Games

Knur and Spell, Nipsy, Peggy and **Billets** are pub games with a common purpose – that being to hit a small projectile into the wide blue yonder, as far as possible, using a stick or club. All were once vibrant and popular games, which now seem to be dying out and could almost be classed as endangered species, in need of care and protection.

George Walker's 'Knur and Spell' illustrates how the knur was knocked into the air from the trippet and how the distance achieved was measured by sticks pushed into the ground at regular intervals.

The knur, knurr, ore, nor, knorr, or ner is the projectile, or ball, originally it is thought, a small knot of wood – then a ball whittled from a piece of box-wood, holly or lignum vitae. I have seen and handled a 200-year-old hand-carved holly knur; it looked for all the world like a small, wooden golf ball, complete with dimples. In the 1900s, Staffordshire players introduced the 1-in pot knur, said to be made of white Wedgewood – the 'pottie' ('dobbie' in the Halifax area) – and this was generally accepted as an overwhelmingly technological breakthrough and taken up by all players. There were glass knurs too, the final small glass ball left after the local glassworks had finished grinding glass for sandpaper. If all else failed, the glass marble from the top of the old-fashioned lemonade bottle would do, at least for practice.

The sticks or bats are anything from 2 to 6 ft long, made of slender ash or hickory, with stout heads of various weights, round-backed with beech and flat-faced with maple or hornbeam, compressed down from 1½ in to perhaps half an inch. They are lovely artifacts, as complicated, efficient and beautiful as modern cricket bats or golf clubs – and were often made, in the old days, by the players themselves. The sticks had different names in various parts of the country; a regional roll call would include 'pommell', 'kibble', 'trip-stick', 'buck-stick', 'tribet', 'trevit', 'trivet-stick', 'primstick', 'gelstick', 'trippitt', 'dogstick' and 'cudgel'.

In the late 18th and early 19th centuries, the knur was knocked into the air from what was sometimes called a 'trippet' – a flat piece of wood or bone, laid in a small depression in the ground. George Walker depicted the game, imperfectly, in 1817, in Yorkshire. You can see from his illustration how the trippet, or 'spell', worked and how the distance achieved was measured by sticks pushed into the ground at regular intervals. I'm a bit concerned for the welfare of the three people standing behind the striker, not to mention the fellow standing directly in the line of fire, who looks as if he is about to get a knur straight between the eyes, but Walker was more interested in picturing costume than the niceties of Knur and Spell play.

There were four other possible ways of getting the knur into the air to get a clout at it – out of the hand, which is self explanatory; off the club, which meant resting the knur in a small depression on the head of the club, then tossing it in the air; and off the pin or off the spell, which require further explanation.

The mechanical spell, which seems to have been introduced in the late 19th century, is a fearsome-looking device rather like an inverted, iron rat-trap, with four spikes on its underside, so it could be fixed firmly in the ground. On top, there is a small cup, powered by a spring which can be tripped with a flick of the club or stick, to throw the knur in the air to a predetermined height. I've seen spells displayed as exhibits in museums and outside pubs as conversation pieces, but I don't think anyone would use them any more for a serious match – they can take anything up to half an hour to set correctly, and even then they are temperamental. Latterly, everyone seems to have gone 'off the pin', which is a sort of gallows affair, with a spike in the ground and a noose for the knur (see p. 106). Purists might argue that this is really **Knur and Sling**, not Knur and Spell, but the old name is still used indiscriminately.

There are two separate and distinct games played – **Long Knock** and **Scores**. In Long Knock, each of the contestants has, say, 20 hits, or 'rises', in batches of five. The winner is the one who hits the furthest on a single shot. The record is said to be a knock of 15 score 14ft by Joe Machin at Barnsley, in 1899. In the same year, Fred Moore achieved 18 score 12 yards, 1ft 8in at Lightcliffe, Halifax, but the knur hit the top of a stone wall and bounced on, so this is discounted by some pundits.

Scores calls for power and consistency. The field is marked out in concentric arcs of 20 yards and the match is decided over 25 to 35 rises, again split into groups of five. Only completed scores count, so if you hit the pottie an inch short of the 9 score line, you would still only score 8. A group of five rises might look like this:

$$8 : 8 : 8 : 0 : 7 = 31$$

Here, the player has cleared the 8 score line (160 yards) with his first three hits, missed altogether with his fourth shot and got past the 7 score yard line with his last shot. In 1854, William Sutcliffe, the licensee of The Royal George, Midgley, West Yorkshire, had 367 scores in 30 rises, a record which stood for a long time. Eventually, Joe Machin beat it. In one contest, in 1901, Machin, in his third series of five knocks, got:

$$14 : 15 : 15 : 13 : 13 = 70$$

a record that is unlikely to be bettered.

These matches were serious, professional affairs, with large sums of money riding on them and further betting throughout the contest. They were usually played downhill and downwind, in large fields or on the open moorland. Each player, or 'laiker', had an assistant and together they would prepare the 'spell 'oil' – the hitting ground – within the statutory 2 yards of the referee's peg; first the surface was levelled with a spade and buckets of ash, then the spell was adjusted so that it threw the knur to a consistent height and length. Only when the knur dropped regularly on a peg placed ahead of the spell would the laiker be satisfied. He then put in a heel peg and a foot peg, to make sure he would take up exactly the same stance each time. Clubs were chosen with great care, using different stick lengths, head sizes and weights and even different faces for various weather conditions – there were 'soft' or 'kind' heads for sunny days and 'hard' heads for dull days.

One of the great laikers between the two World Wars was Joe Edon, of Barnsley, who had backers who would challenge anyone. There are extraordinary stories of his contests; in one year he took on Walter Smith, the local champion of Greetland, near Elland, Yorkshire, and beat him. Smith went to Barnsley and lost again, then the third game took place in Greetland and all the villagers' money went on their man – some said there was as much as £500 involved. They lost. 'Greetland were skinned that day', said my informants, in hushed tones.

Knur and Spell all but disappeared from public view soon after the Second World War, although there were always players willing to put £50 or more down to back their prowess against a challenger and, if you were in the know, you could usually find a match, somewhere up in the Lancashire or Yorkshire Moors.

Then, in the early 1960s, at The Spring Rock Tavern, Greetland, the landlord, Jack Driver, started chatting with some of his older taproom regulars and eventually, with their encouragement, staged an exhibition day as a charity event, to raise money for the West Vale Old Folk's Treat Committee. One of the day's three contests was between Ned Helliwell, a 78-year-old and once 'undisputed Lancashire and Yorkshire champion', who hadn't played competitively for 30 years, and Walter Smith, Joe Edon's old adversary, who was then a 72-year-old and 'a little rusty'. They played ten rises each. Six hundred curious spectators turned up and saw Halliwell win.

There was a great leap forward in public awareness in 1969, when *Calendar*, the Yorkshire Television local magazine programme, took an interest, introduced a trophy and brought in cricketer Freddie Trueman (who had never heard of Knur and Spell until then) to present the show and have a go at the game. This time, the lanes to The Spring Rock were jammed with cars and extra police had to be called in to deal with an estimated 5000 spectators. Over the next few years, outstanding players re-emerged from old strongholds of the game, like Colne, in Lancashire, Grenoside, near Sheffield, Dodworth, near Barnsley, as well as Upper Calderdale villages such as Greetland, Stainland, Norland and Barkisland. It proved impossible to sustain the momentum – the contests for the title of World Champion in the late 1970s seemed to get bogged down by a combination of bad weather, bad luck and bad temper. In 1979, in a qualifying match at The Red Lion, Stainland, the Yorkshire players accused the Lancashire contestants of taking unfair advantage of weather conditions and wind speeds – they also complained that the cowpat count in the field of play was far too high. There were mutterings – although not proven – of sharper practice – treading potties into soft ground so they couldn't be found.

There was, by the way, an unnerving catalogue of malpractice in what you might call 'professional' Knur and Spell – subtle altering of heel or toe pegs so that the laiker's swing went microscopically out of line; sending children out with a second marked pottie, so that it could be dropped quietly, then 'found' beyond the original, which had been trodden out of sight; smearing a pottie with Brylcreem so that it swerved on impact off the face of the club – when you talk to some of the old timers, you begin to wonder if there ever was a straight game!

There have been some praiseworthy attempts to revive the game in Yorkshire. In 1991, there was a charity Knur and Spell match at Otley Cricket Club and a challenge match, with just six invited players, sponsored by Webster's Brewery, at The Bradshaw Tavern, Halifax. Both were unsuitable locations, with walls running across the line of fire, and nasty crosswinds making it difficult to follow the line of flight, but it was nevertheless fascinating to see the experts at work – the long, intricate preparations, the Zen-like contemplation prior to a shot, and an explosive yell as the club face struck the knur into the far distance.

Nipsy is a simpler version of Knur and Spell, played only in Yorkshire and especially in the Barnsley area. Even there, the game is sometimes called Tipcat, while in Lancashire and around Castleford and Brighouse in Yorkshire, there is a very similar pastime called Peggy. They all form part of a group of sports known at various times and in various parts of the country as **Bungs and Barrels, Stick-in-the-mud, Bad I'th'wood, Piggy, Cat, Catty, Trip It and Miss It, Tribet and Trippet, Dab, Peg, Trip, Kit Kat, Cat and Kitten, Whacks, Waggles, Cat and Dog, Peg and Stick, Munchers** and **Hornie Holes**. All are, or were, children's games stolen by adults and transformed into pub games.

The nipsy is the projectile – a small piece of lignum vitae, egg-shaped, with a nose or snout at one end. This is placed on the smooth top-side of a house brick, then smashed on the nose with a nipsy stick so that it flies into the air and can be hit. The stick is a carved-down mattock or pickaxe handle of hickory, just short of 3ft long, with the handle taped to enable a secure, one-handed grip, and a flattened spade-shaped head. The distances achieved in Nipsy are more modest than those expected in Knur and Spell and are measured in plain yards or metres, by means of a long piece of rope marked off with metal tallies and tethered to an iron spike fixed on the edge of the striker's base. All the materials for this game are fairly easy to obtain – perhaps that is why it used to be known, jocularly, as 'poor man's golf'.

Nipsy was primarily a miners' game. Thirty years ago, there were 50 teams in two leagues in the Barnsley region of South Yorkshire, nowadays they are down to six teams playing in a single league – two from The Engineers at Brough Green, two from The Wellington at Athersley, one from Worsborough Dale Club and one from The Ring O'Bells, Silkstone. Matches are on Sunday mornings, starting at 10.30 am and finishing neatly at opening time. The season starts on Easter Sunday and goes on until September.

The game has seven players to a team and each player has seven hits, or rises. The teams' total yardage is totted up and whichever team has the highest total wins the match. An average single shot could travel between 90 and 130 yards. Anyone missing or mis-hitting a rise in league play would have a nought put against his name, so consistency, rather than strength, is important. The highest individual total

Selwyn Schofield of Elland, a past champion of Knur and Spell, sets up ready for action. Strictly speaking, this version of the game should be called Knur and Sling.

score from seven strikes is 1159.2 yards, by Frank (Yank) Lenthall, in a match against Keith Steeples, who also hit over 1093.6 yards. Locals reckon this was the finest game of Nipsy ever seen.

A variation of Nipsy, known as Long Knock, is also played, but the record single rise is a matter of dispute. In 1962, Joe Cook claimed a hit of 208 yards at The Pheasant Inn, Monk Bretton, near Barnsley. According to reports in the publicans' newspaper, *The Morning Advertiser*, Mr Cook, a school caretaker, practised for hours and used what was described as a 'golf technique'. He was reputed to be writing a book on the game, but I have been unable to trace either the book or the author. If he did achieve 208 yards, it was certainly a stupendous hit. A few years ago, a World Individual Long Knock Championship was organised in Worsborough. there were 27 entrants, and the winner had a hit of 149.8 yards, which brought a lot of derisory comments from the old stagers, who could remember 'lots of 200-yard-plus knocks'. The dispute continues unresolved, and will remain so unless someone comes up with authenticated newspaper reports.

My late father used to play Peggy as a child in the back streets of Rochdale, shortly after the First World War and, from his tales, I had always assumed that it was a Lancashire game, closely related to Yorkshire's Nipsy. In fact, I now have to admit that they play Peggy in Yorkshire.

There was a Peggy league in Castleford, Yorkshire, inaugurated at The George and Dragon, in 1969. In the same year, the Castleford Historical Society organised a finals day for the leagues on Bank Holiday Monday in August, at the Queens Park Extension.

Peggy is very similar to Nipsy, although the stick used is smaller, usually made from a cut-down broom handle. A 2½in wooden peggy is placed on an approved building brick, bashed on the nose and clouted while in the air. A player is allowed three goes at a rise, but if he makes contact with the peggy in the air, the shot must count. In Castleford, they had six players in a team and three 'innings' per match. Yardages count in all games of Peggy, of course, but there is a crucial additional rule which distinguishes the game from Nipsy. Once a rise has been struck and has landed, the captain of the

striker's team can 'offer' the opposition a given number of strides to reach the peggy from the brick. If he accepts the offer, and one of his team can reach the peggy in the offer number of strides (or less), then that yardage score is void for the striker's team. Obviously, the striker's captain must try to make an offer his opponents can't refuse, but can't achieve, so the whole business involves dangerously fine calculations of distance. Each team also has a specialist 'strider', or 'jumper', who should have long legs and a great deal of energy.

In 1975, the Brighouse Round Table organised what was described as a Lancashire versus Yorkshire War of the Roses, with 32 teams. The final was between Batley (Yorkshire) and Ashton (Lancashire) and it gives me great personal satisfaction to report that the Lancashire team won.

Billets may have disappeared now, although only a few years ago it was played occasionally up on the high moorland above The Robin Hood pub at Cragg Vale, near Mytholmroyd, or down in the valley on a factory recreation ground.

The billet is a gently-curved piece of hard wood – boxwood, holly or hawthorn – about 5 in long. They were cossetted, when not in play. Some experts kept their billets at the bottom of a manure heap, others swore by pickling them in old ale or rum – it must have been an aromatic game! The club is about 4ft long and has an 8in cylindrical head, with a shallow groove cut laterally across it. The billet is balanced on the groove, rather like a drooping sausage, then tossed in the air and hit away. Distances were measured in scores, as in Knur and Spell, but the highest-ever billet rise, by Henry Horsefield in 1882, was only 11 score. Nevertheless, Billets contests attracted some of the best Knur and Spell players before the First World War and the prize money, side stakes and even off-course betting reached astronomical sums. The first prize was often a copper kettle.

They still have the Billets tackle in The Robin Hood, but it is kept in the attic where it gathers dust. The present landlord has never seen the game played and doesn't seem particularly interested, but has heard vague tales of Billet players 'round Castleford way'. The tales could be true, of course – on the other hand, it may well be that people are confusing Nipsy or Peggy with Billets.

A game of mixed bowls in progress at Saltdean, Brighton.

Background

The bowling green was once considered a great asset to a pub and was advertised as such. Sadly, although you can often see the advertisements, still picked out in stone, wrought iron or stained glass, the bowling green, all too often, has been lost – a victim of road-widening schemes, extensions to pubs or, most frequently, an expansion of car parks.

Faded photographs in local history books tell their own sorry tale. I particularly regret not seeing the green at The Wilton Arms, Denton, near Manchester, which had a surplus double-decker tram parked alongside, acting as a grandstand for spectators. The landlord, Oswald Knight, had his own name, the pub's name and the words 'Bowling Green' proudly painted in large letters where the adverts used to be when the tram was operational. Oswald, tram, bowling green and pub are, alas, long gone. There are, of course, still hundreds of pubs with bowling greens, but the losses, particularly in the last 25 years or so, have been grievous.

Bowls is a venerable pastime, which has been traced back to Ancient Egypt, Greece and Rome. In the Middle Ages, in Britain, the target seems to have been a cone, or stick, rather than the now-familiar jack. There is a tradition that biased bowls, another distinctive feature of the modern game, were developed after an incident in Goole, Yorkshire, on 31 March 1522, when the Duke of Suffolk – obviously involved in an away match – delivered a bowl with such ferocity that it shattered into pieces. The Duke dashed indoors, sawed off an ornamental ball from the foot of his host's bannister, and biased bowls were born.

Old Bowls

Southampton Bowls Club claims to have the oldest bowling green in the world, originally laid out in 1187; it is said that some form of bowls was played there in 1220 and it was in regular use for the game in 1299. They have an annual competition, the Knighthood Tournament, first played on 1 August 1776 and still trundling on. It usually takes place on the first Wednesday in August and goes on for some time. Competitors send two bowls to a jack which rests on a penny. One point is gained for each bowl that player has nearest the jack; the game goes on until someone has scored 7 points, a process which can take up to three days. The winner is dubbed with a 'knighthood' of Southampton's Old Green and thereafter has to be called 'sir' – at least while he's on the green. Old 'knights' are in attendance throughout, wearing traditional dress – top hats, frock coats and campaign medals inscribed 'win it and wear it'.

There is what might be described as a rival organisation, playing a game they call **Old English Bowls**, on a green in the old tilting yard protected by the walls of Lewes Castle, in Sussex. The pastime was first noted there in 1639, and the members of the Lewes Bowling Green Society still have some 40 sets of 200-year-old bowls – matched pairs of heavily biased spheres, each some 4½in in diameter and weighing 1lb 12oz. The 10oz jack is also biased and a further hazard is that the natural Southdown turf green, which covers an area of roughly three-quarters of an acre, has a pronounced slope to it, as well as many small hummocks and depressions. Bowling here begins from a point marked by a 'trig' – a small rubber disc (it used to be copper) and, after the first end, the winners can roll the jack anywhere within the green. The next end starts from the trig again, which meanwhile has been moved to where play finished previously. A game is won by the first player to get to 11 points.

Tom Paine, writer, polemicist, radical and an active witness to both the American and French Revolutions, was an excise officer in Lewes from 1768 to 1774, and a member of the Lewes Bowling Club. One of his biographers claimed that it was after a game on the green at Lewes, and a drink or two in a nearby pub, that Paine had the inspiration for his greatest work, *The Rights of Man*. I like to think that the inspiration occurred in The White Hart Hotel, which is the headquarters of the Lewes Bowling Green Society today.

Then there's the matter of Sir Francis Drake and the game of bowls he is said to have completed on Plymouth Hoe, before dashing off to deal with the Spanish Armada on 19 July 1588. I know this story to be true, since I clearly remember a large, coloured poster of the event on the wall of my primary school, but some writers have pointed out that a) the game was then illegal, b) there was no bowling green on the Hoe at the time, and c) no sane military commander would have delayed action, given the strategically precarious position the country was in at the time. On the other hand, there are those who would defend the legend with three counterblasts – a) a number of biased bowls of the era have been dug up on Plymouth Hoe, b) Drake is known to have liked the game and c) it was perfectly sensible to stay in port, since conditions were unsuitable for setting sail and he needed more time to assess the Spanish fleet's numbers and destination. Furthermore, bowls relaxes the mind wonderfully . . .

The Old English Bowling Association, which comprises nine teams scattered around the Portsmouth area, claims to be still playing the game that

Drake is supposed to have enjoyed on Plymouth Hoe. In places like Alverstoke, Emsworth, Bosham, Hayling and Titchfield, they use very heavily-biased bowls on wide, flat grass rinks, aiming at a jack which must come to rest within a box marked out on the grass. In a league match, there are 12 players to a side, divided into four rinks with three players playing two 'woods' each. The games consist of 25 ends.

The Association used to have pub teams, but now plays on club greens or on special park greens. I don't think that the bowlers of Southampton, Lewes and Portsmouth have ever got together to see if they could sort out a common set of rules to enable an Old Bowls national championship to take place – come to think of it, they're probably better off enjoying their own tranquil games at home.

Modern Bowls

Southampton, Plymouth, Lewes and Portsmouth apart, it is often uncertain which game is being referred to when you come across historical references to bowling, since the term was used indiscriminately to mean either bowls, ninepins or skittles. What was Charles Cotton philosophising about in *The Compleat Gamester*, in 1674, when he wrote: 'A Bowling-green or Bowling-alley is a place where three things are thrown away besides the Bowls; viz, Time, Money and Curses, and the last ten for one'?

Whichever game it was, the Authorities didn't approve and, until 1845, an edict of Edward III's, dating back to 1361, was erratically evoked in various forms to inhibit the game. Edward had been anxious to keep people's attention focussed on archery; subsequent Authorities wanted to keep people, especially the lower orders, away from gambling, drunkenness and similar diversions. It was thus made illegal for 'inferior' people to play bowls, and that included every sort of 'artificer or craftsman of any handicraft or occupation, husbandman, apprentice, mariner or fisherman, waterman or any service man'. The penalty for disobedience was a 20 shillings fine, but the law was relaxed at Christmas when the people were allowed to play, but 'not in their master's house or in their master's presence'.

Naturally, there were always ways round the law. If you were rich, it didn't seem to matter and in later years, if you paid State protection (i.e. if you paid cash for a licence) you could have your bowling green. A landlord in Bury, Lancashire, had a bowling green laid outside his pub in 1821 and had to pay a £100 licence fee for the privilege – a great deal of money in those days. Hundreds like him thought it money well spent, and did the same thing. Of course, at those prices, only the well-off landlords of pros-

perous pubs, with wealthy customers, took the plunge.

The great leap forward came when the prohibitive law was repealed in 1845; from then on, breweries often provided new pubs with bowling greens and even the lower orders were made welcome. The greening of Britain began.

There was, and is, a South–North divide, into **Lawn Bowls** (the flat green game), played all over the country, and **Crown Green Bowls**, which you will find mainly in the Midlands and the North West.

The object of the flat green game, indeed the object of most bowls games, is to get your bowls nearer to the jack, 'kitty', or 'cot' (the target bowl) than your opponent's. Whoever has his bowl nearest the jack after an end – everyone's bowls having been dispatched – gains a point. If there are two of your bowls nearer than the best of your opponent's shots, you get 2 points, and so on. The jack is a small, unbiased, white ball, 2½in in diameter. Bowls are known as 'woods', although these days they are much more likely to be made of plastic or hard rubber than lignum vitae. The woods are biased, and can vary from 4¾in to 5⅛in diameter and 2lb 12oz to 3lb 8oz in weight. In singles matches, each player has four woods which he bowls alternately with his opponent and the game is 21 points up.

The green itself should be pancake-flat and square, with each side between 33 and 44 yards long, and divided up into broad strips, or 'rinks' 19 to 21 yards wide, one rink being divided from another by lines of tautly pegged-out green twine. Games are played up and down the rinks, with up to six or seven matches possible on a green at any one time.

These are just the essential details, so that the species might be identified. The wonderful complications of green speeds, drawing, guarding, trailing and driving shots, spin, arcs of delivery, gradations of bias and the rules of specific games I leave to more specialised textbooks.

The other game is Crown Green Bowling, played mostly in Lancashire, Greater Manchester, North Cheshire, North Derbyshire, North Wales and Yorkshire. It is called Crown Green Bowling not because of royal decree, but because the surface of the green slopes up to a central point, or crown, which may be anything between 8 and 19in higher than the sides. In addition to that, every green has its own peculiarities – perhaps a steeper slope from crown to edge on one side than the other, individual troughs, hollows, bumps, rough patches, or characterful wrinkles. The expert players, so the theory goes, like to go and preview the green that they are due to play on – preferably after heavy rain so that they can mentally map out the complicated geography of the green from the pattern of puddles on the grass.

There is an interesting theory that, in the old days, the rich used to bowl in alleys – narrow, flat, grassy rinks, confined between hedges, often within large gardens attached to great houses. Their descendants are the lawn bowlers. The working class made do with rough old ground, like the Potsherd Boolers of Tyneside. From these conditions, the crown green game emerged. Although both games look similar, they are in fact very different; one writer, admirably biased in favour of crown green bowls, said that the games are 'as much alike as a Mothers' Union beetle drive and a pontoon school on the Holyhead boat train'.

Instead of operating up and down parallel rinks, the crown green bowlers follow the entertaining principle of the 'roving jack' – which means they can play anywhere on the green, as long as the jack, once dispatched, travels a minimum distance of 21 yards. In practice, this means that most amateurs tend to play corner-to-corner, which can be quite unnerving for a newcomer since it seems certain that this dangerous choreography will result in collisions, acrimony and melodrama somewhere in the middle of the green. It never seems to happen. The professionals, on the other hand, will use every inch of the green to their best advantage, bowling long if they think their opponent cannot cope, or short and along the edges if that seems a good idea. In winter, I have even seen them make use of patches of mud to create problems.

The jack, variously addressed in the North as the 'chitty', 'monkey', 'block' or 'little 'un', weighs 23oz and is biased, as are the woods. A player's skill in manipulating the jack is vital. In the lawn game, it is merely a target, but here the advantage of jack and first wood is enormous. Because the crown greeners have the intricate problems of the green to fight, and use only two woods, bowling tactics are less complicated than on the lawn green, with a smooth surface and four woods per player. There are few regulations about the size and weight of crown green bowls – experts and professionals often have several pairs, of different weights for different conditions, although on average they all tend to be lighter than lawn green woods.

When I first watched the crown game, from a tactically-sound position between the bar and the green, the bowlers used to follow something called the 'Blackpool rules', which allowed a second go with the jack if they weren't happy with the first – and 'stamping', which was a very strange dervish

dance around the wood as it travelled towards the jack. I am not sure if this flat-foot stamping was supposed to clear deviant blades of grass, or waft the wood onwards by means of compressed air, but it was certainly very startling to watch. The ruling body put a stop to it in 1981.

The normal game is 21 points up, but the professionals play 41 or 51, and have been known to have marathons of 71, 81 or even 101.

There's been a long history of betting money on the game. At the turn of the century, *The Sporting Chronicle* was full of advertisements and challenges: 'A bowling match will take place at the Chat Moss Hotel, Glazenbury and the Farmers Arms, Padgate, between Robert Nunney and Novice and the brothers Roberts. Today, Wednesday July 16, game 61 up. First half (31 up) to be played at Chat Moss, comm 2.00pm. The other 30 to be played at Farmer's Arms, 4 o'clock J Baron, prop.' And, 'A match will take place today between two Blackpool gentlemen, for £40. Neither bowler to send a wood before they start.'

The rich tradition of professional bowling has been preserved at Westboughton, near Bolton, where the panel of experts continues to meet, either at Westhoughton Reform Club or at The Red Lion, every day of the year except Sundays, Good Friday and Christmas Day. If it snows, they brush a clear swathe across the green and continue to play. If it is foggy, the referee shines a lamp over the jack and the players bowl at the lamp. If it is sunny, they sweat. If it rains heavily, they throw, rather than roll the bowls through the puddles. The players must endure the elements, the pressures of play – and the betting, advice and barracking, which begins from the moment the first jack is rolled and continues vociferously, until the end of the match. Perhaps to relieve this pressure, the players *and* the referee have been known to bet as well.

There are wonderful, probably apocryphal, stories of skulduggery and artifice surrounding the game.

Players measure out distance with their feet as a first calculation, and one player was reputed to wear a size eight on one foot, with a nine on the other, to be used as and when he thought fit.

There are tales of elastic tape-measures stretched or left on demand. When the greens were dry and fast – 'on fire' – they used to dip a rag in the lees of a glass of stout and rub the restraining mixture on the woods.

On cold days, players used to carry hot baked potatoes in their pockets to keep their fingers warm.

A terrible storm caused a flash flood one day in

Bowls.

Blackpool – park benches floated and the players had to wade in to see where their bowls had landed . . .

If Westhoughton is 'Valhalla', then The Waterloo Hotel, in Blackpool, is 'Wembley' for the crown green bowler. There are dozens of matches on the green at The Waterloo throughout the year, but the important one is the September Handicap, which began in 1907 and has continued annually ever since. There are 2048 entrants (selected 18 months before the event), so that 11 rounds produce a winner. The game is 41 up and if you can get tickets for the last two days, I'd like to know who your contacts are. There's a lovely, if somewhat dated, story about The Waterloo and it concerns a bowler from Huddersfield who said: 'I used to dream of taking Jane Russell to the Savoy and doing things that are unprintable, but now I'm older and wiser, my ambition is for a fairy godmother to grant me a couple of wishes. One, to win The Waterloo and two, to celebrate with halibut and chips at the Lobster Pot.'

Indoor Bowls

There was a time when historians were rather keen on the 'crucial date' – the special moment when, with the benefit of hindsight, it was possible to pinpoint an epoch-making swing in social, political and economic forces. I offer as a modest contribution to any such future debate, the date of 1 April, 1973. It combined, uniquely, April Fools' Day and Mothering Sunday. It saw the introduction of the iniquitous VAT and the termination of the Carlisle State Management Scheme. It also marked the end of Table Bowls as a strong, competitive public house game.

The pubs of Carlisle had been nationalised during the First World War by Lloyd George, in an attempt to enforce sobriety among the local munitions workers. After the War, the scheme continued and bright young architects, who may or may not have been puzzled by a brief which asked them to design pubs which would not foster excessive drinking, went to work with planning the much-acclaimed new buildings. The results, according to travellers who ventured north, could only be compared with post offices or station waiting rooms. As the years passed, the city, and many of its pubs, decayed and acquired a dusty, listless and flyblown look. In 1973, the then Conservative goverment dismembered the scheme and split the properties among the private breweries.

Whatever else may be said, the pubs were large and several of them were able to find room for Table Bowls. The new owners, however, obviously thought that such space could be more effectively used to pack in keen and profitable drinkers, and so the game, which had been played in the area for at least 50 years, made a quiet tactical withdrawal to the clubs of Carlisle, where it can still be seen and savoured today.

Billiard Table Bowls is played on a normal, full-sized billiard table, with a set of eight miniature lignum vitae or plastic, variously biased bowls each approximately 1½in in diameter, and a jack about half an inch across. The scoring and tactics are almost exactly the same as the larger outdoor version – the player or side having a bowl nearest the jack scores 1 point. Should two or more bowls played by the same individual or team be nearest, a further point for each bowl is added. The maximum a side may score in an end is therefore 4 points. There are eight players in a league team and each pair play nine ends in a match.

The jack and bowls are not rolled from the hand, but trundled down a vital extra piece of apparatus, an 18in wooden chute, grooved down its top surface and rested in play, slanting from the top of the end cushion down to the playing surface.

Table Bowls has a mystique and a satisfaction all of its own, a unique distillation of the charms of Billards, Bowls and the taproom. You must not push the bowls forcefully on their way, but let them roll, dictating speed and distance by how far up or down the chute you start. The jack must reach the top half of the table, and should come to rest at least 12in from the top or side cushions, otherwise it is 'dead' and your opponent takes over. If any of the following bowls touch a cushion, they are taken off the table and out of the game. The bias on the bowls adds to the fascination of the game – you must manipulate the chute to allow for this, since you cannot roll straight at the target. The knack is to quickly size up distance, speed and curvature, and sort out the advice from the vociferous experts. 'Give it more land', 'keep it tight', 'too heavy', 'too light', is the varying advice – obvious when you have time to think about it but confusing for the novice. One thing you should always remember is to 'shift your chute', so that your opponent cannot make use of your carefully-computed angles. It is hardly surprising that one veteran, searching misty-eyed for words to express his hypnotic addiction to the game, told me that Table Bowls was once 'the captivity of Carlisle'.

The final day in the reign of the game, at the pub I happened to be in, was a sad occasion. The players mournfully admitted that the tables had become rather dilapidated and, incredibly, the home table advantage, with its minute bumps and bruises on the slate bed and patched-up holes in the baize, had become an embarrassment to serious league

A game of Irish Road Bowls in progress. Although it is illegal to play games on public highways in Britain and Ireland, on special days in Cork and Armagh, no-one seems to mind.

competition. The final nail in the coffin was the prediction that draught bitter would be going up from 11 pence to 15 or 16 pence per pint and on the last night of State Management, the barrels had run dry and the final toasts had to be drunk from undignified bottles of light ale.

Table Bowls continues to be played in some pubs and clubs in London, although I have not yet discovered any league organisation. Here, they use slightly larger bowls, all with the same strong bias, but the principles of the game remain exactly the same as they are in Carlisle.

You may come across other indoor translations of bowls, such as **Carpet Bowls**, which comes in two versions. The first is **Scottish Carpet Bowls**, which is played on a raised 'table', 9in off the floor, 22ft long and 3ft wide, with unbiased bowls aimed at a 'target', as in **Curling**. The second, carpet bowls, is played to a jack with biased bowls, on a 30ft × 6ft carpet, rolled out on a normal, smooth floor. These versions are sometimes played in pubs – I have come across a couple of examples which close their restaurant annexes twice a week, to make room for the bowlers.

Short Mat Bowls, it is said, began in Belfast when an outdoor match was rained off and played in a local church hall instead, in 1926. It is played exactly the same way as flat green bowls, on a 45ft × 6ft mat and is now getting more and more popular in the whole of Ireland and the UK.

Road Bowls

Of course, you don't necessarily have to have a green, a carpet or a table to play bowls, you can simply use the road. On 4 August 1739, a farmer from Croydon bet that he could roll a bowl from his home town to London Bridge, a distance of 11 miles or so, within 500 throws. He won his bet, with some 55 throws to spare. They were still playing an odd version of this game in England up until the 1940s. In 1954, Mr Patrick McGuinness, then a sprightly 76-year-old and the licensee of The Three Crowns Hotel in New-castle-upon-Tyne, issued a challenge to the world. He was, he said, the former English champion of 'potsherd bools' and reckoned he could still take on anybody. No-one rose to the challenge, probably because the details of the game were somewhat obscure by then.

In 1914, Mr McGuiness had sent a 'bool' some 226 yards which, for want of any evidence to the contrary, we can take as a record. The Croydon farmer had averaged 45 yards per throw, but was working under more difficult conditions.

The grooved bowls used in **Road Bowls** were made from a vitreous substance used to line the furnaces of the local glassworks, and they weighed anything from 18 to 54 oz. **Potsherd Bools** was played on Newcastle's Town Moor and other convenient open spaces. Distance, rather than accuracy, seemed to be the name of the game. Each bowler had an assistant, or 'trigger', who tried to point out the best line to throw – hard ground was best, since the ball would roll on rather than stopping dead. Since the opponent had to throw from where the shot finished, a further trick was to 'put him on a soft trig', from where he would find it difficult to bowl. Players were handicapped according to average match results. It's interesting that the word 'trig' crops up again here, as it did in the Lewes game.

At the same time that Mr McGuinness issued his challenge to an unheeding world, in 1954, the Bol-Chumann na h'Eireann (the All Ireland Bowl Playing Association) was set up to regulate Road Bowling in the Republic of Ircland. The game was already old and, it is thought, may have been brought to Ireland by English or Scottish weavers in the 18th century.

The new organisation simply set out to legalise and codify proceedings, and perhaps moderate the drunken rowdiness which previously accompanied it. The iron ball, or 'bullet', is a standard issue 28oz projectile, about 2¼in in diameter. There are usually two competitors and the object of the game is to cover the course – a winding stretch of road anything from 2 to 5 miles long – in the least number of underarm throws. Players are graded and each has his own band of supporters, who encourage their man, and – according to one report – indulge in 'an unrefined type of psychological warfare' against their opponent. Bets on the result are taken and naturally, there's drinking before, during and after the game.

County Cork has 104 Road Bowling clubs, with not far short of 2000 registered players.

In Northern Ireland, the game is based in Armagh; the Armagh Bowling Association, founded in 1952, was replaced in 1963 by Bol-Chumann na h'Eireann Northern Branch, which now claims about 500 members, in six clubs.

The branches, North and South, combine to arrange the annual All Ireland Championships, which provides an interesting contrast in styles – the Armagh players throw the 'ground bullet' (a fast run-up followed by a low, fast throw) and finger-spin the ball round corners, while the Cork men occasionally like to 'hinch', or 'loft' high throws across corners, or even over buildings. Both styles also employ a guide, or 'shower' for each player, who goes ahead to indicate a favourable line for the throw. If shower and thrower are in tune, the ball will trundle to a stop between the shower's outstretched legs.

Playing games on the public highway is not permitted, so Road Bowling is, of course, illegal, although acknowledged and tolerated by the Authorities in Cork and Armagh. There's the occasional quiet game in the Borders region of Scotland – very low-key, because the police don't approve. You can also catch the odd game in Dagenham, Kent, within the confines of the Ford car plant there, played by Irish exiles who have been there since the 1920s, when the plant was set up and imported Irish labour.

There are versions of Road Bowling played in the Netherlands, Belgium and Germany and these countries, together with Ireland, have been contesting occasional European Championships since 1969 – the present Road Bowling European Champion is Dan O'Halloran, from County Cork.

Pétanque

There is a plaque on the wall by the tree-shaded boules terrain up the hill from the harbour of La Ciotat, near Marseilles, which honours the fact that the game of *Pied-tanque* was invented there in 1910. *Pied-tanque*, now known as **Pétanque**, is today the second most popular sport to cycling in France and, even more remarkably, has, in the last 15 years or so, become the fastest-growing outdoor game associated with the British pub.

Pétanque developed in Southern France from an earlier boules game, called *Jeu Provençal*, an energetic affair involving the hurling of nail-studded wooden balls over distances ranging from 16 to 23 yards, at a smaller wooden jack, or target ball. The story of the transmutation of *Jeu Provençal* into Pétanque would bring a tear to the most cynical eye, so it is probably too good to be entirely true. It is nevertheless well worth telling . . . Jules le Noir, so-called because of his black beard, as well as his fierce expression when concentrating on *Jeu Provençal*, eventually grew old and crippled by rheumatism and so could no longer play his beloved game. He was reduced to watching impotently from the sidelines of the terrain at La Ciotat, scene of his former triumphs. A friend of his, Ernest Pitiot, took pity on him and while waiting to play the long game, entertained Jules by engaging him in a more modest knock about off the main pitch – they threw, from a small circle scratched in the dust, at a distance of a mere 3 yards or so. Some hard-hearted spectators scoffed at the game and called it *Pieds-tanques* – Marseilles slang for 'feet tied together' – and the name stuck. Others watched, and eventually joined in. Eventually, Pétanque became what you might call a *jeu sans frontières* and spread to over 30 countries, while *Jeu*

Provençal remained a local pastime where it had always been, down in the deep south of France.

During the course of research for a previous book of mine on pub games, in the early 1970s, I came across Pétanque, which had strayed across the Channel to Essex and was being played in half a dozen pubs which had banded themselves together into the Braintree Pétanque League. The first British club to affiliate to the Federation de Pétanque et Jeu Provençal, the official governing body, was the Cressing Club de Pétanque, originally called the Chingford Club de Pétanque, from Essex, in 1966. Essex clubs picked up contacts with French café and club teams, especially in the Le Touquet area, and cross-Channel friendly matches were arranged, even in those early days.

The British connection came about, of course, through British holidaymakers who saw Pétanque played on gravel, sand or bare earth in sun-baked village squares and on camp sites in France, and eventually plucked up the courage to join in. Some even braver souls purchased sets of boules, brought them home and risked ridicule by playing on pub driveways and car parks, under the scornful eye of British natives used to playing in rain with biased composite bowls on manicured grass. This was almost the exact scenario which resulted in the formation of the British Pétanque Association (B.P.A.) in 1974, when Maurice Abney Hastings, plus wife and friends, returned from a camping holiday in Britanny and decided to precede their Sunday lunchtime drink at Sam's Hotel, Shedfield, Hampshire, with a little gentle exercise using their newly-purchased boules on the gravel drive of the cricket club opposite the pub. They were joined by other customers and the game caught on and became a regular Sunday institution. Abney Hastings became the President of the B.P.A. and I expect there will be a plaque at Sam's Hotel, eventually, just as there is at La Ciotat, near Marseilles.

The energy, skill and speed with which the B.P.A. organised the game in Britain rivals that of those Victorian administrators who sorted out all the green grass games in the last quarter of the 19th century. In 1974, the same year as the tentative Sunday morning experiment at Sam's Hotel, the B.P.A. got itself affiliated to the Federation de Pétanque et Jeu Provençal. National Championships were held at Sam's Hotel in 1975 and a British team was dispatched to the World Championships in Quebec, Canada. Perhaps their most breathtaking coup of all was to stage the World Championships themselves, with great success, in Southampton, in 1979. Along the way, they picked up media coverage ranging from local and national

Pétanque players in Mollans sur Ouveze, Drome, Provence.

press to network television, and sponsorship from a variety of firms and organisations. Today, the B.P.A. has regular full-time officers, a magazine, a regional league structure, a national team and a national coaching system, plus a second Four Year Development Plan, approved and funded by the Sports Council.

The B.P.A. can supply a list of hundreds of affiliated pub and club teams, divided up into regions which now cover the south and east coasts, plus the Midlands and Wales. If you look at their map of conquered territory, it looks as if a tidal wave has swept in from the south-east corner of Britain, and is now lapping at the land just north of the Watford Gap. An ambitious tyro boulist could, with the help of the BPA, graduate from local pub team to local, regional and national championships, take part in the Grand Prix contests and find himself in one of the national teams taking part in World Championships in exotic locations – a British team has appeared at every World event since 1975.

However, one of the great joys of Pétanque is that you can play without taking it too seriously and there are many teams and individuals all over the country that don't bother to affiliate and have no ambitions beyond a pleasant game, a pint or two and good company. If you have never played, then you have missed a treat and should put the matter right immediately by finding a pub with a piste, terrain, bouledrome or pitch. You don't need elaborate facilities to play Pétanque – any patch of hard ground will do. The only surface that isn't much good is grass. Many breweries have encouraged their pubs to find the space to play, and have put money into the game, mainly, I think, because they think Pétanque is the sort of pastime which will attract rather up-market customers who will spend a bit more than the domino or crib players, during the course of a session.

The old Provençal boules, made of wood and plated with nail heads, gave way – in the late 1920s – to spheres of phosphor bronze, and then, latterly, to steel coated with zinc, nickel or chromium. The best competition boules you can buy today are made of stainless steel, are 2.75 to 3.1in in diameter and weigh between 1lb 6oz and 1lb 12oz. They can be striped with various patterns, or plain. All serious competitions insist that the boules used should be stamped with a registration number and their weight – amateur British players attempting a *concours de boules* in foreign fields, have been known to get the two figures mixed up.

The boules are thrown at a small, wooden target bowl (1 to 1.2in in diameter) which bowlers call a 'jack', but boulists refer to as *la blique*, *le cochonnet*,

le gari, *le but*, *le kiki*, *le pitchoun*, *le petit* or *le petit ministre*. In France, it is left as natural wood; in Britain it is often painted white so that it can be seen in the gloom, mist and rain of a typical summer's day.

You can play a singles match, which is known in France as a *tête à tête*, a doubles match (*doublettes*) or triples (*triplettes*). In singles or doubles, each player has three boules, in triples, which is the game most often played in league competitions, each player throws two.

Whichever game you play, the basic principles remain the same – after tossing a coin to see who starts, the *cochonnet* (jack) is thrown by the first player, who must stand in a small circle only 12 to 18in in diameter, scratched in the gravel. There is only just room for the average pair of feet within a circle of that size and it is this feature which produces the extraordinary, statuesque ballet poses which distinguish Pétanque from all other boule or bowl games – no matter what sort of shot you are attempting, your feet must remain firmly rooted to the ground, although the body can sway like a tree in the wind. The *cochonnet* must come to rest between 19½ and 33ft from the circle and 3ft 3in (in some areas 1ft 7½in) from any obstacle such as a shrub or tree, or the edge of the terrain. The basic positional and scoring rules of the familiar British bowls game apply, and the aim is to get your boules nearer to the *cochonnet* than your opponent's – you earn a point for every one of yours nearer than its closest rival, so in *triplettes*, an end may be won with anything from 1 to 6 points. A game is usually 13 points.

In Pétanque, the throwing sequence is different to bowls, and has been known to break beginners' hearts. The player who has thrown the *cochonnet* then throws the first boule. At this point, the opposing team takes over, and throw their boules until they get one closer to the *cochonnet* than the original throw. If that first throw was a good one, and the boule rests snugly next to the *cochonnet* (this is called *un biberon* or *un tetard* – a baby's bottle or a tadpole), then it is quite possible for an inexperienced team to dispatch all their boules without ever getting a closer shot and therefore losing an end to a single opponent's boule.

If and when you find that you are landing the odd boule successfully near to the jack, you may want to join a more sophisticated and experienced league *triplettes* team, which will probably have an interesting and traditional division of labour. One member of the team will be *le pointeur* (the pointer), who specialises in getting the boule as near to the *cochonnet* as possible; next comes *le tireur* (the shooter), whose job is to get opponents' boules out of the way; lastly, there will be *un milieu*, an all-rounder, who can perform every task well and has an eye for tactics – he'll almost certainly be the captain. *Le tireur* performs the most spectacular and dramatic work, especially if he can pull off the high trajectory mortar shot known as *un carreau*, when he hits a boule next to the jack, knocks it out of harm's way and leaves his boule exactly in the spot where the original one was – this is the sort of explosive stuff that raises cheers or curses from the crowd, depending whose side they're on.

I have always believed that if a thing is worth doing at all, it is worth doing badly and I enjoy my Pétanque mainly, I think, because it inevitably reminds me of sunshine, and the sound effects – the click of boules, the crunch of gravel – help to conjure up fond memories of foreign holidays. I've even acquired a new vocabulary, to cope with my lack of skill. I expect *un palet courant* (a poor *carreau*, which, having hit its target, rolls on too far), I usually *fait un narri* (make a very bad pointage), and I invariably hit *un gratton* (an unfortunate stone or bump on the pitch which unexpectedly deflects an otherwise good boule). However, one thing that hasn't happened to me yet is to be 'fannied', which means losing a game 13–0. In Britain, such an achievement is greeted with jolly sporting cries of commiseration – in some French clubs I'm led to believe that they have an old painting of a *fin de siècle*, plump lady of pleasure, called Fanny, throwing up her rear skirts. The losing team have to kiss her backside. It certainly isn't cricket.

One small postscript – occasionally the British boulist is accused of bringing an alien and 'foreign' game into the hallowed ground of the British pub. The B.P.A.'s response to this is a startling claim that boules, not bowls, was the game played by Drake and friends prior to defeating the Spanish Armada, and therefore, they have merely re-imported a game which was traditionally British.

Petanque is steadily gaining popularity in Britain. This game took place at The Royal Oak, Bovington Green, Marlow.

Steel Quoits has always been a popular game in the north east of England – these Newcastle pit men were sketched in the early 19th century.

Background

The game of **Quoits** is ancient, and no-one can possibly know for sure how, when or why it began. So, in the absence of any specific evidence, speculation rules supreme.

In the north east of England, many of today's players believe that their game originated in the Olympiads of Ancient Greece, as an early form of discus throwing. From Greece, they say, it travelled to Rome and from there reached these shores at the time of the Roman Conquest. At this point, it is claimed, an interesting form of class distinction emerged – the officers played with specially-made, bronze quoits, while the troops, whose take-home pay did not run to such luxury, made do with discarded horseshoes. A case of putting the quoit before the horse, one might say.

Another theory which I am fond of, but cannot prove, assumes that, having invented footwear for the horse, Man did not rest content, but soon adapted the shoes for his own impractical purposes, and began throwing them at a pin, stake or hook, for recreation and amusement. The game of **Horseshoes** could have been brought here by invaders or settlers from Jutland or the Low Countries – a suggestion backed up by the fact that the Boers in South Africa and Dutch settlers in America and Canada still play it. Horseshoes, then, according to this story, came first and then developed an offshoot called Quoits. At the Dunnottar Quoiting Club near Stonehaven, in Scotland, some of the members subscribe to yet another story. Quoits, they say, was invented by James IV, who encouraged his soldiers to relax and pass the time before major battles by throwing horseshoes at an iron pin stuck in the ground.

Whichever tale you favour, the two sports of Quoits and Horseshoe Pitching seem to have been inextricably linked in their pre-history. Nowadays, they are quite distinct. The other thought which occurs is that all the explanations advanced are very insular, and cheerfully ignore what additional evidence might be scattered across the rest of Europe. We must wait, perhaps, until the data for the 'Quoits and Horseshoe' section of the *Atlas of Traditional European Games* has been pieced together, before we jump to any more conclusions.

Quoits

The first definite historical reference to Quoits in Britain comes from punitive legislation of 1361, when Edward III, concerned that his loyal subjects were dissipating their energies with enjoyable games rather than keeping in trim for more war-like activities, decreed that they must 'use bows and arrows or pellets or bolts and shall learn and practise the art of shooting'. In future, they were 'not to meddle in hurling of stones, loggats and coits . . . and other games of no value'. **Archery**, in spite of such legislation, continued to decline until it was taken up as a harmless sport some 500 years later. The 'games of no value' – bowls, skittles and Quoits – continued to prosper.

Quoits emerged from the mists of near-myth at the end of the 18th century and enjoyed considerable – and well-documented – popularity throughout the 19th century. The basic principle of the game remained as simple, as it always had been – iron rings were thrown at a distant pin in the ground. Regional and house rules, however, varied enormously. The throwing distances to the 'mark', 'pin' or 'hob' ranged from 11 to 21 yards; the weight of the quoits varied from 5 to a scarcely-credible 23 lb; the number of players in a team was recorded variously as between two and 24, and the points required for game could be anything from 11 to 61.

The game soon became associated with the pub, but early in the 19th century clubs were formed specifically to play it. In a brilliant study of quoiting within a 20-mile radius of Stirling, in central Scotland, N.L. Tranter notes that there were 21 clubs in this comparatively small area, between 1831 and 1840. The Darlington Quoit Club, in what is now known as Cleveland, claims to be the oldest organisation of its kind in England, having been founded in 1846 – and it has been playing ever since.

Gradually, the pubs and clubs were drawn together and, in the 1880s, the game was codified. In the North East, representatives from the local clubs – Darlington, Darlington Borough, Durham Elvet, Eston, Guisborough, Middlesbrough, Erimus, Middlesbrough Ayresome, Stockton, West Hartlepool Recreation, Middlesbrough Teesside, Newcastle Tradesmen and the 'Raglan' West Hartlepool came together at The Castle and Anchor pub, Stockton-on-Tees, and later at The Princess Alice, Middlesbrough, and formed the Association of Amateur Quoits Clubs for the North of England. They agreed on a list of 15 rules, which have been more or less adhered to in that part of the world ever since. The rules were published in *The Field* on 23 April 1881, and the ensuing publicity brought in enquiries from Hungerford, in Berkshire, North Shields, Brighouse, in Yorkshire, Worcester, Aberdare, Coddenham, in Suffolk and Cheltenham. Everyone who adopted these regulations agreed on a size of quoit – no more than 5lb 4oz in weight, no more than 8½in diameter outside and 5½in inside, no more than 1¼in high and made of malleable iron. The pins or hobs were to be placed in 'tempered clay ends' to project no more than 2 in. The throwing distance was 11 yards.

This was the game I first stumbled upon 20 years ago, at the back of a splendid pub at Corbridge-on-Tyne, just south of Hadrian's Wall. At first, I thought I must have come to the wrong place, since I could see no sign of a pitch. The clay beds were covered with wet sacks, which were planked over because they weren't in use at the time, and there were beer crates stacked over one end and a car parked at the other. It wasn't until that evening that everything was cleared away and the game was revealed.

The northern pitch consists of two 3ft × 3ft beds of clay, each enclosed in a timber 'box' sunk into the ground. The surface of the clay is smoothed-out so that the whole bed is flush to ground level and plumb in the centre of each bed is an iron pin, some 2 or 3 in proud of the clay. The two pins are 11 yards apart and the game consists of throwing quoits (two per player) from one bed to the other, aiming to circle the pin or hob (for 2 points), or at least to land closer to it than your opponent (1 point). The quoits are thrown alternately and, when all four of them have been cast (an end), both players walk to the target bed, tot up the score, pick up the quoits and then throw again, this time back towards the first bed. Some pubs have two or more pitches, side by side, so the action during a league match is busy and continuous. The game is usually 21 points up, although sometimes 11 or 15, if it is a casual match. There are eight people to a team, paired individually with opponents, and at the end of the match the points are totalled to work out who has won.

Such a breathless scamper through the rules of the game does it less than justice. The lore, language and tactics of Quoits are endless and intriguing. The clay surface of the beds, for example, must have the right composition, consistency, surface and treatment. Blue clay is preferred – other kinds tend to stick to hands and clothes. In the old days, even on a good pitch, a boy was employed to clean the quoits after each throw. The clay is an important ingredient in the game because the fact that quoits can be made to stick on edge in the bed is an important factor, in the more skilful tactics which experts bring into play.

The quoits themselves used to be handmade locally. A Northumberland blacksmith, who no longer played the game, but grew misty-eyed as he recalled the 'ring o' coits' in his younger days, gave me his recipe. The quoit, as he made it, began as a round bar of mild steel, 18½in long and 1⅛in thick.

This was ringed and fire-welded. One side was hammered flat, the other bevelled, or rounded. All you needed then, he said, was 'a good file and a lot of bloody energy'. The end product measured 5in across the hole, weighed 5lb 6oz or 6lb and had a finish of either chrome or silver. The quoits were made in pairs, and were lovingly cared for by their owners, who had often saved up for months to buy them. The shape of this sort of quoit has been compared to the bottom of a wine glass stem, a flying saucer and a discus with a hole punched through it. Traditionally, the upper plane is called the 'hill', the bottom plane the 'hole' and, instead of tossing the coin to decide who has first throw, a quoit is flung in the air and the call is 'hill or hole' instead of 'heads or tails'.

Styles of throwing quoits vary from region to region and even from player to player. As long as you begin your throw from the right place, alongside the near pin, there are few regulations. In Corbridge, a two-paced run-up was allowed and the favoured throw was from between the legs and out of the open hand. Elsewhere, the throw, after the same two-paced run, seems to be underarm from the right of the body. The experts will tell you to hold the quoit in the hand, at the angle you wish it to fall in the box, and to make good use of the thumb, the ball of the thumb, the tips of the fingers and the wrist. The trajectory is important too, and good quoiters will have practised length as assiduously as bowlers in cricket. You are allowed to walk up to the box between throws, to assess the situation, but in some of the stricter clubs they will not allow you to carry your second quoit on this expedition, since a quoit thus transported has passed the length of the pitch and has been 'played'.

Every placing of the quoit, on or near the hob or pin, has a name, as important and meaningful to the quoits player as the names of field placings for the cricketer. Some, like the 'ringer' or the 'front-toucher', are fairly obvious, but the origin of others – the 'gater' or 'face-gater housekeeper', 'hillway', 'Q quoit' or 'Frenchman' – is obscure.

The ringer would appear to be the best shot to go for but, in sophisticated play, this is not necessarily the case, since an experienced opponent might land one on top of it and cancel your score. A player going first will usually try for a gater, which will defend the hob against his opponent's first throw and will give him the chance to knock the gater over the hob and convert it into a ringer with his second shot. In most situations, the throw which ends flat, or 'hole', is preferred; if the quoit lands 'hole-up', like a saucer, it can be bounced and flipped over, or even off the pin, by an accurate shot on the edge of the lip.

Quoits was a game played in both the industrial and rural areas of Britain. These agricultural workers in Essex seem to be enjoying their game.

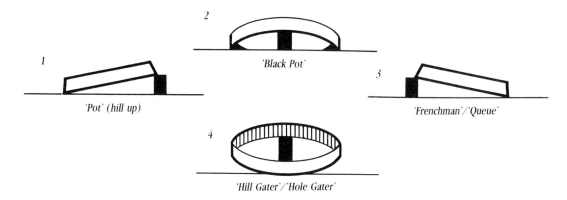

1

'Pot' (hill up)

2

'Black Pot'

3

'Frenchman'/'Queue'

4

'Hill Gater'/'Hole Gater'

In league matches, the thrower has a helper, called a 'bibber', a 'shower-up' or a 'coach', who stands at the target bed and shouts advice and encouragement. He is sometimes equipped with scraps of paper, which he uses to mark out the exact spot where he wants the quoit to land. He often remains crouched over the clay in an apparently suicidal position, until the quoit thuds into the clay, often only inches from his hands, head or feet. Frequently, the lay of the quoits after an end is very close and the distance between quoit and pin has to be measured with tape, cigarette packets or, in important matches, with straight-legged compasses. At key matches there is a 'trig man' – his job is to watch the throwers' feet and call out foot faults. A marker chalks up the score, point by point, while the referee will only be called upon if there is a dispute.

The fortunes of Quoits have fluctuated considerably during this century. After a decline following the First World War, the game flourished in the 1930s – especially during the Depression, when working men had too much time and too little money. Many players became almost professional during this period, travelling the North to supplement their income with cash prizes from Quoits contests. An additional prize for the big annual contests, in the villages of the Yorkshire Dales, was a copper kettle, and a 'five kettle man' was a hero of his time. At Beckhole, in the North Yorkshire Moors, not far from Whitby, they continue to have an annual Open Handicap Contest, on the first Saturday in August – the eagerly-contested first prize is still a copper kettle. After the Second World War, the game almost died out, although strongholds, like Darlington, never gave up. There have been several 'revivals' of the game, although this is a term which irritates some veterans who argue that they have never stopped playing.

Nowadays, the future looks bright – there are thriving leagues in Yorkshire (Zetland, Danby and District, Whitby Indoor, Lower Dales), Durham

(Spennymoor, Birtley and District, Vaux, Sunderland), Northumberland (Northumberland, Coastal, Glendale) and Cleveland, as well as individual country pub teams and specialised clubs, like Darlington and Hawkeys Lane, North Shields. The National Quoits Association was formed, with the encouragement of the Sports Council, in 1986 and has revived inter-league competitions and a World Championship for single players and pairs, held at the Beamish Open-Air Museum and sponsored by Newcastle Brown, in July each year.

The chairman of the National Quoits Association, Peter Brown, his secretary, Alan Burton, and the members of the committee are, in a quiet but determined fashion, planning a revolution – they want to contact other quoits players and organisations in Britain, the rest of Europe and beyond, and eventually restore the game to its rightful place, in the Olympic Games. As a step along the way, they are also considering an 'Alternative Olympics' in Europe, involving sports such as Quoits, skittles and Pétanque.

However, there is a problem on their own front doorstep, so to speak, in that other parts of the U.K. play a game of Quoits to an 18 yard, instead of an 11 yard, throwing distance, and use quoits of various sizes and weights, which would make them 'illegal' in the North East's scheme of things. This is the 'long game' which A.P. Herbert, in his novel *The Water Gypsies*, describes at The Black Lion, Hammersmith, between the wars:

'An ancient, heroic, dignified game, like something in the *Iliad* or an English *Aeneid*. The quoits were massive pieces of iron, weighing, in the best matches, some sixteen pounds. At either end of the ground were square pits of clay, and in the centre of them a small buried peg. The matches were a series of single combats; each man had two quoits, and the game was twenty points.'

It has always been dangerous to say that a pub

Quoits in North Yorkshire. The points are being assessed by the referee, using a pair of straight-legged callipers to measure distances between quoits and hob.

game is dying out, but I think it may well be that the traditional 'long game' is no longer played much, if at all, in England. It has certainly disappeared from London. Twenty years ago they were still playing at The Angel, in Braintree, Essex, but now there is just a memorial stone at the back of the pub, recording the fact that the All England Championships were held there in 1927. The clay pits are still there, although barely discernible, and the present landlord has rescued a single rusty quoit, which he discovered buried in the undergrowth. What I find especially sad – and unnerving – is that I visited The Angel in the 1960s when they *did* play, and I met one or two of the veterans. They used to have an annual international match, when a team of Scottish quoiters descended upon the East Anglian club, consumed a great deal of whisky and usually beat the English team out of sight. The Angel also staged the News of the World Individual Knockout Cup, which was played to 32 points up. When I spoke with them, they were running out of opponents, as Essex quoits beds disappeared beneath layers of asphalt for new or enlarged car parks.

There *are* Quoits leagues to be found in Suffolk – the Hadleigh and District Sunday League and the Stoke-by-Nayland League, which plays on summer Saturday evenings, for example – but they play with comparatively small, lightweight quoits and a ringer is removed as soon as it has been thrown, which obviously results in a different tactical game. The circular clay beds are 18 yards apart, and slope gently towards the thrower.

The ancient long game still survives, though, in Scotland and Wales; those two countries hold international matches, but can no longer find English teams to compete, although I suppose, with some adjustments on both sides, a sort of compromise could be reached.

Tranter's research in Central Scotland showed that there were 45 active quoits clubs within 25 miles of Stirling at the end of the 19th century. Now, there are perhaps a dozen clubs in the whole of Scotland continuing the great tradition under the auspices of the Scottish Quoiting Association. Until 1955, the team and singles championships were thrown at 21 yards, but in that year the SQA decided to reduce that distance to 18 yards, to 'conform to common practice' in Wales and parts of England. The first international against England was played at Parkhead in 1930, and they continued sporadically, as we have seen, until the 1960s. The first Scotland versus Wales game was at Merthyr Tydfil in 1931 and that fixture now takes place in Scotland or Wales on alternate years.

The Bwrdd Coetio Cymru (the Welsh Quoiting Board) was reformed in 1979, having faded away some 20 years previously. Nowadays, it is affiliated to the Welsh Sports Council and has a small grant to help run the game. Again, there are no more than a dozen clubs, based mainly in Dyfed and Powys. They play the long game and have always thrown at 18 yards.

In the big game, the annual tussle between Scotland and Wales, teams consist of 12 players on each side, listed in seeded order and matched in singles games with their opposite numbers. The games are played to 21 points up; the final result is arrived at by totting up the aggregate scores of all the games.

The long game is very impressive to watch. At 54ft from bed to bed and with tiny hobs, flush with the clay, it must be difficult to see, let alone hit the target area. It is not enough to achieve distance and accuracy, for the momentum of a heavy quoit will often bounce it from the clay – the ideal throw appears to rise no higher than eye level and, miraculously, seems to glide rather than fall sharply from the top of its trajectory. A ringer (here only 1 point instead of the North East's 2) is almost unbeatable on a peg which is flush with the clay, so a favourite, safe, tactical ploy is the shot which lands just in front of the hob and protects it by its mere bulk.

There are folk tales of the phenomenal accuracy achieved by some of the older players – tales of quoiters who could ring a drawing pin, or encircle a gold watch without damaging it. At the Dunnottar Quoiting Club, they still hold a night-time Candle Contest – a lighted candle is placed by the hob and the object of the game is to put out the candle, either by landing the quoit on it, or getting so close as to snuff out the flame with the draught of the falling quoit. The winner is the person who achieves the 'distinction of extinction' the most times out of ten shots.

You may come across a game of Quoits in England, Scotland or Wales played on grass. (They call it **Sward Quoits**.) Although quoit beds can be unobtrusive – sometimes invisible out of season to the untrained eye – the initial construction and subsequent maintenance and protection of the vital clay beds can call for a great deal of time and trouble on the part of the local team and the landlord. In some areas, matters are simplified by organising the game on any available patch of grass. Some pubs actually prefer such simplicity and an arrangement like this is obviously more convenient for the organisers of special annual events, such as a horse fair or an agricultural show, where a Quoits match is part of much larger entertainment.

In Sward Quoits, the two hobs are simply driven into the ground 11 or 18 yards apart, painted white and perhaps left projecting a little higher than usual. Once the ground around the hob becomes too cut up and rough for play, both pins are simply pulled up and moved to another patch. Sward Quoits calls for cunning play - obviously a great deal depends on the ground, which may be soft and wet or hard and dry. The experts size up the situation at a glance, and adapt their play accordingly.

Horseshoes

The approved horseshoe pitch is reminiscent of a Quoits terrain, in that there are two circular beds, one at either end of the pitch, but they are filled with sand instead of clay. The peg in the centre of each sandpit is made of steel, 12 to 14in high and inclined towards the thrower some 3in from the vertical. The pins are 40ft apart, often with a 30ft tee for ladies. The horseshoes should weigh 2lb 8oz and be 7⅝in long, 7in across at the broadest part, with a 3½in gap between the 'calks' (toes, or heels, to you and me).

Each player has two shoes and the object of the game is to ring the peg or get one or more of your horseshoes nearer to the peg than your opponent's. Only the top ringer counts after each end or innings has been thrown - you get 3 points for a ring, 4 for ringer, plus nearest shoe. A singles match is 50 points up, a doubles 21. These rules come from the National Horseshoe Pitchers Association of America, which was founded in 1921 and is still going strong in 45 American states and six Canadian provinces. The game came back here from the other side of the Atlantic in fairly recent times, and has enjoyed limited popularity in Essex, although the leagues that once ran in places like Clacton and Colchester, in the 1970s, seem to have petered out.

Essex is still the place to go for Horseshoes, though, for in 1979 Peter Kinsella introduced the Irish version of the game to Harlow. It has proved to be extraordinarily successful and he now finds himself president and chairman of a league involving over 40 pub and club teams, operating in three divisions. 'Horseshoes,' says Kinsella, 'is not so much a game, more of a disease' in Harlow.

The Anglo-Irish rules would appear to be much the same as the American regulations already outlined, although there are minor differences in some measurements - the pin here is only 8 or 9in proud of the sand and is vertical. The pins are 33ft apart, but the throw is from a concrete slab 7ft behind the pin, so the length remains at 40ft, although in Ireland, the distance is 36ft. They play three games to 21 points, with teams of four, in the Harlow League.

Peter Kinsella has had contacts over recent years with Horseshoe Pitching teams from Bedford, Luton, Lincoln and Somerset, but now thinks that the game may have died out in those areas. He still has contacts with Southern Ireland, though, and on one memorable occasion took a Harlow All Stars team to play the All Ireland Champions, from Donegal. They staged the match on neutral ground - the Isle of Man - and I'm sorry I missed it, for it must have been quite a weekend.

I suspect that the sort of Horseshoes they play at The Queen's Head in Bulwick, Northamptonshire, is typical of the amiable, free translation of the American game which has taken place in some areas of Britain. A group of Queen's Head customers visited the States a few years back and were taken with the pastime which seemed to them to be played and enjoyed in everyone's back yard. They now have a competition at their pub, based roughly on the American rules, each New Year's Day. The pitch is 30ft long for everybody, they use English shire horseshoes from a local farrier and play to only 7 points per game, since the event is a knockout doubles competiton and if they went up to 21, it would 'go on for days', according to the landlord. The Americans have a rule which says that to count at all, a shoe must be within a shoe's width (7in) from the pin. The Queen's Head pitchers don't bother with such niceties and will allow a score from any distance, as long as the shoe is nearer than an opponent's. It sounds like a pleasant way to see in the New Year.

Rings and Things
Rings

One of the earlier pieces of printed evidence about darts, quoted in several of the books on the subject, comes from the unlikely pages of the Stationer, Printer and Fancy Trades Register of 1 June 1901, where '322 Ring Boards, Dartboards, and Parlour Cricket' were advertised for sale. You could re-interpret that sparse entry and claim that it represents evidence that ring boards were marginally more popular than dartboards at the turn of the century. I think Rings was squeezed out by darts, sometime between the two world wars. Parlour Cricket is another story.

Just prior to the Second World War, a cloud of researchers for the social investigation that subsequently became famous as Mass Observation descended upon the Lancashire town they code-named 'Worktown' (it was Bolton). Their report, *The Pub and the People*, reads oddly - like an anthropological analysis of a primitive tribe. Perhaps its distant and detached style sprang from a desire to evolve a new 'scientific' method – or maybe the researchers all came from south of Watford and had never come across 'real' people before. *The Pub and the People* chronicled the fading of traditional native pastimes, including Rings, or 'Quoits', as the explorers called it. There were a few largely ignored and unused boards left in Bolton, but one old gentleman told them what their use was. There had been players, he remembered, who, having completed a normal game, could throw five rings into a gill (½ pint) glass from 6ft away, or could stand at one end of the bar and ring all the beer pump handles, finishing off with the small tap on the strong ale barrel. It appears that the old man could only recall the encores, not the actual game, a point overlooked by the eager researchers.

I move with reasonable freedom about the North West of England, and know enough of the language to be able to communicate, and I hear the same story, 50 years on. Many pubs had rings boards, not dartboards, up until the 1920s and '30s and, if you get yourself into quiet taprooms in places like Salford and Oldham, they will tell you tales similar to those told by the old gentleman of Bolton. I'm fairly certain, too, that Rings was widespread throughout the country and not just confined to the North West.

Some pubs preserve the rings board to this day, but as an ornament rather than a useful piece of equipment. At The Rose and Crown, Kirkhampton, in Cumbria, the landlord found a rings board behind some barrels in his cellar, when he first moved into the pub in the mid-1980s. He liked the look of it, so he cleaned it up and hung it on a wall in the pub. The board has hooks numbered from 1 to 13 and the old locals said the main game was to score 31 exactly, using five rings. They told the landlord that the game was fairly widespread 'in the old days'. Today, only the 'occasional tourist' asks to have a go.

This bears out what I discovered myself, 20 years ago, working on a previous book on pub games. There were mentions in local papers of the odd board, each one 'the last of its kind' . . .

In 1952, customers of The Ferry Boat Inn, at Harwich, in Suffolk, appealed in vain to *The Morning Advertiser* for opponents. They had a '50-year-old' rectangular board, 16in square, with 13 hooks. Each player threw six rings, each 3½in in diameter. The object of the game was to travel 'twice round the pegging board' (i.e. a cribbage board) from which I deduce that you had to score 121 to win – a much longer game than the Kirkhampton veterans recalled. The nickname of the Harwich pub was 'The Dooley' and they called their game the 'Dooley Rings'. Now, the board and the pub are no more.

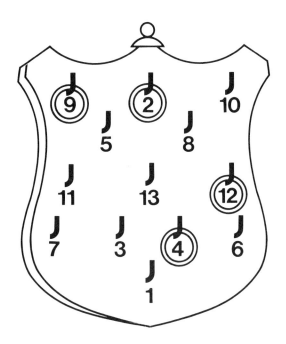

Standard Rings board

At The Hampshire Hunt Inn, at Cheriton, near Winchester, they used to have a 100-year-old circular board, again with 13 hooks. The players threw 4in diameter rings, six to a turn, and the game was, once more, 121 up, finishing exactly. One unusual rule of the Cheriton school said that three consecutive rings around the same number won the game outright.

In the days when the game was popular in Lancashire, the main exercise was 'twice round the board', following the numbers in sequence, from 1 to 13, then repeating the whole thing. Doubles, that is, two consecutive rings on the same numbered hook, counted. Thus, if you got double 5, your next throw would be at number 11. I met a man in a pub once who, hearing of my interest in games, gave me his set of six Lancashire rings; the throw he demonstrated, at a blank wall, was hard and flat at the 'board', rather than a skimming action, the more natural thing to do. He donated the rings to what he hoped was a worthy cause because there was nowhere left in his locality where the game could be played.

The game survives in its most organised and vibrant form in two quite separate locations – Ventnor, on the Isle of Wight, and Dagenham, in Essex.

In the Ventnor Rings League, the boards have 15 hooks and the serious game here, played on Tuesdays from September through to spring, is 201 up.

There are six players to a team, who play in three sets of pairs, best of three games to a match. You must 'get out' exactly, finishing with the score you need – no more, no less. They also play 'round the board', this time each of the six players in a team playing a singles match with his opponent. This game is from 1 to 15, 15 once more, then 1 to finish. All games are from an 8 ft throw, but apart from the throwing distance, there are no rules on how to throw. Some throw flat from the palm of the hand, others from a darts-like grip. Even underhand lobs are known and allowed.

Some people tend to treasure sets of rubber rings, handed down from generation to generation. Others swear by the new technology of the plastic ring. The old rubber rings are eagerly sought after, especially if they still have 'VL' stamped on them, denoting their Ventnor League provenance and status – sets of these drooping veterans have been known to change hands for £40 to £50. The plastic rings have to be softened – for years, it is said – before they are fit for play. Methods of treatment vary – they are stretched round bottles, left in the sun, even kept for years in back pockets.

No-one knows how long the game has been going on the Isle of Wight, although they have photographs of winning teams in the 1920s, hanging on the walls of the Ventnor Social Club, a central venue for the game.

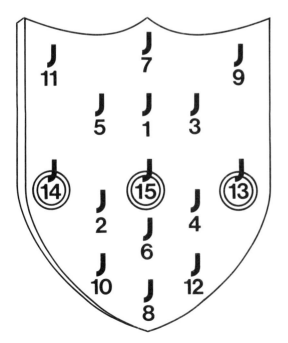

Isle of Wight Rings board

I rather suspect that the Dagenham game may have been an Irish import into Essex – just as Road Bowling and Horseshoe Pitching were. The South East Sussex Rings League uses a smaller board than the Ventnor folk – there are 13 numbered hooks, instead of 15. The main game is different, too, and is 600 points up, with eight players to a team, each member throwing six rings to a turn. The finish must be exact, ending up with four consecutive 1s – a very odd ending to a game. There are 16 clubs in the League, but no record, as yet, of a team going back to County Cork to take on the local champions there.

Those waiting for the game to make a comeback in their own local can speed matters up by buying a board. I have one, bought from a children's toyshop (which may be where the game came from in the first place, perhaps via the funfair). It is called the Standard Tournament Rings Board and is still commercially manufactured. It comes together with six rings – rather flimsy affairs compared with my old Lancashire rings – and a rule book. According to this source, the singles game is 301 up, the pairs 501, each match to be the best of three games – it seems to me they've probably got it confused with darts.

Ringing the Bull

There are some startling claims for the ancestry of **Ringing the Bull**. Its invention has been credited to the Romans, largely, I suspect, to provide an explanation for the game's widespread but sporadic distribution. Then there is the Crusader connection – the famous pub, The Trip to Jerusalem, tucked into the cliffs below Nottingham Castle, was reputedly a meeting place for Christian warriors either on their way to, or on their way back from, the Holy Land. There is a Ringing the Bull set in one of the pub's many rooms and therefore, runs the legend, the game dates back to the Crusades, and was either taken to, or brought back from, Jerusalem.

The game, wherever it came from, is simplicity itself. I first came across it in Warrington, Cheshire, in the late 1960s. An upturned metal hook was screwed into a block of wood fixed in the centre of the taproom wall, at about the same height above the floor as the bull on the adjacent dartboard (i.e. a few inches short of 6ft). A metal ring, 1½in in diameter, was hanging from the ceiling by a long piece of string, 7 or 8ft from the hook. The object of the game was to swing the ring onto the hook – you moved back with the ring, to a distance of about 12ft from the hook, and pushed it away, pendulum fashion, aimed at the target.

The locals, playing a casual game of 20 throws each, in between ordering pints and filling in betting slips, made it look relaxed and easy. I soon found

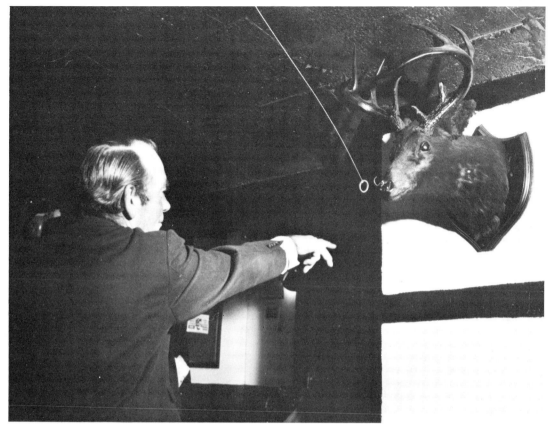

An unusual version of Ringing the Bull, which should be called Ringing the Stag, I suppose. There is yet another version, known as Ringing the Warthog's Nose.

though, that like all pub games, it required special technique and skill, bred by years of practice. My first 20 throws produced nothing but a madly-gyrating ring and a debt of half a bitter to my indulgent opponent. Eventually, with professional advice – 'always stand in the same position and aim at a particular feature on the wall that will bring the ring's parabola into correct alignment' – I started to hit the target, not frequently, but at least more often.

I was then treated to an exhibition of further sophistication. The good players could throw successfully with a left-handed or right-handed swing, while some could make the ring circle the playing area twice before landing on the hook. One expert stood next to the hook, with his back to the wall, and threw the ring away from him – it returned and smacked him firmly in the middle of the forehead. A miscalculation there, I feel. There were people, I was told, who could ring a cigarette-end impaled on the hook, without disturbing the ash. That particular fantasy was not actually demonstrated, but I did believe assurances that the house record at the time was 38

consecutive successful throws. This was achieved at a pub called The Crown, the only pub in Warrington still playing the game at that time. Just before the Second World War, I was informed, there were seven or eight pubs with the game. It may well be that no-one plays Ringing the Bull now in Warrington, since the town has been knocked down and rebuilt in the last 30 years.

Middle-class writers on middle-class pubs tended to write off Ringing the Bull as an ancient and dying pastime. Eric Delderfield, chronicler of the pub sign, mentions an inn called The Wooden Ender, at Ardleigh, in Essex. Although the pub's name was apparently derived from the baulk of timber which protected the sides of the cattle pond across the road, the sign actually shows the game of Ringing the Bull in progress. It is no longer played there and Delderfield says of it, 'once universally popular, but now played in only a dozen inns in the whole country'. Michael Brander's *The Life and Sport of the Inn* is similarly gloomy on the subject: 'Another very localised and simple alehouse game, quite possibly

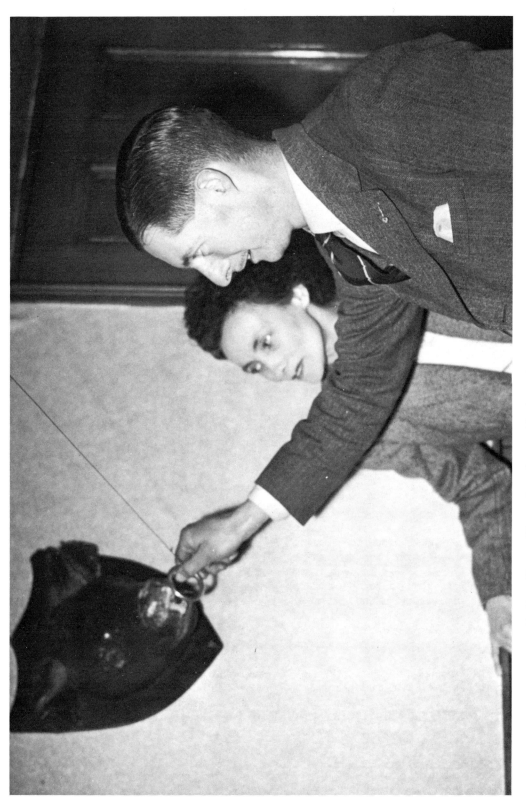

Mr George Wayne, of The King's Head, Lewes, lifts the ring from the bull's nose after a successful shot.

of very ancient origins, was known as "Ring the Bull". By 1900, this . . . was to be found in a few alehouses in country areas.' Yet again, a saloon-bar view of what might or might not be happening in the public bar. The truth of the matter is that Ringing the Bull has *always* been played in hundreds, rather than dozens of pubs, and nowadays it is enjoying a revival and is more widespread than ever. I'm reminded of the holiday visitors to a seaside pub in Suffolk, who saw the bull ring at rest, with the ring settled on the hook – and asked the landlord if it was a device for holding up the building.

For some reason, most pubs which have the game are convinced that it is rare. I must have come across it in at least 40 locations and been told each time that it is 'unique', and I've collected the names of at least three times that number of pubs which play. Most places use it as a casual pastime – at The Trip to Jerusalem, the landlady says that her customers try to ring the bull 'from different parts of the room'; at The Daneway Inn, an old boatmen's pub near the Sapperton Tunnel in Gloucestershire, the landlord challenges customers to a casual game of 'best of ten throws' – the loser has to put £1 in the blind box; at The Merry Monk, in Rochdale, they have a go in between darts matches. Everywhere you go there is a peculiar brand of local one-upmanship – you are encouraged to give the game a try, then a regular comes along and shows you how it should be done. Some players indulge in strange psychological tricks, like twisting the cord before they hand you the ring, which means that it is almost impossible to get the ring on the hook. There's actually no need for all this foolery, since every pitch is different and home team advantage is insurmountable.

I'm not at all sure about the Roman or Crusading ancestry of Ringing the Bull. The earliest specific reference to the game I've found, courtesy of Rob McGee, pub historian extraordinaire, comes by way of a dramatic tale which unfolded in January 1869, at Stalybridge, Cheshire. Police Constable Wadsworth, patrolling the town one evening, saw, through a window from Chapel Yard, a bunch of boys, whom he judged to be 16 or under, playing cards in The Globe Inn. Upon entering the premises, he found that the patrons were indeeed underage – and that the landlord had also allowed men to play Bull-ringing for beer.

At The Pineapple Inn, in Shaw, Greater Manchester, they have a boisterous but extremely well organised Bull Ring match each Boxing Day. Its history stretches back into the mists of time – 1976, to be precise – when a customer, who is a long-distance lorry driver, brought the game back from Newark,

Nottinghamshire, where 'every other pub used to play'. In Shaw, the game is a knockout contest of 16 rings up (21 rings up in the final). There are ten goes to a turn and a scorer by the chalkboard notes how many throws each player has had and how many rings have scored. Immediately before each game, the players are allowed three practice shots – if, during the course of a game, they inadvertently drop the ring, rather than throw it, a shout of 'dropped ring!' allows the error and another throw. The contest of Boxing Day, 1990, went on from 1.30 pm to almost 5 pm and was eventually won by John Stevens, the landlord – he's won it three times in the last four years, but swears he never practises from one year's end to another. The target is a bull's horn and the ring is from a bull's nose – the abattoir is not far down the road. There are free beef-sausage hot dogs during the interval.

A modern, porcine adaptation of Ringing the Bull, called **Pig Snout**, was manufactured in the mid-1980s by an elusive organisation called the Little Pub Company. A life-size fibreglass model of a pig's head is mounted on a green wooden shield and fixed to the wall – it looks like a rather odd sporting trophy, or something that has escaped from the display in a butcher's shop. There is a cord string from the ceiling, but instead of a ring on the end, there is a solid rubber object, reminiscent of the ferrule from the bottom of a walking stick. The targets are two-pence pieces balanced on the pig's nose and ears. You get 2 points for knocking off the nose coin, 1 point for each of the ear coins and the game is 11 points up.

Pig's Snout is available in several pubs up and down the country – most appropriately, perhaps, in The Sow and Pigs, Toddington, Bedfordshire.

Indoor Quoits

You will find, if you dig deep enough into the collective folk memory of the public bar, traces of Rings throughout the land. Ringing the Bull, too, has been – and is being – played nationwide. When we come to **Indoor Quoits** though, the story is quite different; this is a game of limited but vaguely-defined distribution along the debatable lands of the Welsh/English border. I've tried sticking pins representing Indoor Quoits in a map, and find that they cluster thickest in Powys, with substantial overlaps into Hereford and Worcester and Gloucestershire. Having said that, although the game is recognisably the same throughout the region, there are always differences of opinion and interpretation to take into account.

There is great confusion about the actual game. Timothy Finn, in his book on pub games, published in 1966, called the game **Dobbers** – a name I've come across nowhere else. In my first book on pub games, which came out in 1976, I concentrated on the rules and regulations of the Evesham and District Quoits League, which at that time was flourishing – although then, as now, I called the pastime Indoor Quoits, mainly to distinguish it from the outdoor version. Recent editions of *The Good Beer Guide* have specifically mentioned **Evesham Quoits** in places as widespread as Broadway, in Gloucestershire, and Bretforton in Hereford and Worcester. If you go into a pub where they actually play, they simply call it Quoits, sometimes Table Quoits.

The quoits board is roughly 18in square, and is laid flat on a small table raised about 2ft 6in from the floor. Within the wooden board are two scooped, concentric circles, with a central, sturdy, bolt-headed spindle, called a 'spike' or 'peg'. There is usually some form of netting behind the board, to prevent the quoits from overshooting and causing alarm and consternation elsewhere in the pub. Many of the boards, especially those in Gloucestershire, are painted red, green and black, with a polished brass spike and have a distinct fairground look about them – a kind of faded, garish elegance. Others are simple, functional and undecorated. There is at least one board cut from stone, at The New Inn, Pembridge, and another, perhaps legendary monument, carved in marble, reputedly somewhere in the city of Worcester.

The quoits are made of rubber, very much like the Lancashire rings described earlier, although within the territory, they vary in size, thickness and weight. In some areas, they are painted white on one side and left black on the other. A ring which pitches black-side-up is 'dead' and does not score, no matter where it lands.

All this information should make it obvious that Indoor Quoits is a brilliantly-miniaturised, domesticated form of the much older outdoor game – instead of the hob and the clay bed, there's the spike and the board. The rules concerning the 'hill' and the 'hole' on the heavy, metal quoits correspond exactly to the white and black sides of the rubber rings. There is one interesting difference between the two games – Outdoor Quoits, although now largely confined to certain areas, notably North Yorkshire and East Anglia, was once universally played in England and Wales. The indoor version, as described, has never strayed far from Offa's Dyke.

There are several different games to be played on the quoits board. In most pubs, the basic scoring system is uniform – the spike counts 5; the pan, which is the sunken circle around the spike, scores 2, while an outer circle registers just 1 point. It is well to check the local house rules. Teams in Evesham used

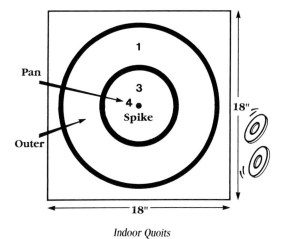

Indoor Quoits

to play 5:3:1, then changed to 4:3:1 to make for closer games.

Nowadays, the boards in Gloucestershire and Hereford and Worcester tend to be isolated and used only in the individual pub to pass away a couple of minutes. League play has retreated to the hills . . .

The most rewarding area to explore, for both the landscape and the game, is Powys. There is, for example, the Presteigne League on Monday nights in winter and the Knighton League on Tuesdays in summer – the same dozen teams play in both. The Standard game is from 1 to 13, not, as you might think, in round-the-board fashion, but more like the darts game of Scram. There is a special scoreboard, with the numbers 1 to 13 on it, each number hidden or revealed by a small sliding panel called a 'card'. Once you have a number, scored by any combination of quoits, it is yours and barred from your opponent. Whoever scores the most points wins – it may not actually be necessary to close all the 13 cards, since one player or another may be already too far ahead to be pulled back by what is left. There are six players to a team in a league game and a match consists of six singles and three pairs games.

In Gloucestershire, they call this game **Stick**. It runs from 1 to 10 and you can elect to 'stick' on a score before you've thrown all four quoits. If you go over the required score, you're 'bust' and lose everything gained from those four quoits.

In Powys, they throw 8ft 6in from the board. Go south to Evesham and the distance is 9ft 3in and the main game quite different. League and cup matches consist of three pairs, playing 121 up and six singles of 61 up. You must finish on exactly the number required. If you bust your score, you cannot throw unused rings and must wait for your next turn. This game is sometimes called **Round the Board**, meaning that it is scored round a cribbage board – very confusing for darts players!

Some leagues are very strict about the style of throwing. In several areas they differentiate between the 'pitchers' and the 'throwers' – a pitcher basically operates underarm, and an expert can have two or three rings spinning on the spike; a thrower comes overarm, crashing the rings down from head height in a straight trajectory for the spike. This is not a matter of mere aesthetics – players must elect which style they are going to adopt at the beginning of the season – and must keep to it. There are cups and prizes at the end of the season, not just for winning teams, but for the best pitcher and the best thrower of the campaign, not to mention the player with the highest number of spikes and the most pans.

There are variations away from the rigours of league play. One such is called **Spikes Up** and tends to be played by the hot-shots, for money. The first thrower goes for as many consecutive spikes as he can; if he scores four with his first four quoits, he retrieves them and carries on until the successful sequence is broken. His opponent has to top his score, which often gets into the 20s and 30s. The tension in a big game can be high, with most of the pressure on the second thrower.

There's a less pressurised, more casual game for four players, using an ordinary pack of playing cards. Each player is given a full suit of cards – clubs, spades, diamonds or hearts – laid face-down in front of him. He discards three cards from his suit, without turning them over or seeing what they are. Now the rest must be turned up, one at a time, and as each card is revealed it must be 'scored' on the quoits board. A king counts 13, a queen 12 and a jack 11, so court cards can cause problems. The plain cards require their numerical equivalent and an ace scores 1. A throw is, as usual, four quoits. The winner of the game is the player who scores and therefore disposes of all his cards first.

There are party tricks, often performed after league matches and as closing time looms. Any suitable projection in the pub becomes a case for treatment – pump handles, bottles, beer glasses, coat pegs, and even the four legs of an upturned stool in an exhilarating, extravagant display – just like the old days in Bolton, as described by the old man to the curious researchers from Mass Observation.

The history of Indoor Quoits remains elusive. Occasionally, someone who is interested in the game turns up a reference to some 15th- or 16th-century ordinance, usually encouraging archery and condemning prostitution and Quoits – and great excitement ensues as the ancestry of the game moves back

500 years. I'm fairly certain that all such references apply only to the outdoor game. My theory is that Indoor Quoits was invented by someone's great-grandfather, in the latter half of the 19th century, in Brecon, Builth Wells, Ludlow, Hereford or Worcester.

Suffolk Quoits and Caves

I am a haunter of those shops which sell junk, bygones and collectables and have a roomful of battered, old pub game artifacts which some people might dismiss as 'rubbish' and others praise as 'antique'. One of the rarest pieces is a thick, wooden, circular board, perhaps 18in across. It has a 1in batten of wood underneath and to one end of the circle, so that the whole thing will sit on a low table and slope towards you. Once upon a time, it was painted white and was divided up into shapes by thin black-painted lines – a circle in the middle, four broad segments radiating from the centre. It gets the occasional dusting, but looks a bit neglected now. The scoring figures on each area are barely legible. This rather forlorn, but to my eyes beautiful, object is a Suffolk quoits board. Twenty years ago, on patrol in East Anglia, I saw one or two in pubs, usually produced from behind the bar as a curiosity. I don't recall one ever in play, although the rules of the game were explained to me.

It was perhaps too simple a game to survive. You threw four flat rubber quoits at the board, from a distance of 8ft or so, and scored whichever number was painted on the segment in which your quoit landed. Anything that crossed or touched a line did not count – which must have caused endless arguments, and made the game more a matter of luck than judgment. The game was 21 up.

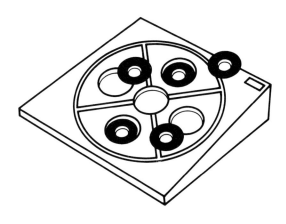

Caves board

In 1930, the landlord of the Black Boy, in Bury St Edmunds, patented a game which he had invented, called **Caves**. It was manufactured commercially and, until comparatively recent times, enjoyed modest popularity in pubs of the region – Lowestoft seems to have marked the furthest distance of its travels. The patent specification shows that he was not in fact inventing something new, but improving on the existing and frustrating pattern of the old Suffolk Quoits board: 'Instead of having only numbered ruled partitions on the flat surface of the Quoit board (placed on the ground or the table) our present invention consists of a Quoit board wherein are made a number of cavities within the ruled partitions. By this means a player, instead of throwing a quoit within a numbered ruled partition for the purpose of scoring will, by our present invention, have to throw a quoit within one or other of the cavities, for the purpose of scoring.'

The board is 16in square – slightly smaller than the Indoor Quoits board of Powys or Gloucestershire. It slopes at a very gentle angle towards the thrower, exactly as the old Suffolk board used to do. The five circular depressions, one in the centre and four around the board, are half-an-inch deep and 3½in in diameter – just about right for the thick rubber quoit to rest comfortably within. Five rings are thrown, from a range or 8ft 6in. A ring must settle *exactly* in a bed to score 1, 2, 3, 4 or 5 points, as indicated. A maximum, near miraculous, score would thus be 15 – a second quoit in a bed already filled does not count. The game remains at 21 up, sometimes 31, and occasionally, it is claimed, 61.

The Caves board may well have represented an improvement on the original flat board, but it never became very popular and certainly never caught on outside Suffolk. I doubt whether any now remain on view, let alone in play – they're probably all quietly appreciating in value in Suffolk antique shops.

Caves was invented in the 1930s by the landlord of a Suffolk pub, to replace the old Quoits game using a flat board.

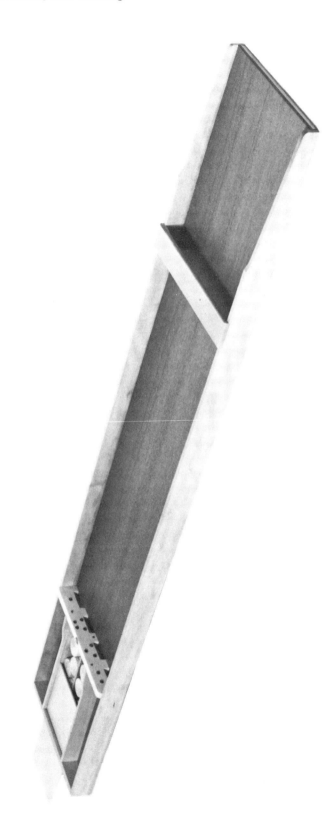

The Dutch version of Shuffleboard – Sjoelbak – which is occasionally found in British pubs. It is an extremely popular game in Belgium and the Netherlands.

Shovelboard and Shuffleboard

It has always been a matter of some regret that I have never been able to get hands-on experience of a 16th- or 17th-century shovelboard. They were enormous tables, up to 30ft long and you shoved, or shuffled, flat metal weights along acres of polished wood to reach critical points at the other end of the hall. There are several of these old tables still around, in various old houses or museums, but of course they are there to be looked at, not played upon - most frustrating.

In the long gallery of Astley House, near Chorley, Lancashire, there is a shovelboard table, 23ft 6in long, perhaps 3ft wide, supported by 20 fat legs. The whole surface is constructed of 12 × 3in pieces of wood, laid like a sort of herringbone parquet floor, but smooth as glass. There are a couple of metal weights on display in a case mounted on a nearby wall. Herbert Cesinsky, the architect who reported on the condition of the hall in the 1920s, for Chorley Corporation, noticed that the table had been sawn up, to get it into the newly built gallery in 1666, then stuck back together again; he dated it back to c1570.

There is another splendid example of a monster table, this time 30ft long, in Norwich Museum; it belonged originally to the Pastons, Earls of Norfolk, and was kept at Oxmead Hall, Norfolk, until 1732, when the second Earl died owing so much money that the entire contents of the house were sold to pay his debts. It was probably at this time that the landlord of The Black Lion at Buxton, a few miles from the Hall, bought it and allowed his customers to play. Benjamin Strutt described the table formerly at Chartley Hall in Staffordshire, which was 'ten yards, one foot and one inch long, made of 260 pieces, generally eighteen inches long, some under a foot - and so accurately joined and glued together that no shuffleboard is freer from rubs or castings'. No aristocratic home, it seems, was complete without one of these masterpieces of the joiner's art; they were, says Strutt, 'in great repute amongst nobility and gentry, and few of their mansions were without a shoveboard'.

We owe the following description of the game as it was actually played, to Mr Strutt, who wrote some extremely long sentences: 'At one end of the shovel board, there is a line drawn across parallel with the edge and about three or four inches from it; at four feet distance from this line another is made, over which it is necessary for the weight to pass when it is thrown by the player, otherwise the go is not reckoned. The players stand at the end of the table, opposite to the two marks above mentioned, each of them having four flat weights of metal, which they shove from them one at a time alternately: and the judgment of the play is, to give sufficient impetus to the weight to carry it beyond the mark nearest to the edge of the board, which requires great nicety, for if it be too strongly impelled, so as to fall from the table, and there is nothing to prevent it, into a trough placed underneath for its reception, the throw is not counted; if it hangs over the edge, without falling, three are reckoned towards the player's name; if it lie between the line and the edge without hanging over, it tells for two; if on the line, and not up to it, but over the first line, it counts for one. The game, when two play, is generally eleven; but the number is extended when four or more are jointly concerned.' We can assume that the game was like bowls, in that one could knock an opponent's weight out of the way and out of a scoring position. We can also assume that what made the game exciting was the betting that accompanied it.

Henry VIII was famous for his destructive tendencies, concerning both wives and monasteries - he also lost at an extraordinary variety of games, including **Shovelboard**. The privy purse expenses of 1532 show that in January of that year, a Lord William won £9 from the King at 'Shovilla Bourde', and 'my lord of Rocheforde won of the King at Shovilla Bourde and betting at the game £45'. While all this was going on, the general populace, of course, was forbidden by law to play the game at all.

Strutt's famous book was first published in 1801 and by that time, Shovelboard had been abandoned by the aristocracy, who had taken to playing billiards instead. The huge, old shovelboard tables were cut down to a more practical domestic size, or broken up, stored away and forgotten, or sold off. Those that remained in play were in pubs, which is where Strutt actually saw one, on one of his 'rare' field trips 'at a low public house in Benjamin Street, near Clerkenwell Green, which is about three feet in breadth and thirty nine feet two inches in length, and said to be the longest in this time in London'. The game, said Strutt, no doubt with an involuntary shudder of distaste, was 'now considered as exceedingly vulgar and practised by the lower classes'.

I live in hope that one day I will find a 'low' public house, full of the 'lower classes' still playing this vulgar game, but I've been searching for many years now with not so much as a hint of such a precious find.

In the early 1900s, Shovelboard re-emerged as **Shuffleboard** in California and soon caught on throughout the United States. American-style Shuffleboard was played not on a table, but on the ground, with a new scoring system and novel tactics, but the pieces and general principles remained much the same as before. Eventually, the new game developed in two distinct directions – as a game played by well-heeled passengers on the decks of ocean liners and as an indoor table game in amusement arcades.

In both versions of the game, the target areas were divided up into several numbered scoring sections, instead of the old notion of trembling on the edge of the table. I've never travelled on an ocean liner, so I've missed out on this branch of the family tree, but back in 1967, I *did* see the American version of this ancient English pastime reintroduced into this country and *The Morning Advertiser* described the game aptly as 'a cross between shove ha'penny, billiards and curling, played on a table 10 to 8 feet long'.

There was, as I recall, a British Championship held at The Kingsway Tavern, in London. A few years later, at the Alexandra Palace, London, during an Amusement Trades Exhibition, there was a magnificent table on display, courtesy of the American Shuffleboard Company ('the hallmark of American craftsmanship for more than three decades') – a splendid, glistening 9ft table, with electronic pingate control and scoreboard and winking fluorescent tubes. The game did catch on, briefly, in a few pubs in London and Birmingham, but not enough to notice.

The second prong of the foreign Shuffleboard invasion came from the Low Countries, especially Holland, where yet another variation on the old game has been popular for at least a hundred years. *Sjoelbak* (let's call it **Dutch Shuffleboard**) is an extraordinary combination of the Mississippi and Trou Madame versions of Bagatelle (qv). There are 30 wooden discs, looking a bit like slightly oversized draughts, and they are pushed under the bar and along a 6ft wooden table, to score by passing through one of four numbered arches. Slipping one piece into each of the four scoring slots (scoring 1: 2: 3: 4) doubles their value, so there is some considerable encouragement to go for all four targets, rather than concentrating only on the four-slot.

Once you have got over the awkward beginner's stage, when all the pieces seem to lodge in an impenetrable jam outside the arches, Dutch Shuffleboard is an absorbing game. In Holland and Belgium, it is taken very seriously and there are regional, national and international contests. There have been several attempts to launch the game in Britain, but with only limited success so far, although there have been sporadic sightings of play in London, Birmingham and West Yorkshire.

Summer Ice

There is a long-standing, these days fairly amiable, dispute between the Scots and the Dutch as to who invented the sport now called **Curling** – a form of Quoits or bowls, played with stones on ice. The Scots claim that the game depicted on 17th-century, Dutch winter landscape paintings uses frozen clods of earth, whereas the Scots have always used stones. I mention this only in case you feel the need to foment a quarrel between the races about the significance of clods and stones. The game was effectively codified by the Duddingston Curling Club, in Edinburgh, in 1795 – these were the rules polished up and sanctified by the Royal Caledonian Curling Club in 1838. Curling was a pub game only by virtue of certain houses that simply turned a hosepipe on their back yards in winter, to create an impromptu and irregular rink. The real game is largely played on artificial indoor rinks.

There was, however, an interesting development, given the charming name of **Summer Ice**, at one time played all over Scotland, but now confined to a handful of villages near Loch Katrine, in Perthshire. The Summer Ice track, rink or board, is very much like that in Shovelboard or Shuffleboard – it is a wooden table, 25ft long, 2ft wide, with a highly-polished surface. As the name suggests, Summer Ice offers frustrated curlers an indoor game out of season – the missiles are called stones but are bulbous, flat-topped pieces of steel weighing about 3lbs each and propelled up the table by thumb and finger power. The aim here is not to pose the stones trembling on the far edge of the table, but to get them into a small circle marked in the surface of the wood – a concentric target reminiscent of the curling target. The inner circle, the 'bull', so to speak, is the same size as a stone – 2½in across. In a sense, the game is rather like bowls, so you get 1 point for each of your stones nearer the target than your opponent's. Play is fifteen ends and the game can be singles (four stones each), doubles (three stones each) or rinks, or teams of four playing two stones each.

The Aberfoyle Summer Ice League includes teams from Gartmore, Kippen, Bucklyvie and Aberfoyle. Oddly, the matches begin in September and finish sometime in March; even more oddly, a local story claims that the game was brought to Scotland by Irish labourers working on local railway tunnels in the 1880s, whereas all logic suggests that the Scots simply adapted Curling and brought it indoors. Robert Telfer, the skipper of the Aberfoyle Summer Icers, reported that he had seen the game while on holiday in 1987, in Hartford, Connecticut, USA. He was told that the game had been played there for many years and had been introduced into the area by Scottish immigrants – the only difference seemed to be that the surface of the American table was covered in very fine crystals. Some of the Aberfoyle players remember being visited, years ago, by a team from Coatbridge, near Glasgow. The visitors turned up wearing grocers' aprons, since their home table was covered in rice flour, to help the stones slide.

Shove Ha'penny and Push Penny

Shovelboard was a game on the grand scale and there can't have been many pubs able to accommodate a 30 ft-long hulk of timber and still have room for customers. **Shove Groat, Slype Groat** and **Slide Thrift** were various names given in the 15th, 16th and 17th centuries to a smaller-scale version of the game, played on a conveniently-sized portable board and using coins instead of weights. (A groat was a silver coin, known from 1351 and worth four pence.) It must have been an enjoyable pastime, judging by the number of times the Authorities felt obliged to ban it and fine people for playing – in 1521, to select one case from many, the Society of the Inner Temple found their members were devoting more time to Slype Groat (and Shuffleboard) than they were to studying their law books. Shakespeare has Falstaff encouraging violence in a splendid mixed metaphor to delight all games players: 'Quoit him down Bardolph, like a shove-groat shilling!'

Apart from historical and literary references, the earliest evidence I have seen for the game was a photograph of a board, actually set in a larger table, which came from Hinwick House in Bedfordshire. The table was mentioned in an inventory of the house's contents in 1582 and, although the board may have been inserted later, it is thought to have been there since at least 1614. The coins with the board were Edward VI shillings. Apparently, the debased coinage was renewed in the reign of Queen Elizabeth I, so the old coins became valueless and were used as mere tokens – I suppose this might be a clue to the first real enthusiasm for the game.

Strutt was very snobbish about Shove Groat, which he said was the same as the 'modern' game (c1801) of **Justice Jervis** or **Jarvis**; this sounds promising, too, since he says it was 'confined to common pot houses and only practised by such as frequent the taprooms'. The playing area of the board was 3 or 4ft long and 12 to 14in wide and was divided latitudinally into nine equal partitions, or beds. Each bed was marked with a number from one to nine and the game was not quite the one we know today as

Shove Ha'penny. 'Each of the players provides himself with a smooth halfpenny, which he places on the edge of the table, and striking it with the palm of the hand, drives it towards the marks; and according to the value of the figure affixed to the partition wherein the halfpenny rests, his game is reckoned; which is generally stated at thirty one, and must be made precisely; if it be exceeded, the player goes again for nine, which also must be brought exactly, or the turn is forfeited . . .' – I'm not quite sure that I understand the last bit, but going for a score of 31 in nine numbered beds sounds interesting and can, of course, be played as an entertaining variation of the basic game on a contemporary Shove Ha'penny board.

Even more of a challenge was an ingenious translation of Cribbage, played on a board with ten numbered beds – 'they play with four halfpence, which are considered as equivalent to so many cards at cribbage; and the game is counted, in a like manner, by 15s, sequences, pairs and pairials, according to the numbers appertaining to the partitions occupied by the halfpence.'

A hundred years or so on from Strutt's report, one James John Hissey came upon another game, clearly from the same family, in the course of an interminable 432-page ramble through the pubs of the eastern counties, which he published in 1917, under the title *The Road and the Inn*. The game, spotted at an anonymous pub, was a new one to Hissey and he described it in some detail: 'This consisted of a long smooth board placed flat on a table, the board being marked by horizontal lines, some two inches apart, with figures at their ends. Each player, in turn, placed a penny at the foot of the board, which he struck with the palm of his hand, so that it slid along towards the top, and the score was calculated from the figure at the end of the line where the coin stopped, he whose penny stopped by the highest figure being winner. Two or more men played the game, and there was always the chance that later players might, as at bowls, for better or worse, disturb the position of the pennies already on the board, or even drive them off it, so that they did not score. I noticed that the game was in request for most of the evening. If there were only two players, then each player played six pennies each – one penny at a time in turns.'

Apart from the fact that Strutt's game was played with halfpennies and Hissey's with pennies, they're obviously very similar pastimes. It is a great shame that neither gentlemen could bring themselves to talk to the taproom players, much less ask for a game – had they done so, we would have had a much clearer picture of precisely what was going on.

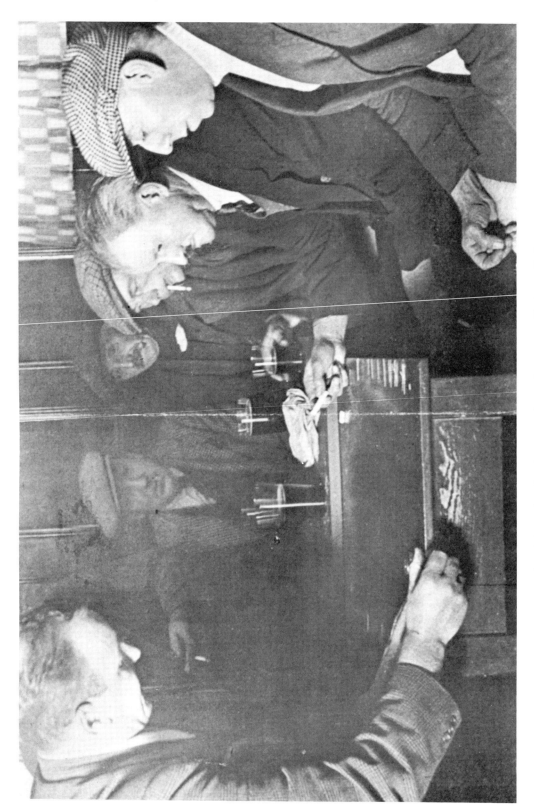

A shove ha'penny board in play in a southern pub, I presume (the beer is flat!)

Similar games today use old pre-decimalised halfpennies, which are shoved and pennies, which are pushed. I suppose you could say that both coins, like groats and Edward VI shillings, are now debased – they're certainly not legal tender. (I should perhaps explain, for the benefit of young readers, that there were 240 pennies to the pound and therefore 480 halfpennies; the 1d piece was much larger and heavier than today's 1p piece and the ½d was the same size as the shilling, which you probably called a 5p piece until it disappeared, in 1990. Come to think of it, the ½p piece has gone the way of all useless coppers, too.)

The standard shove ha'penny board illustrated reveals the ancient design. In earlier times, it would probably have been simply chalked or scratched on a wooden table, but from the 1920s onwards, the pattern became uniform, as the boards were commercially manufactured and encouraged, like the standard dartboard in later years, by publicans and breweries. The board is usually about 24in long × 14in wide. The far end has a raised semi-circular ridge to stop the coins sliding out of play and into oblivion on the bar floor. Underneath the near end, a narrow baton of wood is screwed, to butt up against the table edge and keep the board firm and steady in play. The scoring surface is divided into nine equal beds, 1¼ in in breadth; on either side of each bed is a small square, used for scoring.

The object of the modern game is to propel the coins up the board, in the time-honoured way, one at a time. Each player has five coins per turn and for every coin which ends up exactly in a bed, a chalk mark is made in the appropriate scoring square. The game is won by the player who gets three coins scored in each of the nine beds. If you get *more* than three in a bed, the extra points are given to your opponent, if he needs them. The only exception to this is the final winning point, which must be scored, and not received, to win. In Guernsey, where they play a lot of Shove Ha'penny and stage an annual island championship, they insist on five coins in each bed, which – they claim – adds to the skill and complexity of the game.

There are learned – and sometimes heated – disputes about the relative merits of teak, mahogany, slate and even marble or glass for the board, and everyone seems to swear by a different cleaning and polishing agent for the playing surface – I've heard petrol, paraffin, French chalk, beer and black lead discussed and I am suspicious of all of them since they may be mentioned merely to confuse, while keeping the truly effective formula a secret.

As always, you must find out what the house rules

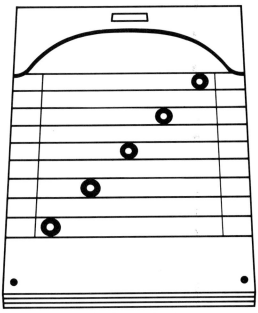
Shove ha'penny board

are about a scoring shot – in some places, only a coin mutually agreed to be in the exact centre of the bed will score; in others, it will be allowed if it can be separated from the line by a sheet of paper's thickness. Some elaborate and expensive boards have brass strips sunk beneath the surface of the lines separating the beds. In case of dispute, these strips can be raised from one side – if the coin is disturbed, it is not considered 'true' and does not score.

There are many styles of 'shoving', the commonest being to strike the coin poised on the edge of the board with the heel of the hand – what the chiromancers call the Mount of the Moon. Some players use the palm of the hand, others the side of the thumb joint or the tips of the fingers. Each style has its elegant and effective devotees.

There still seems to be a reasonable supply of old halfpennies, although they actually went out of official circulation in this country in 1974. John Jacques & Sons, who have been catering for games players one way and another since 1795, sell a set of five original old English halfpennies for £1. Alternatively, you can still find them fairly easily in junk shops and at flea markets. It is usual to mill-off one side of each coin to a perfectly featureless, smooth finish; convention dictates that it is the tails side which thus disappears – there is a lingering pub rumour that defacing the monarch's head is still a capital offence. If the worst comes to the worst, you can buy official shove ha'penny discs, which are rather boring artifacts that look a bit like washers.

141

An outdoor version of Shove Ha'penny being played by London youths, in 1959.

Back in 1973, a Shove Ha'penny enthusiast from Oxford wrote a column in the *Daily Mirror*, claiming that the city had 28 teams from 25 pubs and clubs in the area. He doubted whether any other area in the country could match that, with the possible exception of the Channel Islands. At the time, there might have been counter claims from other regions, such as Gloucestershire, Hampshire, the East End of London and County Durham, but as far as today is concerned, I am not so sure. Although, if you comb assiduously through the close-knit columns of *The Good Beer Guide* or *The Good Pub Guide*, you will find many pubs, nationwide, offering Shove Ha'penny as one of the house attractions, I get the impression that the game is in steep decline. Certainly, the Durham League, once a lively and important organisation, has collapsed through lack of support, although individual pubs keep the board tucked away and will allow it out in quiet periods, for a few experts to keep their thumbs flexible.

I remember seeing matches in Durham, in the late 1960s, where the experts were wary of draughts from open doors or windows, which could subtly change the atmosphere and temperature and thus affect the surface of the board. There were stories of people actually being thrown out of pubs because they had spilt beer on a board, or used a dampened coin. Players tended to 'build' from the near to the far beds and rarely wasted a shot, nudging, pushing and cannoning so that the best possible use was made from every coin. It seemed quite normal to score a 'sergeant' – three coins in a bed – or to score with all five coins – a 'sergeant major' or 'gold watch'. There were certainly great players in Oxford, too, and it was here, according to games historian Timothy Finn, that the game of **progressive** enjoyed its finest flowering. The coins which scored were chalked, then played again, so that it was possible to build up a break – skilful practitioners could get most, if not all, of the 27 chalks needed to fill the board scored in one break. At this level of play, only a hair's-breadth separates the top performers, so there is a distinct advantage in playing first. To even things out, some pubs insist that the winner of the toss, and therefore the 'shover-off', must use only three coins for his first turn, both players using all five thereafter.

Push Penny is alive and well, and being played regularly in Stamford, Lincolnshire, where they have a Tuesday-night league from September to early April, with two divisions of nine teams each, plus innumerable singles, doubles and threesomes knockouts, not to mention a World Championship, held during the Stamford Festival at the end of June, or beginning of July. Most, if not all, of the best players in the world come from Stamford, although they do get challengers coming up from Hastings, from time to time. A winter Tuesday in Stamford is the time and place to see extraordinary skills on display.

They still make their own boards in Stamford, usually from mahogany, sometimes oak. Stamford craftsmen are always on the look out for unwanted shop or bar counters, free of faults, cracks, joints and knots. The push penny board looks exactly like the shove ha'penny track already described, except that the nine beds are slightly larger, to accommodate the pennies; three old pennies laid side-to-side along the length of the board will exactly cover two beds. The scoring areas are called the 'grass' in the Stamford area. Boards may look the same, but they vary enormously in the way they play – some are slow and need a heavy hand to get the pennies into the far beds, while others need the slightest touch on the coin to send it smoothly skating up the board. Knots can be obstacles which have to be worked round; the grain of the wood can take a coin in extraordinary curves along the board's surface. All in all, home-board advantage is so strong that a visiting league team will consider it an achievement to get a draw and a triumph to actually win, while solo matches and certainly the World Championships, have to be played on neutral boards. Obviously, boards must be carefully looked after – they are usually kept in bags resembling felt pillowcases, in a cool room in the pub and are brought out only an hour or so before a match.

Three old pennies are used, with the tails-side milled flat and then polished to a good finish. There will usually be a heavy one, a 'middling' one and a light one, so that different shots can be achieved – a heavy penny will hold firm and a light one can be bounced back from it, or the heavy one can go 'through' a light one and push it up the board. The technology and philosophy of penny pushing can be quite mind-boggling and has to be seen to be believed.

Isle of Purbeck Shove Halfpenny

There are some odd goings-on in and around the Dorset village of Corfe Castle each Shrove Tuesday. When the church bell strikes noon, several young men trot across the road from The Fox, carrying large glasses of beer, while several older men appear to be trying, not too seriously, to interrupt their progress and make them spill their drinks. Some time later, all the men emerge amicably from the building opposite the pub and start kicking a football about in West Street up to a piece of common land called The Halves. Later still, a token force goes by car to the site

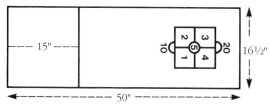

Isle of Purbeck shove halfpenny board

of Owre Quay, in Poole Harbour, carrying the football and a pound of ground pepper; the pepper is ceremoniously presented to the landowner.

All this is in fact the Annual General Meeting of the Company of Marblers and Stonecutters of the Isle of Purbeck, whose medieval ancestors cut the Purbeck marble for Salisbury, Winchester, Worcester and Lincoln cathedrals and Westminster Abbey. The young men with the beer are apprentices seeking admission to the Company and the business with the football and the pepper is an assertion of their collective ancient rights of way, from the quarries to the harbour from which the marble used to be shipped out – the pepper is 'rent' for use of the now non-existent quay.

The Isle of Purbeck was once a remote area, almost cut off from the mainland by tidal inlets and rivers. Today, it is a popular tourist area, centred around the attractions of Corfe Castle and Swanage; a modern road system has rendered the name a mere geographical and historical oddity. Another legacy of its former isolation, besides the activities of the Marblers and Stonecutters on Shrove Tuesday, and perhaps not unconnected with those worthy men, is the unique Isle of Purbeck Shove Halfpenny board and game. This involves shoving halfpennies in the usual way, but on a board much longer than usual – anything from 4ft 6in to 5ft 6in long and 16 to 18in wide – the target is a numbered area, as shown in the diagram. This particular example comes from the Red Lion in Swanage.

No-one knows how, when or where the 'long board' first saw the light of day, although locals will tell you that it was invented about a hundred or so years ago by the workers in the quarries, to idle away the time when the weather was too bad to work or cut stone. These men, it seems, were formidable drinkers, who were in the habit of taking their entire week's annual holiday in the pubs of nearby villages and towns, where playing and betting on Shove Halfpenny was one of the major attractions. (They spelled it Shove Halfpenny and not Shove Ha'penny, by the way, and I feel these regional niceties should be preserved.)

There is a rival theory about the origin of species

of the long, or Swanage board, entertainingly put forward by games historian Timothy Finn, which suggests that it came from Shuffleboard as played by sailors, and then passengers, on the decks of ships. He argues that Swanage was, in the old days, more open to influence from the sea than the marshy hinterland, and the marking and scoring system in both games are striking similar. More research is called for – but in the meantime let's consider the rules of this wonderful pastime.

The main game played, in league, knockout cup, team and individual contests throughout the season, is 101 up, best of three legs. The scoring is as obvious as the illustration suggests, except that the numbers are not actually indicated on the board, but have been stored up in folk memory. Local etiquette demands that each halfpenny must lie at least an ⅛in within the lines of its bed to be 'good'. This rarely causes disputes when regulars play, although each team in a league match elects a sort of arbiter, or 'touch judge', whose collective decision is absolutely final. In casual games, if there is any query, an unused or non-scoring coin is stood on edge; if it will fit within the problem gap, then all is well. Lastly, coins which fail to reach the line across the board some 15 in from the playing end may be retrieved and shoved again.

The 'long boards' need a great deal of tender loving care – perhaps that is why the game has never travelled far from its home territory. The preparations for a game look deceptively casual – the board is brought out, set on its table, casually squirted with a soda siphon and rubbed down with kitchen roll or paper napkins. This is, in fact, only the final, simple cleaning process which has been preceded by years of preparation, for the boards only attain true perfection after generations of sliding coins and smoothing hands. When new teams enter the league, old boards have to be found for them – brand new ones would never match up to the exacting requirements of expert play. Each board has its own peculiarities and they all have marginally different dimensions, although the 'football-pitch' scoring area remains much the same. Some are mahogany, others beech or teak, some are fast, some slow, and all have hidden obstacles which are found only by experience. As with Push Penny in Stamford, home-board advantage is very strong and serious individual competitions have to be played on foreign territory.

The coins, too, can vary from pub to pub. The oldest I saw, during an admittedly brief tour of inspection, were 1906 English halfpennies (which could be a clue to the game's actual vintage), but Guernsey, Jersey and Irish coins were also used. All of them were wafer-thin with sliding mileage, and be warned that if you accidentally knock one on the floor and it gets dented, chipped or otherwise knocked out of true, you will have to spend the whole of the next day rubbing down a substitute on a piece of slate.

The actual technique of the older, wiser players seems to be to go for the 20s, in the top quadrant, until the 101 hoves into view, then to adjust accordingly, so that the exact number needed to get out can be scored. For the novice, or even a moderately experienced refugee from a normal Shove Ha'penny board, the first half hour or so on the 'long board' is a weird experience. The coins seem to float endlessly along the glassy surface of the board, curving inexorably away from the target area. I'd like to see a reciprocal contest between the Penny Pushers of Stamford and the Long Board Shove Halfpenny Men of the Isle of Purbeck – and I'd always put money on the home board.

The Swanage league season runs from October to March, usually on Thursday evenings and there are currently 15 teams involved. During the tourist season, the boards and coins are carefully stored away and as a casual stranger you would know nothing of the game's existence, unless you took the trouble to ask.

Caroms

Caroms (sometimes spelt Carroms) is a relatively cheap, do-it-yourself game of finger billiards, thought to have been first played in Egypt and Ethiopia, but codified over a hundred years ago in India. The All Indian Carrom Federation, based in Bombay, has laid down the latest and most comprehensive set of rules. The game is also played in the Yemen, Burma, Switzerland and the occasional British pub.

I don't know how the Swiss connection was established, but it was from Switzerland, in 1987, that the latest attempt to convert the British was launched. It is called *Carambole* over there and it is claimed that 300 000 people play. André Knuchel, the Swiss champion, was flown over to demonstrate his finger-flicking skills at The Sun, in Castle Street, Reading, but it doesn't seem to have caught on – the regulars at the Sun are still playing Shove Ha'penny, skittles and bar billiards, but have not succumbed to the new game. Back in 1973, there was another attempt to bring Caroms into the pub games pantheon, coming this time from India, via Cheshire. An Englishman who had lived and worked in India, brought a board home with him and played, just with family and friends. His son later set up a company to make and market the game and enjoyed some modest success. The net result of all this effort, over almost 20 years, has been that one or two pubs have boards, but keep them more as a curiosity than anything else, perhaps waiting for the odd Swiss, Yemeni, Burmese or Indian customer to drop in.

Caroms is usually played by two players, who face each other across the board. The playing surface of the board is smooth and flat, about a yard square, with ridged edges and a stringed pocket at each corner. Each player has nine counters, or 'men', which are hardwood discs, one lot painted white, the other black – they are set out for the beginning of a game as shown in the diagram, with an extra piece, the red 'queen', in the centre and the white pieces in a Y-shape, the stem of the Y facing the first player to shoot off. The final piece in the puzzle is the 'striker', which is a disc, initially placed between the parallel lines (the base lines) in front of the first player, then flicked off with finger or thumb at the target men. The aim of the game is to pot all your men, and the queen, before your opponent can. Your score is the number of pieces your opponent has left when you have cleared your pieces – exactly the same principle as the old pre-snooker game of Pyramids. The game ends when one player has amassed 29 points and a match comprises the best of three games.

Toad in the Hole – and Near Relations

Besides being pushed, pennies get thrown. In fact, there is a whole family of games involving the pitching, tossing or throwing of coins, or discs, into a slot cut into a bench, chair or box. The most elaborate and curiously-named of all these games is **Toad in the Hole**, played only in a quite narrowly-defined area of East Sussex around Lewes and Newhaven. It is a game of some antiquity but no written history, and it faces an uncertain future.

The toad is a thick, heavy, brass disc, about 1¼ in across; there are four to a set and they are sometimes numbered and stamped with the name of the pub, but never dated. Mrs Mary Hufnet, whose family kept The Ram Inn at Firle through several generations, from 1908 to the '80s, says that the toads there used to be William IV pennies, then the customers tried lead tokens and finally arrived at brass discs, which they confusingly called 'coins'. At The Royal British Legion Club in the High Street of Lewes, they still play the game enthusiastically and have half a dozen differently weighted sets of brass discs – some people prefer heavy ones, some light, rather like darts players. The Fountain at Plumpton Green has ruthlessly cut through all these problems and simply requires that customers should use their own ten pence pieces.

The hole which, with a bit of luck, skill or judgment, the toad goes into, is enshrined within a specially-made wooden box on four legs. The upper surface of the box slopes gently towards the thrower and has a rounded headboard at the far end; a thick sheet of lead covers the surface, and this is pierced with a central slot, or hole, and unfolds into a narrow trough along the front edge. There is a drawer underneath this lead crust, to catch the toads which drop through the hole.

The object of the exercise is to toss the toads, usually over a throw of 8ft or so, into the hole. In Mrs Hufnet's day, the first player threw two toads, his opponent followed with three and thereafter each had four per turn. A player scored 2 points if he managed to get the disc into the hole and 1 if the toad rested on top of the lead crust, but didn't roll into the trough. The game was 31 points up, scored on a cribbage board and, when a player got to 28, he could only use three shots to get out; at 29 he was allowed two shots and at 30, just one. It was at this point that Murphy's Law of the bread always falling butter-side down was demonstrated – needing exactly 1 point to win, a player would invariably plunge straight into the hole and bust his score by getting 2. If he got all four toads in a normal turn into the hole, he won the game outright, there and then.

These were the rules according to Mrs Hufnet, in the days when there was a Toad in the Hole league and the game was much more widespread than it is today. Nowadays, you will find that, more often than not, the game is not taken at all seriously and people make up the rules as they go along – some places use only three toads and score 3 for a hole and 2 for a top. Worse still, there are pubs which keep the game merely as a curious piece of decoration and the only time it ever gets played is in quiet periods when tourists ask for it.

Toad in the Hole has now become a museum piece – literally, for there are examples in both Hove and Horsham museums, taken from pubs which no longer had any use for them. On the other hand, the customers at The Royal Oak, at Shoreham, just along the coast from Firle, were so taken with the game that one of their number has made a brand new box and set of discs and the locals seem to enjoy it.

A farmer and local historian, Mr Aubrey Charman, remembers seeing a more elaborate version of Toad in the Hole back in the 1920s, somewhere around Alfriston. The table, or box, had not one, but five holes of different sizes, distributed like the five spots on a dice, and the coins which went through the holes would slither down into an open-numbered compartment, like a miniature version of the

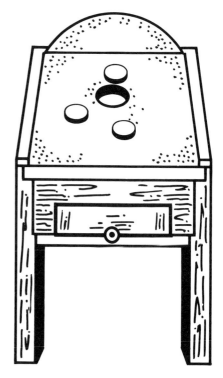

Toad in the Hole

arrangement you see at the near end on a bar billiards table. This multi-holed version of Toad in the Hole is known in workmen's cafés and bars in other countries. It is called *Tonspel* in Belgium (there is an example in an 'inn' in the Bokrijk Open Air Museum, in Limburg), *Jogo do Sapo* in Portugal and *La Rada* in the Catalonian region of Spain.

Not quite so far afield, in Norfolk and Essex, they have a game called Pitch Penny, the **Penny Game, Penny Seat, Penny Slot, Tossing the Penny** or **Penny in the Hole**, all of which involve throwing pennies across the room and into a hole carved in the seat of a high-backed settle or wooden bench.

Until comparatively recently, several pubs had much-prized sets of fat, heavy pennies dating back to 1797, the year when George III is reputed to have temporarily banned the game; perhaps the thought of the royal head rolling around the taproom floor struck him as a shade undignified. Heavy copper coinage can be quite damaging to the stoutest wood-

An unusual version of Toad in the Hole – transportable, for outdoor use.

work, especially when it rains coins for generations around one particular spot on the bench. Often, the area immediately around the slot would become so splintered and worn that it would be reinforced with a harder wood, leather, or even with a lead sheath. A lead panel was often added to the backrest of the bench, again to protect the woodwork. This added another dimension of skill to the game since it became possible to bounce coins off the back of the bench and into the hole. The Pitch Penny corner became a distinctive and popular part of the Norfolk pub repertoire.

There were, of course, legendary heroes of the game. Timothy Finn noted the name of Palmer Claxton, of St Germans, near Kings Lynn, who, in the 1960s, was considered the undisputed champion for miles around. Before Claxton's time, there was Nat Gooch, one time licensee of The Fox, Great Bradley, near Newmarket; he had been blinded by an exploding ginger beer bottle while serving with the army in Ireland, in the 1920s, but this extraordinary misfortune did not prevent him from running his pub and performing remarkable feats with flying pennies. In the 1930s, it is said, he once pitched three consecutive 12s in succession, a feat which has never been repeated.

It has to be reported that Pitch Penny has suffered a sad and steep decline. First, the valuable pennies vanished, then the drawers underneath the bench disappeared, and finally, the benching was ripped out in a frenzy of redesigning, to make the pub more 'comfortable'. By a supreme irony, Watneys, the firm which sponsored Finn's first book on pub games,

bought the local brewery and closed down the venue of old Palmer Claxton's exploits in St Germans.

East Anglia is a deep and mysterious territory for pub games and it may well be that Pitch Penny survives in pubs that I've not yet discovered – but my impression is that it has survived in less than a handful of places.

The late Oscar Watefield, landlord of the Lifeboat, at Thornham, on the north coast of Norfolk, revived the game in the 1960s to such great effect that his pub became known as the 'Penny House'. He withdrew his precious George III pennies from circulation and substituted a set of 13 brass discs of roughly the same size – the game in those days was usually played with four players to a team, each member throwing 13 discs, best of three legs for the match. The hole was 2in wide at the top and the throw was roughly 7ft. Nowadays, The Lifeboat is run by Nicholas and Lynn Handley, and Pitch Penny is as popular as ever. You still throw 13 brass discs with 'one foot on the fireplace', and the prize for all 13 holed in one go is a gallon of scotch. The Lifeboat is a busy pub and at peak times there isn't room to swing a cat, let alone pitch a penny, so if you want to play, it's best to go at a quiet time – perhaps mid-afternoon or a winter's day. You can try for the scotch – last won 40 years ago, by the way – or just pitch to decide who pays for the next round.

At The Rose and Crown, Snettisham, landlady Margaret Trafford also encourages the game. Here, they use 12 old pennies and the prize for all 12 holed is a single bottle of scotch. It was actually won as recently as 1989 – but generations had previously tried and worn a hole in the brick floor of the throwing area.

At the curiously-named Jackson Stops, at Stretton-on-the-Fosse, in Lincolnshire, they have a game which looks like Pitch Penny, but which they call **Gnurdling**. Their rules, pinned on the bench, read thus: '13 Gnurdles to be pitched at a 2¼in diameter hole, the number thrown in each subsequent throw is the remainder from the preceding throw after deducting the number passing through the hole from the number pitched.' I think this makes some sort of sense, but I wouldn't swear to it.

The Bull, at Langley Green, in Essex, was built in 1800 and they reckon that Penny in the Hole has been played there since the day the doors first opened, judging by the hole worn in the stone flags, where generations of penny hurlers have stood. They play the Gnurdling variation of the game, in that a player throws the whole set of ten pennies provided, one by one, then retrieves the ones that haven't gone down the hole for his next turn. The winner is, of

Pitch Penny

course, the first player to sink his full quota of of ten pennies. It is one of those games easily missed if it isn't actually being played, since the hole in the floor is covered by a carpet and the hole in the bench is hidden under a cushion.

If you should develop any aches and pains while strenuously dealing with Penny in the Hole at the Bull, there's a doctor's surgery there on Wednesdays – the surgery is the public bar and the saloon is the waiting room.

Pitch Penny has several close relatives – **Pitchin' in t'Pot** (translation from raw Yorkshire = Pitching in the Pot) and **Leathers** (pure Lancashire) are two of them, though I would not be at all surprised to find that there were more. Pitchin' in t'Pot was, at one time, popular in Huddersfield and was revived at The Spring Rock Tavern, near Elland, at the same time as Knur and Spell. The pot was a 4in long section of a

4in diameter drainpipe, stood on a pub bench and the discs were 2in across – circles stamped out from the thick fibre belting of woollen mill machinery. The players, three to a team, had six discs each and every one potted scored a point.

Leathers may now be a matter of pub archaeology, rather than a living game. They used to play in a pub near my home – The Morning Star, in Shaw – and within living memory, pub gamesters would give the Bull Ring a go in The Pineapple (see p. 129) and then walk past the station and up the hill to The Morning Star to play Leathers. Ringing the Bull is still played on Boxing Day at The Pineapple, but no one bothers with Leathers at The Morning Star, although it is a splendid neighbourhood pub. However, the bench with the hole and the drawer and a couple of old leathers (again, discs cut from mill belting – cotton mill belting, of course) remain.

Leathers was the Lancashire version of Pitch Penny – in both games, a drawer under the bench caught the succesful missiles.

'In that hand, pal,' all hands on the table for a game of Tippet at The King William Inn, Tunley.

Background

In 1869, Mr Henthorne, the landlord of The Commercial Hotel, in Shaw, Lancashire, was provoked into betting with a group of his regulars that he could run up the hill to The North Star, a pub in the neighbouring hamlet of Crompton, and back, in under 15 minutes. He succeeded, with 2 minutes and 45 seconds to spare, and collected an undisclosed sum from each of his disgruntled customers. I don't think anyone ever tried to bet on the run again, but it just goes to show that you never know when and where such 'pub bets' have occurred.

Any gambling game can be dangerous, depending on the company you keep, but on the whole, the amounts of money involved in pub games and wagers are not crippling – in fact, you may find yourself gambling merely to determine who pays for the next round of drinks. It is as well to recall, however, the immortal words of the American con man, Wilson Mizler, who said, 'There's a sucker born every minute and two to take him.' No doubt Mizler would have been shrewd enough not to accept the 'finger in t'clog' bet on offer in pubs in Colne, Lancashire, in the 1930s – a regular customer would draw a line on the stone-flagged taproom floor and bet an unsuspecting visitor that he could jump further from the line, holding the outside edge of his right clog between right hand finger and thumb. The visitor, naturally, was invited to try first and would risk rupture and breakage trying to jump as far as possible forwards from the line, clutching his clog all the while. When his turn came, the challenger would jump *backwards* from the line – a considerably easier physical feat – and collect his winnings.

In 1674, Charles Cotton summed up gambling as 'an enchanting witchery, gotten between idleness and avarice'. I acknowledge that gambling *is* a disease we all suffer from, to a greater or lesser degree, but nevertheless I feel no qualms about listing under this chapter heading some pub pastimes, ancient and modern, in which the spice and point of the game is the money riding on the result. In some cases, they are games of pure chance and the element of mental or physical skill involved is negligible – this makes many of them illegal which, for some people, makes them even more attractive.

The Football Pool

There are no definitive guidelines as to what makes a 'good' pub, since there are so many personal preferences and prejudices to be taken into account. I tend to rely on the 'notice board test' – if there is a board, aflutter with pieces of paper announcing darts, dominoes, crib and pool teams and fixtures, coach trips to Ostend to sample Belgian beers, local taxi firms, dubious postcards from abroad, charity raffles, old newspaper cuttings, and a **Pontoon Football Club Pool**, or some such, then the chances are that you are in a good pub with plenty of regular customers and a strong community spirit.

This Football Pool is not the Littlewoods or Vernons variety, offering a million pounds for eight correctly-forecast score draws, but a locally-organised collective bet on the goals scored week-by-week by teams in the English and Scottish Football Leagues, as the season progresses from late August through to early May. The pontoon club table is a large sheet of paper which contains a long list of teams; next to each team is a space for a customer's name, then comes a line of boxes for recording that team's goals over a four- or five-week period. Many local newspapers and local, professional football teams supply their own sheets, but probably the most famous example, known throughout the country, is the blue-printed one supplied by *The News of the World*. The rules of the various competitions vary, but *The News of the World* pontoon is won by the team which first scores *exactly* 11 goals. When a team exceeds 11 goals, the customer and his team start again – in other words, if a team scores six goals in its first match and six in its second, the pontoon goes bust and the unfortunate punter goes back to one goal. Everyone subscribes to take part and the winner sweeps the pool, or a major part of it. There are often small consolation prizes for the lowest-accumulated score and the highest bust, both of which are self-explanatory.

Tippet, Up Jenkins, Spoof and Kannoble

The ancient game of **Tippet** experienced a revival in the 1930s as a direct result of a magistrates' ruling that pub landlords should lock away games equipment on Sundays. Tippet, however, required no equipment other than a single small coin which could be easily concealed from prying eyes. It became a popular sport in pubs in Manchester and Salford, especially on Sundays.

The game is still played sporadically, in a few pubs, not just in the North West, but all over Britain. The rules vary slightly, as rules tend to do, as you wander about the country, but the basics of the game remain the same:

Two teams of three station themselves on opposite sides of a pub table and the two captains, who sit in the middle of their teams, toss for first go. The winning side then pass a small coin from hand to hand under the table and out of sight of their opponents. There is a great deal of banter, chat and furtive movement because the aim at this stage is to hide the position of the coin from the opposing team, by fair means or foul. Finally, the opposing captain says 'hands up' and six closed fists crash down on the table in front of him. The task is to find the coin and the captain may choose to look himself, or nominate his left- or right-hand man. Whoever does the job has a couple of ploys he may try to help clear his mind and examine the blank and innocent faces of the coin-holding team. He can point to two of the fists and they must then be opened – if the coin appears at this stage, however, he loses the point, so what he is trying to do here is eliminate a couple of hands before making his final choice. He may also ask the opposing team to put their fists under the table once more and 'tighten 'em', then bring them back. Unless the coin-holder is an experienced player, the knuckles of the guilty hand will be white with tension and easy to spot. Then comes the final, forensic moment when the questioner opens out his palm opposite the hand that he thinks is concealing the coin and says 'tip it'. If he has guessed correctly, his team takes over the coin and sets about hiding it; if he hasn't opened the correct hand, the original team keeps the coin, scores 1 point and passes it to and fro again. The game is usually 11 points up, and a psychologically-gifted team of bluffers can sometimes win the 11 points straight off.

As I've mentioned, the rules tend to change from area to area. In some parts of the country the game is known as **Up Jenkins** and the guessing team are allowed one or two extra moves before making their final choice. They may demand 'smash 'ems', for instance, and all the bluffing fists must be crashed on the table; if they call for 'crabs', the opposition must raise their hands so that only their fingertips touch the table – the coin must be kept tucked into the palm with the thumb. The command 'church windows' means that the hands must be held up, fingers outstretched and palms facing inwards. The purpose of all these gyrations is to find the coin, but also to make the holder drop it from numb and paralysed fingers. If this happens, the coin automatically passes to the other team.

Spoof is an elimination game of guile and deception for any number of participants, although it is more sensible to limit the number to five or six, so that everyone can be accommodated comfortably around a standard pub table. The unusual feature of the game is that you aim to get yourself eliminated as soon as possible, since the last player left in traditionally pays for a round of drinks.

Let us imagine that six people agree to join in – each individual player has three coins, but may

choose to play none of them, or as many of them as he wishes. On the signal, all six bring one closed fist down on to the table. One by one and in rotation, each player must then hazard a guess at the total number of coins secretly and sweatily clutched by everyone concerned; in our sample game this total could range from none to 18. No-one may guess the same figure as another, so as the game progresses, players may get jostled into choosing numbers that they don't really want. Whoever guesses the right number drops out of the game, happy to sit back and watch the fun, secure in the knowledge that his next pint will be free.

In the final stage of the game, when only two players are left, there are, depending on where you're playing, two ways of ending the game. In the West Country, a variation, oddly called **Kannoble**, demands that the first player's guess is confined to a total that he knows is theoretically possible. Thus, if he holds two coins himself, he cannot guess that there are six left altogether, since his opponent can only hold a maximum of three. His choice is restricted to two, three, four or five.

In general, the rest of the country doesn't bother with such honesty, and any sort of lying and trickery is allowed and approved.

Wheels

Long before **Roulette** and casinos were invented, some European bars and cafés, and some British pubs, had gambling wheels of their own – comparatively crude affairs of wood, suspended from the ceiling or spun on the wall.

In East Anglia, it is called the **Norfolk Wheel** or simply **Twister**. On the Isle of Oxney, between Rye and Hythe, in Kent, there are at least a couple of pubs with a similar wheel, but they refer to the game as **Spinning Jenny**. There are probably no more than 20 or 30 of these wheels still turning, so they should be jealously preserved. Customers in Belgian bars used to play the same game until the 1930s, but now the only example on display in the country is the museum pub, The Black Cat, in Bruges.

A typical Norfolk Wheel is divided into 12 equal segments, painted alternately in black and red, each segment numbered, but the numbers randomly jumbled up. A wrought iron pointer, like an old fashioned one-handed clock, is fixed so that it can rotate freely with a flick of the finger, scanning the 14-in face of the wheel. There used to be two games played, either 100 up, or a short, sharp, single spin for the highest number – whoever got the lowest number paid for the next round of drinks. A blacksmith in Dedham, Essex, used to make the wheels, in the 1950s, for five shillings each, and his work is still extant in a few pubs in Essex and Norfolk.

Twister, however, seems to be a casualty of redecoration, redesign, rethinking – the wheels don't seem to fit into the design of 'modern' pubs. I have an example, bought at a junk shop in Suffolk, which must have graced a pub at one time – it has the numbers 1 to 12, clumsily painted in yellow on a red wooden wheel, but in this case, the wheel itself revolves and the marker is a fixed arrow. Some landlords treasure their wheels, of course, and have them repainted when they get flaky and replaced when they fall down. It's probably as a result of this ceaseless renewal that you find such variation in decoration – one example I saw had the signs of the zodiac squashed between the numbers, another had a feather as a marker. One landlord told me that a genuine Twister should be so patterned that each pair of opposite segments should add up to 12, except for 6 and 12, whose opposite numbers should show 0. Since he had got rid of his wheel a few years ago, I don't know how much credence to attach to the theory.

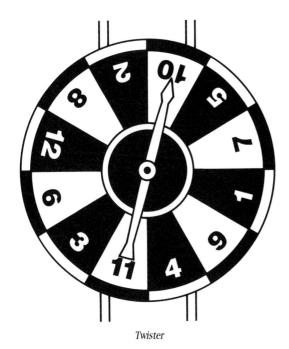

Twister

A new company, which produces a variety of old pub games, has come up with yet another design, a wheel with numbered segments running from 1 to 10 and designs in between the numbers representing pint pots, half-pint glasses, sherry glasses and playing card symbols. This particular Twister, as they

call it, has a gold-painted spinning arrow and the whole apparatus can be mounted from a beam, or simply set up on a table.

I've seen the new version of the old game interestingly interpreted in an Oxfordshire pub – the game goes to 51 up if ten people play, 101 up if five people are involved. You score whatever number comes up each time you have a turn, but the symbols become obstacles – if you turn up a pint, a half, or a sherry glass, you have to buy a drink of the appropriate volume and drink it before your turn comes round again, otherwise you must drop out. The card symbol means that you miss a turn. It is the custom for each player to put £3 in a large jar before the game begins; the cash thus collected is used to pay for all the penalty drinks. Whoever gets the required score picks up any money left in the jar.

Most of the older customers in Twister pubs in Norfolk, Suffolk, Essex and Kent agree on one thing – there used to be sessions with a lot more resting on the twist of the arrow than there is today. On market days £5 and £10 notes and even cattle were spun for and, when the fishing fleet was in with a good catch, all the play was for huge fish filched from the docks. Farmers gambled away sacks of potatoes or vegetables and one drunken carrier was said to have lost his horse, then his cart and finally his cargo, before he decided that he'd had enough. It makes the Oxfordshire £3-gamble seem quite modest in comparison.

In Salford, the Spinning Jenny was not a wheel, but a Victorian toy also known as a Teetotum. It looked like a tiny top and was spun by twisting the upper stem between finger and thumb and releasing it to hum around on a pub table. The top had eight, sometimes ten, flat, numbered sides – whichever number was uppermost when it stopped spinning counted as the score. Like Twister, the game was sometimes 100 up, or sometimes a short, sharp shock of one turn, highest score winning. I was assured, on my last thorough combing of Salford pubs some 15 years ago, that there were one or two places where the Spinning Jenny is still spun, but I must confess that I never came across it; on the other hand, I did meet up with a similar children's toy providing discrete entertainment in a Midlands pub – this was **Put and Take**. This time, the top had five sides, respectively marked out 'put 1', 'put all', 'take 1', 'take all' and 'all put' – a bunch of car workers were passing the time by staking a pound on each throw. Everyone put in a pound to begin with, then they took turns to spin the top – if the spinner's throw ended with 'put 1', he put another pound in the pool; if 'put all' turned up, he had to contribute an amount to equal the existing pool (a damaging throw if the game had been going for any length of time); 'take 1' is self-explanatory; 'take all' scooped the pool and 'all put' meant another pound in from all the players. For once, I was quite relieved that there was no invitation to join in.

John Scarne, an American and one of the world's greatest authorities on gambling games, reported that Put and Take was the second most popular gambling game to poker in the USA, in the 1920s and '30s, but died out because the top was 'gaffed', or fixed, too often so that it could be controlled by an experienced hustler. Robert Graves noted, in *The Long Weekend*, his social history of the inter-war years in Britain, that Put and Take was the fashion-able craze of 1922, when all classes seemed to play the American game at the least excuse - usually spinning the top in a saucer to stop it escaping.

Dice Games

Dice games have been known in England since the 12th or 13th century, and since then we have had eras of manic play, notably in the 17th and 18th centuries. The rattle of a dice box is now a less famil-iar sound than it used to be in pubs, but a surprising number of houses keep a set discreetly out of sight for all except known and trusted customers. I find that I come across the special dice games - **Crown and Anchor, Poker Dice** and **Shut the Box** - much more frequently than the 'orthodox' games, such as **Hazard, Craps** or **Chuck-a-luck**, but maybe that is because I am not known and trusted in enough pubs.

The Crown and Anchor board, which is often an easily-transportable piece of oilcloth or plastic, is marked off into six squares depicting a crown, an anchor, a heart, a club, a spade and a diamond. Each of the three dice used is similarly marked and they

Crown and Anchor board

are thrown by a 'banker', who takes on bets from the rest of the company.

Each player puts his money on the square (or squares) he fancies, the banker rolls the dice and pays evens on a symbol which turns upon one dice, 2:1 on pairs and 3:1 on three of a kind. He rakes in all the lost money and, since there is an advantage in odds in the banker's favour, the bank passes to each player in turn.

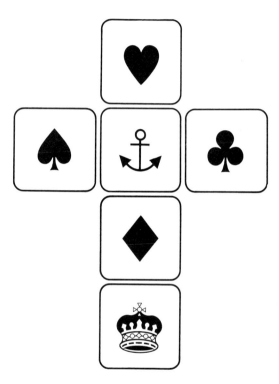

Exploded diagram of dice (not to scale)

As its name suggests, the game originated - and is still popular - among seamen of the Royal Navy and fishing fleets, but the following example of banker's 'patter' actually comes from the Army, 1914–18 vin-tage, where Crown and Anchor was frowned on by the Authorities, but extensively played.

Lay it down my lucky lads; the more you put down the more you pick up. You come here on bicycles, you go away in Rolls Royces. The old firm, all the way from 'Olloway. What about the lucky old mud hook? The old mud hook's badly backed. Any more for any more before we turn 'em up? Lay it down, my lucky lads, thick and heavy. Have you all finished, have you all done? Right, up she comes. Two jam tarts and the lucky old Sergeant Major.

The 'mud hook' was, of course, the anchor, the 'sergeant major' was the crown and the 'jam tarts' were hearts. Give or take a word or two, the same script is still adhered to, 50 years on.

There is an isolated pub in Norfolk where the landlord, his wife, daughter and customers play Poker Dice on the bar counter practically all night long through the winter season. Very little money changes hands; in fact, betting occurs only when a game coincides with a range of simultaneously emptied glasses; the loser then forks out for a round, seemingly without even noticing it, such is the hypnotic fascination of the play. The 'pokey die' are stilled only when a stranger arrives and, once his credentials have been safely established, the conversation, the drinking and the dicing go on. Actually, there is no need at all for all this nervousness and subterfuge – only ten miles away, another publican has applied for, and received, permission from the licensing magistrates to play the game. This scene is probably repeated all over the country. Some landlords like to have everything open and above-board, others are wary about drawing what they consider to be unnecessary attention to themselves. Either way, the game goes on.

There are five poker dice to a set, and each one has its faces marked with an ace, king, queen, jack, 10 and 9, instead of the usual numbers. When it is his turn, each player rolls all five dice at once. He then has the choice of rolling a second time, using all five dice again, or leaving some of them as they fell and re-rolling the rest. A third roll is allowed, with the same options. The object of the game is to build up the strongest possible hand, with the first, second or third roll. The scoring value of the various combinations (*lowest* hand first) runs like this:

highest single die (ace high)	
a pair	
three of a kind	
a sequence	high beats low
a full house (pair + three of a kind)	
four of a kind	
five of a kind	

Once the first player has decided on his hand, play passes on, but the next and subsequent players are only allowed as many throws as the first one took. Thus, if the initial roller was satisfied with his first throw, everyone else has only a single cast of the five dice with which to try and beat him. Whoever ends up with the most powerful hand wins the game and is allowed first roll in the next game.

There is a variation on this standard game of Poker Dice, called **Liar Dice**, very suitable for good liars. First of all, everyone puts an agreed amount in the pool. The first thrower then casts the five dice, but hides the result of the roll from the rest of the players with his cupped hand; he may re-roll as usual, but the re-rolled dice must be shown. Next, he announces his hand, and it is the following player's task to guess whether he is telling the truth or not.

Poker dice (exploded diagram)

The second player may choose to believe what he is told, in which case he rolls his dice and calls his throw, again shielding the actual result; he *must*, however, call a higher throw than his predecessor, whereupon player three has to decide whether he has called correctly. If player two gazes into the eyes of player one, and detects there unease, deceit and guile, he 'sees' him and the hand is revealed; if the original call was false, the unmasked liar pays a 50p piece into the pool and another one to his accuser. If the call was accurate, or *lower* than the dice thrown, player two pays the forfeits. If a following player has failed to challenge, he is afforded an interesting psychological insight into the first roller's mind, for the hand is passed on as it fell, still hidden from the rest of the contestants. Play moves round until consistent losers drop out – if all the players remain tenacious, then some individual losing limit (£5, for example) must be arrived at, to eliminate players one by one, until the last two proven liars are left to contest the pool.

Shut the Box

In this game, the 'box' in question is an open, low-sided, baize-lined tray, with a sequential display of numbers, 1 to 9, along one of the long sides. Each of the numbers has a small, sliding or hinged panel, which can either leave the figure exposed or cover it up. The game starts with all the numbers visible – all that is needed are fellow gamblers, a dice cup and a pair of conventional, numbered dice.

The first player rolls the two dice from the cup into the tray. He is allowed to conceal any number, or combination of numbers, which add up to the same total as that showing on the two dice. Thus a cast of 6 and 3 could be used to close 6 and 3, 9, 1 and 8, 7 and 2, 5 and 4 – any numbers totalling 9. Once a number has been covered, it stays that way and cannot be uncovered and used again. At a certain stage in the game – some say when numbers 9, 8 and 7 have been shut off, others that the numbers left uncovered should add up to 6 or less – you can choose to throw one dice instead of two. The aim of the game, of course, is to 'shut the box' – i.e. to close up all the panels. More often than not though, before you get to that stage, you will find yourself stuck with a combination score that you cannot use and a set of panels that you cannot close. Those numbers remaining constitute your score, and there are two different methods of calculating the damage – some schools read off the figures direct, so that 1, 5, 9 would be 159; others add up, so that the score in this case would be 1 + 5 + 9 = 15. Whoever has the *lowest* score at the end of the round wins the pool. Some people prefer a longer game, which involves players

lects double the stakes from the rest of the school.

Another 'long game' can be played by just two opponents. The first player rolls the dice and shuts the appropriate panels; the second player rolls and tries to open them again. Some boxes have small duplicate numbers below each closed panel, which helps both players to see at a glance which numbers are open or closed as far as they are concerned, and ensures that the situation doesn't become too confusing.

No-one has proved conclusively when or where Shut the Box was invented. Timothy Finn first came across it on Alderney, one of the Channel Islands, as recently as 1964, but quotes a correspondent, a Mr G.H.R. Panting, who saw 'a very old and obviously handmade' version in a pub on Hayling Island, near Portsmouth, years before that. Finn credits a Mr 'Chalky' Trowbridge with introducing the Channel Islands game to England, in 1958, and claims that it was a Norman or Channel Islands game, popular with sailors and fishermen long before that. R.C. Bell says it has been a favourite game among the sailors of Normandy for more than 200 years, but adds, startlingly, that it is also known in Barotseland, a province of Zambia, in Central Africa. Yet another source states that Shut the Box has 'long been popular in Northern France'. These are early days in games research, but I feel that, sooner rather than later, someone will come across some more convincing evidence about the provenance of such a comparatively sophisticated artifact – although the box itself could be a development of a game which may originally have been scratched on a table, or on the ground. In the meantime, most of the boxes found in British pubs are modern, often commercial affairs – Canada Dry produced a board in the 1960s which they christened 'Shutterbox'.

Pitch and Toss

The basic game of Pitch and Toss must have followed minutes after the invention of coinage. Today, we call 'heads or tails' and spin a coin to decide a winner. The Greeks called their game Night and Day, the Romans followed on with *Caput aut Navis* ('Head or Ship') and Henry VIII lost money at 'Cross and Pile' – they were all doing the same thing, using a coin as a two-headed dice. I like the anecdote of the drunken collier of Westhoughton who threw his cap up in the air in a pub and said, 'If it comes down, I'll stay here; if it stays up, I'll go to work.'

In Britain, up until the 1930s and beyond, there were several versions of the game, all highly illegal, all played behind closed pub doors or, in secret places outdoors, with 'doggers out' (lookouts)

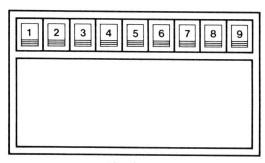

Shut the Box

dropping out when they have accumulated 45 points by the adding up method; in this case, the last player left in collects the money. If anyone actually succeeds in shutting the box, he wins outright and col-

posted to give advance notice of any police presence. Selwyn Schofield saw his first Pitch and Toss school when he was a small child, in the Calder Valley of West Yorkshire – it was part of the preliminary programme before an important Knur and Spell match between two local champions. The young Selwyn forced his way through many legs to the centre of the circle of cloth-capped men and saw, to his amazement, that the floor was covered in silver coins – he ran home to his mother in great excitement and shouted to her that 'all the money in the world' was just lying on the ground.

The Elland game, as seen by Selwyn, was played with two coins, tossed in the air from a small, flat stick or paddle. They used to play much the same thing in Bolton, where it was known as **Two Up**; the call there was 'I'll tail you!', both players put a pound in a cap on the table, one of them tossed the coins and, if two tails came up, the challenger won. If the coins fell two heads, or head and tail up, the challenger lost his pound and had to put another in the cap. Elsewhere, any call was allowed – 'head and tail', 'heads', or 'tails' and the correct call won the game and the money. Scarne describes what he calls the 'Penny Game', 'Two Up' or the 'Penny Tossing Game', which was brought to America by sailors, who had picked it up in Australia during the Second World War.

It is said that many now-respectable Manchester and Salford bookmakers made their initial fortunes by organising games of four-coin Pitch and Toss in the 1940s and '50s. It was played in pubs, but a favourite pre-War venue was the sandhills outside the grim walls of Strangeways Prison. Here, the gambling flourished, while prisoners sent heliograph messages with tiny mirrors to friends, relatives and bookies below. The banker's tosser balanced four coins on the back of his hand, one on each knuckle; the odds offered were evens on one head (or tail), 2:1 on two, 3:1 on three and 4:1 on four. All four coins were tossed into the air at once. A rash of two-headed coins brought the game into disrepute, even among the disreputable, and the successful bankers moved on to greater triumphs.

Fives, a Pitch and Toss game which began with five coins placed on the forearm, was known in Hulme, Manchester, as **Nudger**, which must have been extremely confusing, since 'nudging' was also prostitutes' slang for making their presence felt to customers, in a pub called The Golden Eagle, on Stretford Road. The pub was known as 'The Nudger'. There was also a soft drink, manufactured in nearby Old Trafford, known as 'Nudger'. There was no such confusion in Sheffield, where the game was known

only as Fives, and in the 1920s it led to terrible trouble in the city between the rival gangs, who sought to control the game.

Pitch and Toss, the game where the coins are pitched, then tossed, was very popular with the troops in France and Belgium during the First World War, and enjoyed a new lease of life during the Depression.

A knife, or sliver of wood, known as the 'mot', was stuck in the ground, and all the players involved then pitched a penny at it, from a distance of about 10 yards, the aim being to end up as close as possible to the target. In the more elaborate schools, a circular bed of clay was prepared, with the mot in the centre, rather like the pin in a game of Quoits – the pennies had to stick edgeways into the clay to count. Whoever ended up nearest the mot then gathered up all the coins, including his own, lined them up on his forearm and tossed them in the air. All pennies landing heads-up were his to keep, while the remainder were gathered up by the second nearest pitcher, who followed the same routine. This went on until all the coins were accounted for, whereupon the whole process began all over again. In some schools, the person tossing the coins, having won the pitch, would throw the pennies one at a time, calling 'heads' or 'tails' as he liked and collecting all the coins he called correctly. The pennies, of course, were only the dice, as it were – every toss had side bets for real money and, according to R.C. Bell, who observed this game in Scotland, among pit workers in the 1950s, 'the fivers floated around like toilet paper'.

Pips

Finally, an entertaining flutter from a pub in Essex that should remain nameless – we don't want any curious magistrates or policemen wandering down there, although the pastime is harmless enough.

On 1 December each year, a marrow is put on display on a shelf in the public bar. They have found here, after years of experience, that the marrow may contain no pips or up to 600 pips – the aim is to guess how many, or how few, are packed into the annual example. A large sheet of paper, divided up into 600 numbered boxes, hangs on the wall and it costs 25p to put your name on the number you fancy. On Christmas Eve, the marrow is cut open and the pips counted by a special 'pip-arbitrator', since only mature specimens are allowed. The money collected – £150 – is split up and distributed to the people who have estimated and selected the winning numbers – there are about 30 prizes so there's plenty of cash around for extensive rounds of pre-Christmas drinks.

The Good Old Days.

Background

I will concede that *some* of the old days might have been good, for *some* of the people, *some* of the time.

Prestwich Wakes, which began on 28 August 1832, sounds as if it was a lively do. Records reveal that it all took place by the church outside a pub called the Ostrich, and was intended for 'the edification and improving the Morals of those who may have the pleasure of attending'. There was 'a Foot Race for a Beaver Hat, by six young men who had never won a heat before, followed by an Eating match of 3lb of treacle and Bread, by Three respectable young Men, with their Hands tied behind them, for a Purse of Silver, the Second to receive One Shilling out of the Purse'. In the evening, it was the girls' turn, with 'A Singing Match, by Three young Ladies, to take Three Parts. Each to be presented with a Pair of new Shoes, by a black prince . . .'

The festivities took place over three days with much singing and dancing each evening, but the Prestwich menu was not at all unusual for the period – many towns and villages of early 19th-century Britain had a Wakes, a revel or a feast day, often pub-based, and frequently featuring bizarre events. In Maidenhead, 'five damsels under twenty years of age, chaste in principle, bandy legs and humped backs not being permitted to start', raced for a smock. A similar event on Wandsworth Common promised a race between 'two jolly wenches, one known by the name of "the little bit o' blue" (the handsome Broom girl) at the fag end of Kent Street and Black Bess of the Mint'.

Times change, and I can think of only one example of local annual celebration that preserves some of the lusty old flavour. Egrement Crab Fair, in Cumbria, begins with a lorryful of apples being flung down the main street and continues with a greasy pole challenge (a £5 note at the top); there are foot races down the street and a grown-ups' pram race which involves 'refreshments' in a lot of pubs – the runners' and riders' progress becomes extremely erratic towards the end of the course. There is a lull in the late afternoon and then the whole town goes down to the playing fields in the evening and there, on an illuminated stage, is a 'grinning match' through a horse collar (they call it 'gurning'), a clay-pipe smoking contest, a hunting-song competition, and a worst singer and song contest.

The blast from the past in Egremont is, I must confess, very enjoyable, but I have never really believed in the intrinsic goodness of the old days, partly because I do not subscribe to the view that brutality, malnutrition and poverty are necessarily character-building. There have been many amusements and diversions, commonly associated with pubs, pub-goers and festive occasions, which have now died out because the social climate eventually turned against them. They have not entirely gone, however, and those who would perhaps be relieved to hear that bull and bear baiting have not been heard of in Britain for 150 years, may be shocked to learn that cock fighting and badger baiting still go on.

Lawn Billiards

At the Freemasons Arms, Hampstead, London, they have one of only three Old English skittle alleys left in Britain. Up until comparatively recent times, they had an even greater treasure – the only **Lawn Billiards** court in the entire country. It has now been concreted over, an act of sheer vandalism, carried out in the name of progress, presumably to make room for three or four more cars in the car park. The pitch, I am told, is intact underneath the concrete, so it could be restored.

The Lawn Billiards court was circular, with a kind of apron, giving the whole thing a keyhole-shape – it was made of wood blocks, rather like a parquet floor. All this was placed within a larger circle, 24ft in diameter, made of gravel, which sloped gently to a low boundary barrier. In the middle of the wood-block area was an iron ring, 7¾in across and mounted vertically on a sunken swivel, so that it rotated when struck. The game was played with balls made of lignum vitae; they weighed 8lb each and were 7½in in diameter so that they could just about be coaxed through the hoop. The players used curious cues, 5ft long, with a small metal hoop at the end, to propel the balls around the court and through the hoop – the technique was to hold the pole in such a way that the ball could be levered up and forwards.

The object of the game was to get the ball through the central ring – if you succeeded, you scored 1 or 2 points, depending on how the feat was achieved. In a singles match, each player had two balls; in a doubles contest, everyone had one ball, so in all games there were four balls in play. The balls were brought into the pitch having been fired alternately off the 'shoe' – the bottom of the keyhole of the court. After that, they were manoeuvred from wherever they came to rest. A ball straight through the ring scored 1 point; a ball cannoned off an opponent's ball and through the ring counted 2 points. A normal game was 21 up.

The experts, as usual, could get up to all sorts of tricks, imparting top, screw and side spin on the ball and scoring with drop cannon from impossible angles – since the balls could be thrown in the air, the scope for cannoning was much wider than along the flat plane of a billiards or snooker table. Players'

A cock fight in full swing – a spectacle of cruelty and horror.

balls were also able to hit the rotatable ring in such a way that it was left end-on, instead of face-open to the opponent's next shot, thus effectively closing up the game.

I used to watch the game occasionally, on sunny weekends, in the early 1960s, and marvel at the subtle skills of the players. They called it either Lawn Billiards, **Pall Mall**, or **Mell**, which always puzzles me, since it wasn't played on grass and didn't seem to be the game which Sam Pepys had described in his diary on 15 May 1663 (I was supposed to be studying history at the time and took great delight, then, as now, in becoming sidetracked): 'I walked in the park,' said Pepys, 'discoursing with the keeper of the Pell-mell, who was sweeping of it, who told me of

what the earth is mixed that do floor the mall, and that over all there is cockle-shells powdered and spread to keep it fast.'

It wasn't just a matter of the cockle-shell finish – the Pall Mall court at St James's was one of the largest in Europe at 1000 yards long and today's Pall Mall was built on top of it. The Dutch had a collection of courts; the one at The Hague was built in 1609 and, in 1637, two more were constructed at Leyden and Utrecht – Amsterdam's pitch was made in 1651. All these courts were very long (all over 656 yards) and comparatively narrow. There were posts at each end and a fixed, small gate, or hoop, called an *archet*, in the middle and they used mallets to crack the balls up and down the pitch.

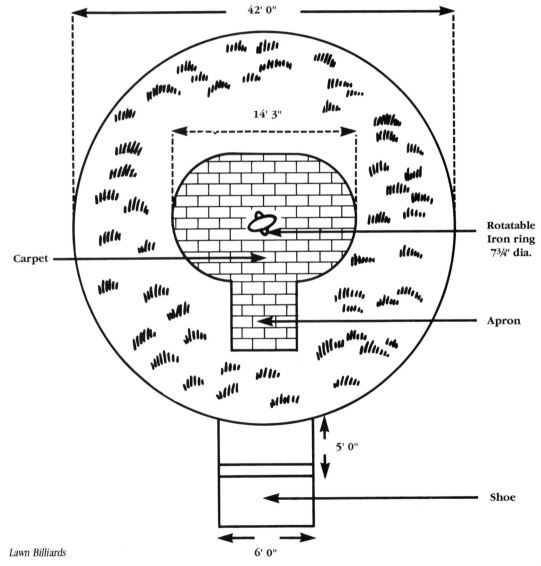

Lawn Billiards

Lawn Billiards at The Freemasons Arms, Hampstead, North London. This pitch – probably the only one in the country – was concreted-over a few years ago, although there are plans to resurrect it.

Pall Mall was scaled down to a more manageable pub-size in the Low Countries, in the 18th century; it was played in much the same way as the original version, on a 22 yard court, usually attached to an inn. They called the new game *kolf*. The Netherlands Kolf Union still comprises some 20 clubs and the Kolf-club Utrecht celebrated its 250th anniversary in 1981. I've seen their court at the St Elogen Gasthuis in Utrecht, but it doesn't look like the Pall Mall I knew and loved.

There is another game, now played in a few villages in the Limburg province of Belgium and notably in the open-air folk museum at Bokrijk, Hassalt, called *Beugelen* which is about the closest ancestor to the Freemasons pastime I have ever seen. *Beugelen* translates loosely as 'at the hoop' and the pitch has a fixed iron hoop in the middle of it; there are four lignum vitae balls trundled about by wooden paddles resembling miniature cricket bats. They say that the game was once common all over Europe and fragmented and isolated examples still survive, not just in Belgium, but in Holland, North Germany, Italy and Portugal – perhaps the Freemasons pitch was the game's northernmost outpost, with one or two

peculiarly British details thrown in. The story obviously needs more work and more research. The first step along the way would be the excavation, restoration and re-opening of the Freemasons court.

Smoking

Clay-pipe smoking is alive and well. In the village of Harpole, Northamptonshire, there used to be three pubs, all of which staged a smoking match on Shrove Tuesday – now, just one house, The Bull, continues the tradition. Eight or 15-in clay churchwarden pipes are used and each competitor has a thimbleful of tobacco, carefully packed by the landlord. They have a couple of minutes to light up, then the contest is simply to see who can keep smoking longest. You must 'show smoke' at the referee's request and, if you need to leave the room, you must leave your pipe on the table – they've been at it for over a hundred years at the pub, so they are wise to all the tricks an unscrupulous puffer might get up to. In the old days, the prize used to be a new spade, but today the longest smoker gets a bottle of scotch for his skills. In 1990, the winner kept his thimbleful of tobacco on the burn for one hour and 20 minutes.

This 1951 photograph of Pall Mall shows Mr Fred Pyle – the then World Champion.

Draughts – 19th-century style.

Background

Churches have hymns, pubs offer board games, ancient and modern, for interested customers. I shall not concern myself here with modern pub diversions such as **Scrabble**, **Mastermind** and **Trivial Pursuit**, except to say that they are available in a surprising number of houses. Chess and draughts need hardly be mentioned either, except perhaps to note that many pubs can supply boards, pieces and opponents. There are one or two places where you can play *al fresco*, the weather permitting, on giant boards on the ground – draughts, for example, at The Linden pub, Longhorsely, Northumberland, and chess at The Castle, West Lulworth, Dorset. The other games described are perhaps less well known.

Merrills (Nine Men's Morris)

Occasionally, you may hear of, or actually see, a **Merrills** or **Nine Men's Morris** board in a pub, especially if you are wandering the North Yorkshire Moors or exploring Stratford-upon-Avon, although they can and do turn up anywhere. If you are new to the game and don't mind being beaten a few times while you learn how to play, take some lessons – you will then have joined the most mysterious and ancient games tradition in the country, in Europe and perhaps even in the world. One thing is certain, **Merrills** reaches the parts other games cannot reach.

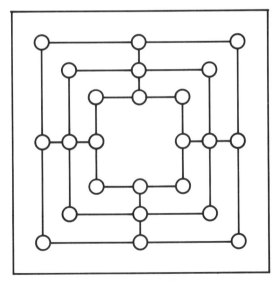

Nine Men's Morris

The wooden board has three concentric squares linked through the centre of each side. This design provides 24 nodal or intersection points arranged in 16 lines of three. Each intersection point has a shallow hole drilled in it, to take a small peg. The two players have nine pegs, or pieces, each.

Play unfolds in three acts, but the object all along is for the players to get three of their pieces into a straight line on the board, called a 'mill'. Once one of them has a mill, his reward is to remove one of his opponent's pieces. Eventually, one of the contestants will be reduced to two pieces and he will have lost the game.

Act One begins with an empty board. Each player, in turn, puts one of his pegs into one of the vacant holes on the board, until both players have thus positioned their nine pieces. If a player contrives a mill during this, or any later stage in the game, he can remove one of his opponent's pieces, providing that piece is not part of a mill. (Pieces within a mill are always safe from capture.) Once pegs are removed, they are no longer of any use and are not returned to the board. It's all faintly reminiscent of noughts and crosses, although only vertical and horizontal and not diagonal lines are used.

Once both players have committed all their pegs, Act Two begins and play goes on with the players taking turns; each time, one piece may be moved to the nearest empty, adjacent point. Again, the point is to manoeuvre pegs into a mill, and then remove an opponent's peg. A player can open up an established mill by moving one of the pieces; the separate pieces are then, of course, open to attack, but if the player successfully closes it again next time round, he is deemed to have formed another mill and can remove another peg from the board. Clever players can contrive a strategy called a 'running mill', where opening up one mill closes another, so every move results in a loss for the enemy. If a player is unable to move any pieces because there are no empty points next to any pieces, then that player has lost the game. Play normally continues until one player or the other is down to just three pieces from his original nine.

Act Three of the drama allows the player with only three pieces left to move one piece per turn to any empty point on the board, no matter where it is. The other player must continue to move in the approved fashion, to an adjacent empty point. Once a player is reduced to two pegs, he can no longer form a mill and has therefore lost.

Each year, in early September, the World Merrills Championship is held at the Ryedale Folk Museum, Hutton le Hole, North Yorkshire. Competitors have been known to come from as far afield as New Zealand and America. The Museum launched the competition building up on a strong local tradition. Folk in the Yorkshire Dales have always enjoyed the game and many local farms kept a homemade wooden board somewhere in the house - sometimes, it must be said, it was reduced to being used as a trivet or a bread board. Local stable lads used to relax by playing Merrills on boards carved on corn-bin lids.

In Shakespeare's time and territory, the same game under its other name, Nine Men's Morris, was played in more dramatic fashion - the 'board' was marked out, to a much larger scale, on turf, and morris ('Moorish') dancers were used as live pieces. Thus quoth the Bard in *A Midsummer Night's Dream* (Act II, Scene 2):

'The fold stands empty in the drowned field
And crows fattened with the murrain flock;
The Nine Men's Morris is filled up with mud
And the quaint mazes in the wanton green
For lack of tread are indistinguishable.'

The Shakespearian connection and quotation are the justification for the revival of the game in Stratford - you will find it in local pubs and souvenir shops.

Merrills is not confined to Britain - it is known and played in countries including France, Italy, Germany, Poland, the USA and the USSR. I have even seen the board scratched in 16th-century monastic cloisters in Dalmatia, on the islands of Hvar and Mljet, and on the Peljesac peninsula, at Orebic - and, unnervingly, in one remote village I visited recently, scrawled in chalk on the roof of a concrete pigsty, with scattered pebbles used instead of pegs.

Fox and Geese

Victorian Merrills boards sometimes had a different configuration of holes drilled on the reverse side, for the game of **Fox and Geese**. Although it is rare, you may stumble upon it in a British pub.

Fox and Geese is an ancient 'hunting' game for two players. Its ancestry goes back to *Hala-tafle*, the 'Fox Game', mentioned in a 14th-century Icelandic saga; it reappears at the court of Edward IV (1461-83), when the royal household accounts include a mention of 'two foxis and 26 hounds of silver overgilt' (i.e. two sets). The Victorian game was also known as **Wolf and Goats**, and slightly altered to produce the game of **Asalto**, or **Officers and Sepoys** - the last name emerging after the Indian Mutiny of 1852.

Edward IV's game had 13 silver hounds. The lesser orders would have had wooden pegs, marbles, or pebbles, set out around the fox like this:

In the illustration shown, one player has the single black or red piece representing the fox; his opponent controls the 13 pieces which are the

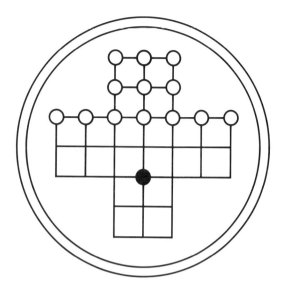

Fox and Geese (old style)

geese. The players take turns - the fox may move one hole at a time in any direction, except diagonally, and he can capture a goose by jumping over it, if the hole immediately behind the goose is empty. The geese may move individually, one at a time, but they cannot jump and capture the fox - they must pen him in a corner so that he cannot move.

After about 1600, four extra geese were added to the gaggle, set out like this:

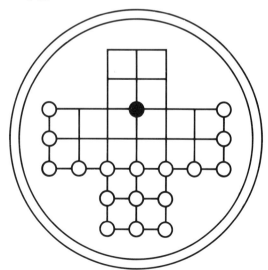

Fox and Geese (new style)

An additional rule deprived the geese of the ability to move backwards. If you are the fox in the picture, you need to capture 12 geese to win the game, since at least six geese are needed to pen the fox in. They tell me that, if the geese are played correctly, the fox must lose – I suspect this is democratic propaganda.

Solitaire

The British legend has it that **Solitaire** was invented by le Comte de Pellison, a French nobleman incarcerated in the Bastille, who developed a new game for one player from the old Fox and Geese board. The French claim that the game was known to the Romans and medieval France, and was then rediscovered by a French explorer in America, who found the Indians playing it. Solitaire certainly became very popular in Europe in the 18th century. The philosopher Leibnitz said that it was the 'perfect game for meditation' – the Germans called it the hermit's game.

One of the crucial differences between the British and European boards is that the European board has 37 holes, points or spaces while the British has only 33.

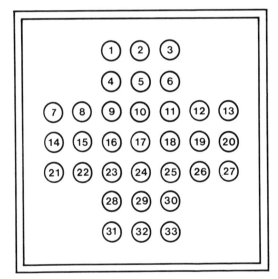

Solitaire board

The holes are not actually numbered; the notation on the British diagram is there to record the solution to the basic Solitaire problem, which is to remove the peg, marble or pebble at D4, then jump one piece over another to a vacant hole in any direction except diagonally. Each piece thus jumped over is 'taken' and removed from the board. The object of the exercise is to clear the board of every piece bar one – which should be left standing in D4.

It is really quite simple:

1.	D2	into D4	remove	D3
2.	F3	D3		E3
3.	E1	E3		E2
4.	E4	E2		E3
5.	C1	E1		D1
6.	E1	E3		E2
7.	E6	E4		E5
8.	G5	E5		F5
9.	D5	F5		E5
10.	G3	G5		G4
11.	G5	E5		F5
12.	B5	D5		C5
13.	C7	C5		C6
14.	C4	C6		C5
15.	E7	C7		D7
16.	C7	C5		C6
17.	C2	C4		C3
18.	A3	C3		B3
19.	D3	B3		C3
20.	A5	A3		A4
21.	A3	C3		B3
22.	D5	D3		D4
23.	D3	B3		C3
24.	B3	B5		B4
25.	B5	D5		C5
26.	D5	F5		E5
27.	F4	D4		E4
28.	C4	E4		D4
29.	E3	E5		E4
30.	F5	D5		E5
31.	D6	D4		D5

Once you have mastered that trick, without consulting your crib sheet, there are more sophisticated variations on the game, including 'balls on the watch' – a ball which must stay put until the final move, or 'dead balls', which must remain fixed until they are captured by the very last move. These delights, and many more, are set out in Ernest Berholt's book *The Game of Solitaire* – recommended reading for insomniacs and anti-social pub-goers.

Backgammon

Once upon an ancient time in the East, a wise man conjured up a board game which symbolised the year. There were 24 positions, or points, on the unfolded board, representing the hours in a day. The half board's 12 points signified the months of the year and the signs of the zodiac. The two players each had 15 movable pieces, totalling 30 altogether – the days of the month. There were two dice, one represented day, the other night. The seven spots totalled

Backgammon – 'an anodyne to the gout and rheumatism, the azure devils or the yellow spleen'.

on each opposing face of each dice were the days of the week and the then-known seven planets of the solar system. The game was called **Nard** and emerged from South West Asia, or Persia. The Moors introduced it into Europe when they invaded and colonised southern Spain.

Medieval Europe eventually expelled the Moors, but adopted the game and called it **Tables**. It dipped from view for a time in the late 15th century, temporarily outmanoeuvred by chess (games came into and fell out of fashion even c1475) and then enjoyed a huge Europe-wide revival in the 17th century, under a variety of names. The French called their version *Tric-trac*, a lovely onomatopoeic description of the counters being shuffled briskly around the board. The Germans, for no discernible reason, called it *Puff*. Spain knew it as *Tablas Reales*, Italy as *Tavole Reale*. In Scotland it was *Gammon*, in England Backgammon.

Strutt summed up Backgammon's rather exclusive properties for middle-class, early-19th-century Britain: 'It has always been considered a particularly respectable kind of amusement, quite fitting for country rectors, and not derogatory to the dignity of even higher functionaries of the Church.' Quite a comedown for a pastime which at one time had been provided for travellers by innkeepers all over Europe, and had been lauded as an 'anodyne to the gout and rheumatism, the azure devils or the yellow spleen'.

I first came across Backgammon, or rather *Trictrac*, 20 years ago in the Plaka district of Athens, the warren of streets and alleyways with souvenir and junk shops, houses and tiny tavernas and restaurants

Black Outer table　　　　　　　　　　　　　　**Black Home or Inner table**

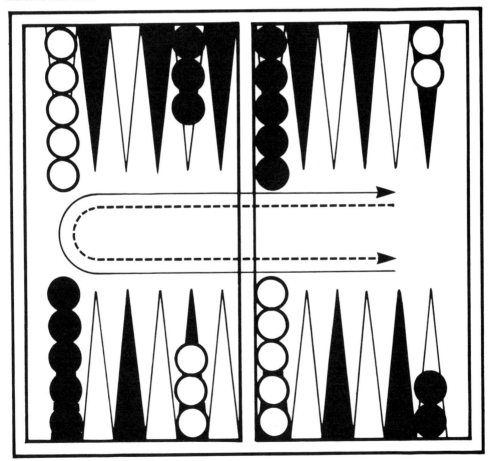

White Outer table　　　　　　　　　　　　　　**White Home or Inner table**

Backgammon board

at the foot of the Acropolis hill. There, *everyone* seemed to play – in the open air, outside bars and at street corners. It didn't look at all respectable – there was money riding on each game, and a great deal of noise from exuberant players and spectators. I bought a board and set of pieces and have played the game, badly, ever since.

You will find Backgammon in quite a lot of pubs, often without instructions, so here are the basic rules:

Most boards come in the shape of a hinged box which, when closed, conveniently holds the pieces and the dice, and when opened up is ready for play. This is the layout to begin the game:

All the pieces are moved around the board along the points according to the throw of the dice; if you are playing white, you follow the direction of the dotted arrow. If you have chosen black, you travel in the opposite direction, indicated here by the solid arrow. In either case, the object of the game is to travel all your own men to your own 'home', or inner table. From there, you can 'bear them off', or clear them from the board, again according to the cast of the dice. The player to bear off all his pieces first wins the game. The inner tables are supposed to be nearest the source of light.

The numbers on the two dice are considered individually. A throw of 6 on one die and 4 on the other is a 6 and 4 move or a 4 and 6 move; one piece may be moved four places then six, or six places then four, or two pieces may be moved, one of them six places, the other four. A double means that you can move the number four times, i.e. double 4 allows 4 + 4 + 4 + 4 moves for one or two pieces. You may touch down on a point which is unoccupied, or one which contains one or more of your own men. If your opponent has two or more men on a point, he is safe from attack and you cannot move onto the point. A single piece left on a point is called a 'blot' and is vulnerable; if you can contrive to land on an opponent's blot, you send his piece off the board and on to the 'bar'. This has nothing to do with buying drinks, but means that the piece is placed on the centre bar which divides the board. When this happens, your opponent must get that piece back into play on his outer table before he can move anything else on the board. If this happens in the later stages of the game, when perhaps you are occupying some of his outer (your inner) points with your men, it could mean that his throws to get back into play are blocked and he loses invaluable turns and has to sit back fuming, while you happily move in for the kill.

When one player or the other has all his men in his inner table, he can bear them off; this means a throw of 1 and 2 enables you to remove a piece from points one and two. A double 2 means that four pieces may be taken off the two point. Even when you are bearing off, you may, if you wish, move men forward, if the throw of the dice allows it, so as to place them in even more favourable positions. If you throw a high number and your corresponding point has no men remaining on it, you may remove a piece from the highest remaining point – in other words, if you have cleared, say, your six and five points and throw a 6 or 5, you can take a man off your four point.

The old method of betting in Backgammon used to be: single stakes if you had 'borne off' all your men and your opponent had managed to get away one or more of his men; double the original stakes (Gammon) if your opponent had not 'borne off' any of his pieces; treble the stakes (Backgammon) if he still had pieces on the bar, or lurking in your inner table.

The modern game has enjoyed a new lease of life since an anonymous American introduced the terror of the doubling cube into the game in the 1920s. This is a large die which has the numbers 2, 4, 8, 16, 32 and 64 on its faces. A player can double the stakes at any time, if he wishes, and his opponent has the choice of accepting the challenge or ducking out there and then, losing the original stake. Once the stakes are doubled in this way, the cube, with the 2 uppermost, is passed along the bar to the player challenged, who can, if he wishes, *re-double* by turning the cube to 4 and passing it back to his opponent. The 'monster', as one player dubbed the gaming die, can keep on bumping up the original stakes until the sums involved are enormous.

Most 'fast action' modern play is also resolved on the points system. The winner gets 4 points for every opposing man left in his inner table or on the bar, 3 points for each one remaining in his outer table and 1 point for each one left in his opponent's inner table. If you play for as little as ten pence a point, and the doubling cube has moved round a few times, you can see that the financial loss – or gain – can be considerable.

I don't suppose the monster will ever appear in a pub – the players would be arrested, for a start, since it would be highly illegal. It's a pity in a way though, that the element of betting has become so important to the game, because the original version provides more than enough action for the average public bar.

If pubs are theatres, then some of them are occasionally theatres of the absurd. What follows is a mere sketch outlining some of the sillier things that go on in or near pubs, ranging from unnecessarily excessive drinking to the continuing theft of children's games, and from the pursuit of excellence in ridiculous challenges, to the enrolment of animals for sport and money.

Drinking Games

If ever we are forced to abandon the pint pot or glass (imperial measure), in order to fall in line with European standard metric measurements, then a large and colourful slice of British drinking heritage will have to be abandoned.

Take Bert Foster, for example, who, in the 1940s, was Oldham's champion black-pudding eater and a man who could shift 12 gills of beer while Big Ben struck noon on the radio. A gill is, of course, half a pint, so what this means is that Bert drank six pints in 12-gill gulps, in approximately 30 seconds. Then there was the Yorkshire Copper Works champion, who took on the top drinker from Coghlan's Forge at The Crooked Billet, Thwaite Gate, Hunslet, near Leeds, in the 1920s. Eight quarts were set out for each competitor and the Yorkshire Copper Works man drank his and four belonging to his opponent – an emphatic victory.

I mention Bert Foster and the Yorkshire Copper Works champion as two modest examples of beer-downing legend, which begins with the deeds and speeds of the Anglo-Saxons, who drank from horns marked with pegs (and took each other 'down a peg'), and goes right up to Bob Farrow, of Diss, in Norfolk, who held the last record for the draining of a pint – 1.18 seconds – in the 1970s.

If the pint is laid to rest, can the **yard of ale** be far behind? A yard is 3ft (90cm) and a yard of ale is a 3ft long tube of glass, with a bulb at one end and a funnel at the other, containing 2½ or 3 pints of beer. They are often seen, empty of course, slung horizontally from the ceiling behind the bar – part of that oddly universal, dust-gathering decor which includes Spanish straw hats, unused pewter tankards, brass hunting horns, model vintage cars and notices saying 'Please Do Not Ask For Credit As Refusal Often Offends'.

The yard of ale and the determination and ability to deal with its contents have a long pedigree, going back at least as far as the 17th century when, according to John Aubrey, one had to drink by the yard to show one was a 'man of fashion'. John Evelyn noted in his diary, in 1685, that the Sheriff Officers and Gentlemen of the Kentish Troop of the Militia in Bromley toasted the King in style: 'His majesty's health being drunk in a flint glass a yard long'. A hundred years or so later, at the inauguration of Hanley Corporation in 1783, it was decreed that there would be no admission to council chamber unless the councillor seeking admittance successfully drained a yard of ale by the door.

Yard of ale champions, unlike councillors, are born and not made, but anyone contemplating a career in this field should practise quietly at home before venturing forth into public competition. First, you have to be physically able to drink 2½ or 3 pints in one long, continuous series of sips; you cannot afford to gulp and then stop drinking, for once you start the yard you must finish it, or give up ignominiously. It is actually a trick glass and, unless you tip it slowly and steadily, sipping all the while, an air-lock will form in the bulb, then break suddenly, sending the beer cascading down the tube, over your face and possibly right down to your socks. Assuming that you can cope with these potential problems, there remains the matter of records to consider. The current challenge would be to improve on the five seconds it took Peter Dowdeswell, of Earls Barton, Northamptonshire, to sink a 2½-pint yard at R.A.F. Heyford, in Oxfordshire, on 4 May 1975. Ten years later, this thirsty individual also managed to down a 3-pint yard in five seconds – at The Royal Oak in Bishops Cleeve, Gloucestershire.

There are regular yard of ale competitions. I suppose one could compile and compete in a sort of nationwide Beer-By-The-Yard Grand Prix, including the event held each April Fools Day at The Holly Bush in Priors Marton, Warwickshire, and the contest organised to coincide with the World Marbles Championship (see p. 180), held outside The Greyhound at Tinsley Green, Sussex, each Good Friday. There is even a pub called The Yard of Ale, in Bishopston Road, Stratford-upon-Avon, Warwickshire, where the landlord is reputedly willing to officiate at in-house competitions, if given appropriate notice.

If the yard of ale is to become a mere souvenir of past glories, perhaps the **European boot** will replace it. The Feldschlossen Brewery, in Switzerland, for example, has a glass boot, wellington-shaped, which holds 2 litres (3½ pints) of beer – examples can already be seen in a surprising number of British bars. As yet, the European boot would appear to be for bar decoration only, but it is *intended* for serious competitive work. It is another trick glass and, unless handled correctly, an air-lock will form in the foot and beer will gush out as with the yard of ale. The solution appears to be to rotate

Here, Mrs Peggie Cunliffe is seen testing her drinking capacity at The Freemasons Arms, Heywood, Lancashire. She took 8 minutes to drain the yard of ale, but enjoyed the drink.

On 19 September 1960, 21-year-old Colin Hogell of Maidstone, Kent, drained the yard of ale in 5 seconds. His audience included the Siamese Ambassador and friends.

the boot slowly through 180°, while drinking steadily from it. I am afraid that, as yet, I have no information on records which may have been set up in past European games.

A stage on from the single pint, quart, yard or boot contest is the team event, known as **schooner racing**. A 'schooner' is the name given to the smooth-sided pint glass, as opposed to the dimpled, handled pint pot – although either type of vessel could be used in a schooner race. Schooner or **boat racing** is a relay team game, usually with 11 to 15 people on each side, depending on whether they are cricketers or rugby players. The two teams stand in more or less straight lines, each individual member holding a full pint poised at his lips. At the signal for off, the first member of the team sinks his pint, then signals that he has finished by holding the empty glass upside-down over his head, at which point number two can start on his pint, and so on. The winning team is the one that finishes its pints first. As the excitement and tension builds, it is not unheard of for an over-enthusiastic team member to forget this simple sequence of events and tip the full pint over his head, then attempt to drink from the empty glass. This, of course, leads to instant disqualification!

Pub crawling, on a restricted-time basis, is very well known, the aim being to drink a pint (or half pint for faint hearts) in a given number of pubs on a predetermined circuit.

Generations of Cambridge University students will recall the King Street Run, which took place on the first and last Wednesday of each full term and involved 'runners' attempting to drink a pint in eight specified pubs, within two hours and without 'any relief being taken'. Each runner was accompanied by a 'jockey' – an experienced runner who was there to buy the beer and carry the entrant home. A distinctive tie was awarded to each successful competitor. The reorganisation and rebuilding of King Street has left that thoroughfare with only five pubs, which has effectively ended the old tradition.

Events like this tend to come and go. The Bell, at Whitchurch, in Hampshire, had a famous beer race, dating back at least 20 years. A team of six, roped together and in fancy dress, attempted to down half pints in all of the village's nine pubs. The event, held around Easter time, used to take a couple of hours, during which time, as one can well imagine, other forms of life in the village came to a temporary halt. However, a new police sergeant professed himself 'not keen' on the event and it was stopped.

At Horwich, near Bolton, there is a race around a dozen pubs each Good Friday – the money collected goes to the Spastics Society. A similar event, the Saddleworth Beer Walk, in villages near Oldham, was revived in 1974 and has gone on ever since, during a Saturday in August; the course is 10 miles and 16 pubs long, and the proceeds go, via the local Round Table, to charity. Perhaps the most startling point about this event is that there is a rule to the effect that any competitor found drunk and disorderly will be disqualified. Since all the competitors are in bizarre fancy dress, rattling collection cans, and extremely raucous, it must be quite difficult to decide who is disorderly and who is not.

Lastly, many local branches of CAMRA – the Campaign for Real Ale – organise beer trails in their own areas. These events don't call for fancy dress or particular speed, but do stress the quality of the beer and offer an award to anyone completing the course within a specified time – the prize is often a T-shirt or certificate of some sort. Included in this CAMRA calendar is the Swiggin' Ale Trail, which calls for half a pint (or a pint) in 13 approved pubs in Wigan Town Centre, and the curiously named Bent and Bongs Ale Trail, which cuts a swathe through 12 pubs and clubs in Atherton and Tyldesley, in Greater Manchester.

Animal Crackers

The Daily Mirror used to have a regular correspondence column for its readers called 'Live Letters', 'conducted by the Old Codgers'; it was essential reading for anyone interested in the sort of problems which emerge during the course of taproom conversation. In February 1977, a Mr Robinson, of Ashton-under-Lyne, claimed to have visited a pub as a boy with his father, where the main attraction was cat-racing. They had not actually seen a race, but had gone home with a poster as proof of the pastime. Unfortunately, the poster had since been lost, but Mr Robinson recalled some of the detail – the cats had to be household pets and cats without tails, whether Manx or not, were barred. The pub, he thought, was somewhere in Kent and was called The Old Jail. A week or so later, a Mr Relph wrote in and exploded the theory in spectacular fashion – he and his brother, he confessed, had had joke posters printed, which were distributed to the unsuspecting public at The Jail Inn at Biggin Hill, in the 1940s. The wording read thus: 'Cat Racing every Saturday Night. Manx Cats not permitted. Held at The Tiger's Head.' Whenever anyone asked where The Tiger's Head was, the response was: 'Five feet from its arse!' All of which goes to show that animals-in-pubs stories have to be treated with a certain amount of caution.

In April 1938, *The Times*, no less, carried a story which is worth quoting in full: 'The Rev Ralph Allport, a Weymouth Methodist Minister, on Satur-

Mice racing, one of the odder manifestations of our love for dumb animals – and betting.

day condemned tortoise racing, which is gaining popularity in South Dorset. The contests take place on billiard tables, the tortoises carrying toy jockeys. Mr Allport said that many public houses in Weymouth were exceeding their legitimate function as places of refreshment. They were being turned into fun fairs, and their proprietors, having exhausted the possibilities of darts and mechanical games as a means of retaining custom, were resorting to silly stunts. Dumb animals which had been bought as children's pets were being dragged out of their environment.' Mr Cyril Frampton, who had introduced tortoise racing, said, 'It is all harmless fun, entirely free from cruelty. We do not allow betting.'

Fifty years on, I think I can safely say that I don't believe Mr Frampton's protestations about betting, although I am sure the tortoises were well looked after. The main point about turning animals loose in a pub has always been to gamble on their performance. I have even seen people bet on which of two flies would be first to abandon a spilt pool of beer.

The Daily Mirror reported a tragic tale in the early 1970s, under the touching headline, 'Randy and Co Nobble the Ladies'. A pub in Bishops Auckland, Co Durham, had made careful preparations for a mouse-race to be staged in the public bar, to coincide with Derby Day at Epsom. There were to be 18 runners, along an 8ft track, with cheese at the far end. Unfortunately, the landlord had housed male and female mice together for a week or so prior to race day. The result was that 15 of the runners became pregnant, while the other three, nicknamed Randy Roy, Speedy Gonzales and Jock McToddy, were too tired to compete.

Slow creatures are often preferred for such quirky races; I suppose the excitement of the race is more drawn out. About three or four years ago, at The Mount, in Stanton, Gloucestershire, a local farmer turned up with a homemade woodlouse-racing track, divided up into six lanes, about 5ft long. Nowadays, spontaneous outbursts of woodlouse racing erupt about six or seven times a year, usually on a Friday evening. Punters bring their own runners in matchboxes - the tray of the matchbox, upside-down, acts as a sort of starting trap at the beginning of the race. There are six races during the course of the evening and all money won or lost in the betting goes to charity.

Beetle racing was once popular at a pub in Evesham. It was begun there by a barman with a vivid imagination, who claimed that it had been a common pastime in his native Derbyshire. The rules were strict - only 'thoroughbred' beetles were used and no common cockroaches were allowed. There were

six runners to a race, each of which cost their owner a six pence entrance fee. The record for the 1 yard course was two seconds flat. Customers brought their own runners, again in matchboxes, but the landlord kept a stable of beetles for any strangers who fancied a race - the winning owner got a pint of beer.

I wondered, momentarily, whether the Evesham barman had served in Italy during the War, for there is a full and interesting account of beetle racing at Anzio, soon after the Allied landings there.

There were plenty of potential winners crawling about in the bottom of every trench so, while their commanders looked cautiously for the enemy, the troops whiled away the time by racing beetles. All the runners were started from an upturned jam jar in the exact centre of a marked circle a yard in diameter. As the starter gave the signal, the jar was lifted and the first beetle to scurry across the line of the outside circle won a great many lire for his owner. Identification problems were solved with military efficiency, by sticking a little flack on each beetle's back, with a blob of well-masticated chewing gum.

Maggots can be raced as well. The Farrier's Arms, Grasscroft, near Oldham, had an inaugural meeting in 1991, along a specially-constructed 1ft long, ten-track course edged by artificial grass and pretty model houses. When the cardboard starting gate was lifted, the maggots crawled off along their tracks, encouraged by the strong light behind them - the theory being that 'a maggot is eager to chase its own shadow'. Some of the creatures were not aware of this hypothesis, and simply rolled around near the starting gate, or jumped over the barrier to join a companion in an adjoining track. It cost £2 to sponsor a runner; the winning owner received a bottle of wine and the takings went to charity. I'm told that this event started in Yorkshire, in 1989 - this doesn't surprise me at all.

The annual World Ferret Racing Championships are claimed (somewhat ambitiously) by The Queen's Head, in Eye, Suffolk, and are staged in late September. There were 30 entrants in the 1990 event; the course is a 30ft length of drainpipe and the record time for completing the course stands at 15 seconds. Owners arrive not just from Suffolk, I am assured, but from the rest of Britain, France and even Australia; the ferrets are, of course, all bred and tamed in Britain. Ferrets are popular creatures in many country districts of this country, and although other pubs have claimed, at various times, to have staged past world championships, at the moment The Queen's Head seems to reign supreme.

Olly, the 1990 World Ferret Racing Champion, enjoys a well-earned pint.

Going For It

The Guinness Book of Records, first published in 1958, was at once a brilliant feat of publishing, advertising and meticulous compilation. It remains the indispensable and definitive work for solving those arguments which spring up from time to time in all pubs, and has legitimised a huge catalogue of oddball human achievements. The pub often seems to be the chosen arena for new record attempts. Not all the examples in this section actually come from the famous reference book, but many of them do and they all retain a faintly bucolic aura.

I was privileged to be around during the early years of **clog-cobbin'** (clog throwing) in this country, when a qualifying round was held in a disused railway-station goods yard at Waterfoot, near Bacup, in the mid-1970s. The action was 'invented' by Mr McCormack, landlord at The Hargreaves Arms at nearby Lumb. There were five members to each team, and teams present from many local pubs, the fire station, the British Legion and the Young Conservatives. Each member had a one-to-one, best-of-two-throws contest with a member of the opposing teams; the longest throw won and the match was the best of five of these contests.

The clog to be cobbed was a massive, malevolent, steel-capped, heavily-studded artifact weighing some 2lb 8oz and it had to be thrown between the legs and down a course marked out in 10ft intervals with housebricks. These were early days and therefore hazardous times for cobbers and spectators alike; it quickly became apparent that the clog must be released at exactly the right time, otherwise it thudded dully straight into the ground or, worse still, hurtled vertically into the air – at this point, the thrower and spectators scattered like sheep, arms protecting heads, until the clog eventually crashed to the ground in a shower of sparks. No-one was injured by a flying clog while I was there, but the actual business of clog-cobbin' seemed to wrench muscles and even dislocated one or two shoulders. Many competitors limped away, holding themselves tenderly and vowing never to clog-cob again.

It may be that Mr McCormack derived his inspiration from a similar, but older pastime, **Welly-throwing** or **Wellie-wanging**, as it is now better known. **Flinging-the-wellington-boot** first saw the light of day in Gerrigong, New South Wales, Australia, in 1971 and has now been strictly coded – the boot must be a size 8 Challenger, made by Dunlop and cannot be altered, weighted or aerodynamically redesigned in any way. The current distance records for men and women respectively are 173ft by Tony Rodgers of Warminster, Wiltshire, set on 9 September 1978, and 129ft 11in, flung by Rosemary Payne at Cannon Hill Park, Birmingham, on 27 June 1975.

There are current entries in *The Guinness Book of Records* for **housebrick-throwing** (146ft 1in, achieved by Olympic shot-putter, Geoff Capes) and **rolling-pin-heaving** (175ft 5in, by Lori La Deane Adams, in the USA), but none as yet for **flat-cap-chucking** which emerged in Leeds in 1978, when it was heralded as 'the finest low-life pastime since pitch and toss' by its publicist and progenitor, an insurance inspector named Jack McHale. Mr McHale pointed out that flat-cap-chucking had a number of advantages over wellie-wanging, not the least of which was that no-one would get hurt if struck by a skimming cap. Distances of over 100ft were already being achieved in 1978, according to reports in the *Daily Mirror*, but evidence has been thin on the ground ever since. **Tripe-skimming**, also mentioned by the *Mirror*, can, I think, be discounted as a serious pub activity.

There are several heavyweight carrying events in the eccentrics' racing calendar. They all tend to start and finish at pubs and were probably invented after the supping of several pints.

The World **Coal-Carrying** Championship takes place at Gawthorpe, near Ossett, near Leeds, on Easter Monday. Contestants race along an uphill course, 1080 yards long, from The Royal Oak pub up to the Maypole, carrying a 1cwt bag of coal. Ladies compete with a 28lb bag of solid fuel over a 100-yard dash.

The British **Bucket-Carrying** Championship may well have disappeared – it was last heard of in 1968, when an eight-man team from The Balaclava Hotel, Blackburn, won the title from The Bay and Horses team from Beeston Rylands, near Nottingham. The bucket, incidentally, was filled with pre-decimal halfpennies and weighed 100lb. I suppose it would be virtually impossible to collect 100lb weight in old halfpennies these days, although I am sure twopence pieces would do the job just as well.

The Oxenhope **Straw Race**, as the name suggests, involves teams carrying bales of straw from pub to pub in the West Yorkshire village, while the Tetbury **Woolsack Race** is an individual event, with each competitor humping an old-fashioned, 55lb woolsack up the steep hill in the Gloucestershire town.

Similarly impressive, although on a smaller scale, was the **Pea-Pushing** Championship, last heard of in the Eclipse Tavern, Tunbridge Wells, some 20 years ago. Few details survive, except that the course involved hands and knees (and nose and pea) progress along a 14-yard, uphill stretch of cobbled road outside the pub.

Barrel-rolling has a long European history, although it was often confined to coopers or brewery workers. As recently as 1979, there was a Burton (-upon-Trent) Barrel Race, won by the Ind Coope Keg Plant team, who narrowly beat the Bass Worthington boys in the final. A record number of teams took part, including 15 ladies' entries and two teams from the Old Chapel Inn, Smethwick. For those who might be frustrated by the sporadic occurrence of official barrel races, there is a current record open to attack – 8 minutes 7.2 seconds over a measured mile, pushing a full 36-gallon metal beer barrel. This was set by a six-man team from the Haunchwood Collieries Institute and Social Club, Nuneaton, Warwickshire, on 15 August 1982.

The **card-throwing** record is held by an American – Kevin St Onge threw a standard playing card 185ft 1in at the Ford Community College Campus, in Dearborn, Michigan, on 12 June 1979.

Most drinkers have flipped a beer mat at one time or another, while waiting for a drink, balancing the mat on the edge of a table or the bar, flipping it so that it jumps and turns over through 180°, then catching it. Dean Gould of Felixstowe, Suffolk, did a bit better than that, flipping an astonishing 102 mats (woodpulp board) at one go in Hamburg, West Germany, on 18 March 1988.

Child's Play

Children's games in Britain have been beautifully and extensively illuminated by Iona and Peter Opie, whose books *The Lore and Language of Schoolchildren* (1959), *Children's Games of Street and Playground* (1969) and *The Singing Street* (1973), are nothing short of masterworks. The Opies have demonstrated, time and time again, that all the

Peanut-pushing – a variation on Pea-pushing.

gloomy pronouncements about the demise of children's games, variously attributed at different times to the arrival of the railway, cinema, motorcar, radio, television and pop music, are uninformed nonsense. The children of the key age group – the eight-, nine- and ten-year-olds – have always retained a huge treasury of old playground games, new to each generation, and kept secret from all but the most perceptive and sympathetic adults. There are some interesting parallels to be drawn here, between the playground and the public bar. Announcements of the death of pub games are made often, and are always uninformed and inaccurate. I'm not sure what the key age groups are in the pub, but the games are still preserved and cherished.

Pastimes which form part of the prolific and mysterious repertoire of children's games often find their way from the playground into pubs and back again, while grown-ups' games are often adopted and adapted by children for their own amusement, in quiet corners or behind the bike sheds.

The various games of **marbles** have been known and played by children and adults all over the world for centuries. Children continue to enjoy a wide spectrum of marbles games, including **Boos-out**, **Bridgeboard**, **Bun-hole**, **Cob**, **Ho-go**, **Holy bang**, **Hundreds**, **Lag**, **Long-taw** and **Nine holes**. Adults content themselves with just one – **Ring Taw** – which can be observed in full flow every year on Good Friday morning, outside The Greyhound Hotel, Tinsley Green, near Crawley, in Sussex. The occasion is the annual British Team and Individual Marbles Championships.

Benjamin Strutt described what he called 'Taw' in 1801, as a game in which marbles were put into a ring 'and he who obtains most of them by beating them out of the ring is the conqueror'. In the marbles world, things don't change much through the years – outside The Greyhound each Good Friday, they still put 49 marbles in a tight group in the centre of a lightly-sanded 6ft-wide, circular, concrete rink and the object of the game is to shoot the marbles out of the ring with a 'tolley', a slightly larger marble used as a kind of cue ball.

The British Marbles Board of Control, established at The Greyhound in 1926, laid down, and adheres to, a strict set of rules. Marbles should be between ⅜ and ⅝in across, while the tolley should be no more than ¾in in diameter, 'otherwise,' say the Controllers, 'you'd have people coming along with tolleys the size of cricket balls'. Tolleys must be 'thumb-fired' – the hand must be on the floor, knuckles touching the concrete, palm upwards and the tolley flicked off the index finger with the thumb.

'Fudging' – moving the knuckles forward to gain an extra inch or so – is cheating. First throw is decided by a 'tolley off' – a representative from each team stands in the centre of the circle, holding a tolley at nose height. The tolleys are dropped simultaneously and whichever one comes to rest nearest the edge of the rink wins the throw.

The games begin with the first player in the team of six firing at the marbles from the edge of the rink. If his tolley knocks marbles out of the circle, but remains within the circle itself, the disposed-of marbles count a point each to his score and he has another shot from wherever the tolley came to rest. It is possible for a skilled player to keep on shooting like this, getting rid of marbles, leaving his tolley in place and building up a considerable 'break'. If the tolley knocks marbles from the ring, but in the process, flies outside the circle itself, the expelled marbles count to the home team's score, but play passes to the opposing team. Sometimes the tolley will shoot across and beyond the concrete without taking any marbles with it, in which case there is no score and the initiative again passes to the opposing team. The most unfortunate shot of all is that which fails to account for any marbles and leaves the tolley in the ring. Then the tolley is vulnerable – if an opponent knocks it out of the ring then its owner is eliminated altogether from the game. The winning team is the one to achieve 25 points first.

For many years, the local 'super-group' was the Toucan Terribles, who won the team championship every year from 1957 to 1974. Their star players were Len Smith and his son, Alan, who between them clocked up some remarkable feats. In 1974, Len scored 15 of his team's points to win the semi-final 25-9; in the final, Alan ran up 24 points to give them an emphatic 25-1 victory.

The Americans began a National Marbles Tournament for children, in New Jersey, in 1922, and their rules were slightly different – the circle was 20ft across and there were only 13 target marbles laid out in the form of a cross, so 7 points won the match. Nevertheless, an American team – a crew of sailors who called themselves the Swede Bashers – managed to adapt and give the Tinsley Toucans a game in 1959. The Sussex lads, captained by 86-year-old George 'Pop' Maynard and starring 52-year-old Arthur 'Hydrogen Thumb' Chamberlain, won 33-16. In 1975, the unthinkable happened when a team from Pittsburgh, specially flown into Britain by Gulf Oil, beat the Toucan Terribles and carried the championship home across the Atlantic.

Ring Taw is a very old game, but I suspect the story put about in Sussex, to the effect that the

The Toucan Terribles were unbeatable in their day, and invariably carried off the World Marbles Championship trophy each Good Friday. This picture shows the 1967 tournament.

A member of the U.S. Navy team – the Grosvenor Gobs – taking the first flick of the 1954 World Marbles Championship.

Tinsley game began in 1600, as a contest between rival suitors for the hand of a beautiful village maiden, is merely a slice of 'fakelore'. I think 'Pop' Maynard might have been able to reveal how and when marbles graduated from playground to pub yard, during his lifetime.

The Toucan Terribles, incidentally, challenged the Cambridge University **tiddlywinks** team to a dual game, in the 1970s. Cambridge had established a dubious claim to be the country's top tiddlywinkers by beating the Duke of Edinburgh's champions – the cast of *The Goon Show* – in an inaugural contest back in 1958. The University trained on Babycham, the Goons on Guinness, or so it was claimed. By the 1970s, tiddlywinks was a bustling, hustling game, with the Prince Philip Silver Wink Trophy on offer in an annual inter-university competition; the Marchant Trophy, for the All England Club Championship; the Guinness Trophy for international matches between England, Ireland, Scotland and Wales; a County Championship, National Pairs and National Singles Championships, not to mention classics such as the Manchester Open (July) and the Hampshire Open (February).

The origins of tiddlywinks are splendidly confused – according to *The English Dialect Dictionary* of 1905, the word 'tiddlywink', besides referring to the game, can mean 'an unlicensed public house, a beershop (particularly in Evesham, licensed before the Beerhouse Act of 1869), a small shed or an unlicensed pawnbroker's shop'.

Just to refresh the memory of those who may not have played tiddlywinks for some time, I should perhaps say that the game involves flicking circular concave/convex plastic counters, or 'winks', with a larger counter, called a 'squidger', into a pot. Matchplay tiddlywinks is an extremely complex tactical battle; games are usually for four players, playing in pairs, flipping six winks each over a firm, felt pitch 2 yards long and 1 yard wide. Experienced players will not necessarily go for the pot, but will try to 'squop', or cover, opponents' winks with their own, thus rendering them inoperative. If the game runs to a 'pot-out', the first player to pot all his winks gets 4 points, the second 2 points, the third 1 point. Partners add their scores together and 1 point is transferred from the losing side to the winning pair; a 'wipe-out pot-out' would therefore be 5–0.

Often, a time limit of 20 minutes is imposed on a game. When time runs out, play goes on until the player who had the 'squidge-off' has had his turn. Five complete rounds of turns then follow. The score is calculated thus: each player receives 3 time-limit points for each of his winks in the pot and 1 point for each of his winks not 'squopped'. Players total these points individually. The player with the highest total then receives 4 points, the next 3, the third 1 – and again the partners add their totals together.

Every year, come September-time, hordes of youngsters gather after school and at weekends around half a dozen ancient horse-chestnut trees, which line the road opposite my house. The kids arrive with a variety of missiles – bricks, stones and lumps of wood – which they proceed to throw into the trees in an attempt to bring down **conkers**. Every year, the police arrive and disperse the children because some irate motorist has complained about children hurtling across the road in front of him, or has had the unnerving experience of spent missiles and dislodged conkers drumming on the roof of his car. It is a tradition which has gone on ever since there were conker trees, a main road, motorists and policemen hereabouts.

A lot of pubs play conkers in season, too, although it's not clear if customers collect the conkers themselves, or bribe their children. At The Green Man, in Little Braxstead, Essex, customers pay ten pence (to the Lifeboat Fund) for a conker and stage an annual knockout competition in November. The landlord of The Brown Cow, in Norden, near Rochdale, Greater Manchester, saves his conkers until Christmas, then sells them at 50 pence each, again for charity, for a contest on Boxing Day. Pride of place on the conker front, though, must go to The Chequered Skipper, at Ashton, near Oundle, in Northamptonshire, where the Ashton Conker Club hosts the World Conker Championship on the village green.

The Ashton Club was founded in 1865 and the Championships are held on the morning of the second Sunday in October. The contest entails none of the arduous preparation, subterfuge, training and skill of children's conkers, since the conkers are collected from trees around the picture-book green by officials. (One year, when the trees failed to produce conkers, supplies had to be flown in from Portugal.) Contestants pick their conkers, already threaded, at random from a bag and the Championship is decided on an elimination basis through fights during the day. The winner receives a cup and a crown of conkers. During the proceedings, odd characters wander about, wearing strange uniforms decorated with garlands of conker-chains and badges. I don't know what the children of the district make of it all . . .

The Annual Conker Championships are held each October in Ashton, Northamptonshire. Entrants must be over 18 years of age, which seems a little unfair on the children of the area.

Over the Edge

There are times when pub-game eccentricity teeters on the edge of lunacy, often during a heatwave or charity drive. Such are the days when you could well stumble across those pastimes which almost defy description, such as **dwile flonking**, **marrow dangling**, **passing the splod**, **rhubarb thrashing**, **conger cuddling** and **Portuguese sardine-racing**, to name but a few . . .

According to the Waveney Rules of 1585, **dwile flonking** is played by two teams of 12 players, although there is great flexibility about numbers – in fact, the longer the game progresses, the more flexible the regulations become. All players are suitably costumed and the general theme seems to be 'rural idiot'. Smocks, ancient floppy hats, straws-in-the-mouth, trousers-with-string-tied-round-them-to-stop-the-rats-running-up, and big boots are popular, though not compulsory accessories.

The fielding team gathers in a large circle, called a 'girter', while one member of the opposing team, the 'flonker', stands within the girter, holding a pole (a 'driveller') on top of which is balanced a beer-soaked dishcloth, a 'dwile' or 'dwyle'. The referee intones the traditional opening, 'Here y' is t'gether', the flonker shouts 'Dwiles away!', the music begins, and the girter joins hands and dances round the flonker.

When the music stops, the flonker has to fling the dwile from the driveller, attempting to hit a member of the girter; a hit to the head is called a 'wonton' and scores 3 points, a body hit – a 'morther' – is worth 2 points and a leg strike, or 'ripper', is just 1 point. The flonker is allowed two shots and if he doesn't score at all, he is 'swadged', or 'potted', which means that he has to drink a potty-full of beer (approximately six pints, depending on local rules), while the circle chants 'pot, pot, pot', and passes the dwile from hand to hand. If the flonker fails to drain the pot in the time that it takes the dwile to be passed round the girter, he loses a point.

When all 12 of the 'batting side' have had a go, the roles are reversed and the girters become the flonkers. Whoever has the most points after two innings wins the match. Those are the general rules, although there are variations. In some areas, the driveller is called a 'swadger' and swadge-copers survive to this day, selling them, as always, by the tardwainer's nard. I owe this last illuminating piece of information to Richard Boston, who conducted a long-running investigation into dwile flonking in his regular column in *The Guardian*, in the late 1970s.

I first saw an exhibition match of dwile flonking on television, probably in the late 1960s, when it was explained to a bemused reporter (Michael Bentine) by a crowd of mad country yokels, in a series called *It's a Square World*. It is now clear to me that this was not a comedy sketch, as I had first thought, but a more or less spot-on report of a game whose origins went back into the mists of time – to 1966, to be precise, when it first saw the light of day at a charity fête in Beccles or Bungay (or both?), under the auspices of the Waveney Valley Dwile Flonking Association. Its invention is credited to a printer and amateur conjurer called Jim High, although he claimed to have picked up the rules from an old farm worker called Amos Thirkell. In 1967, the Waveney Valley Dwile Flonking Association celebrated its first anniversary and applied to the local magistrates for an extension in drinking hours to cover the festivities – the police concluded that the pastime was basically harmless and therefore raised no objections.

The last word on the subject comes from a Mr E. Pearson, who wrote to Richard Boston on the matter, referring him to a fragmentary work in Latin, called *The Memorials of a Ripon*, dating from 1312. Boston's translation (*The Guardian*, 1 May 1976) claimed that 'a chaplain (*capelannus*) called Bill Drunker (*Willelmus Pistor*) was the chief inventor (*inventor principalis*) of a pestiferous game (*ludi pestiferi*) called *Dyngethryfes* – *dynge* meaning to throw or drive with violence, while *thryfes* are savings'.

A great deal more research obviously needs to be done before a comprehensive account of this ancient game can be compiled.

There are several interesting developments from the skittles game referred to as Devil Among the Tailors (see p. 63). Before the First World War, outsize versions of this pastime were known in Germany – the pole was some 12ft high, the ball on the end of the chain was the size of a lawn bowl and the nine pins were about 18in tall. It was a game enjoyed by stout burgers in the Odinwald. Recent British experimentation on the same theme has included **conger cuddling**, last observed at Lyme Regis, in Dorset, where the skittles are humans, bizarrely-dressed and perched on plant pots. The 'ball' used is a 5ft-long conger eel, although I am reliably informed that if congers are not available, 'any other large, dead fish could be substituted'.

An alternative version of the game, preferred by the clientele of The Greyhound, Wargrave, in Berkshire, is **marrow dangling**. Here, the tethered projectile is a large marrow and the skittles wear protective plastic buckets (with eyeholes cut in them) over their heads. In conger cuddling, points are scored for each skittle knocked off, or forced to abandon his plant pot; in marrow dangling the aim is to knock

Conger Cuddling at Lyme Regis, Dorset. 'If you can't find a suitable conger,' say the organisers, 'any big fish will do.

buckets off heads, although a skittle knocked over gains bonus points.

Rhubarb Thrashing has been known in places all over the U.K. Two blindfolded and earplugged contestants, both wearing black bin-liners stand, each in a dustbin. They grasp each other, left-handed, while belabouring each other, right-handed, with large sticks of rhubarb. The first player forced to abandon his bin has lost the game.

Passing the Splod is a two-team relay race. The 'splod' is a large rubber suction device – an inverted rubber cap on the end of a stout pole, normally used for clearing blocked sinks and baths. On this occasion, the splod is plunged into a bucket of water, then pushed firmly onto a teammate's bare stomach, with the traditional cry of 'Splod off!' He wrenches it away with a merry shout, then repeats the process with the next member of his team, until eventually, the splod reaches the referee at the end of the line. There are no regulations about the numbers in each team.

Gordon Green, the landlord of the Neuadd Arms Hotel, in Llanwrtyd Wells, Powys, Wales, is surely in line to gain something like a Queen's Award for Eccentric Industry – he organises the annual World **Bog Snorkelling** Championship, where the com-petitors swim two lengths of a channel cut in the peat bog on the outskirts of town; the Mountain Bicycle Bog Leaping Point-to-Point, over a wild 20-mile course; and the annual Man v Horse v Mountain Bike Marathon over 22 miles of farm tracks, open moorland and forestry roads. There's a prize for the first runner to beat a horse.

Fragmentary and incoherent reports circulate about new sports, or old pastimes rediscovered, such as **Wetton Toe Wrestling**, at The Olde Royal Oak, Wetton, Staffordshire; **Long Rope Skipping** on each Good Friday lunchtime at The Rose Cottage, Alciston in Sussex; the mysterious activities of the **Portuguese Racing Sardines** Club at The Hampshire Bowman, Dundridge, Hampshire, or even the challenge from overseas, the World **Frothblowing** Championship, from Cape May, Washington Mall, New Jersey.

There was an outbreak of **Cucumber Tossing** in Lancashire, in the late 1970s, sponsored by a vodka firm and, as far as I know, there is still an annual contest to drag a Ford Orion car from Ambleside to the top of the Kirkstone Pass, in the Lake District – you will need a couple of friends for this, since each car is pulled by a team of three. The pursuit of eccentricity, it seems, never ends.

Books on pub games: *Inns of Sport* by J. Wentworth Day (Whitbreads, 1949); *Inn Games* (Educational Productions Ltd, 1955; *Pub Games* by Timothy Finn (Queen Anne Press, 1966); *Pub Games of England* by Timothy Finn (Queen Anne Press, 1975); *The Life and Sport of the Inn* by Michael Brander (Gentry Books, 1973): *Pub Games* by Arthur Taylor (Mayflower, 1976).

Guidebooks to pubs: *The Good Beer Guide* (published each year by CAMRA); the *Best Pubs* series, 1989–91 (Alma Books); *Essex Beer Guide* – eighth edition (CAMRA, 1991); *Ale of Two Cities* (Manchester and Salford) (CAMRA, 1989); *Derbyshire Ale* (CAMRA, 1990); *Cheshire Ale* (CAMRA, 1988); *Viaducts and Vaults* (Stockport) (CAMRA, 1991); *The Good Pub Guide* (published annually by Ebury Press).

Books on the history of games: *The Sports and Pastimes of the People of England* by Joseph Strutt, first published in 1801 and updated in 1903 by J.C. Cox (Firecrest Publishing, 1969); *The Compleat Gamester* by Charles Cotton, first published in 1674 (re-issued by Cornmarket Reprints, 1972); *Cassell's Book of Indoor Amusements, Card Games and Fireside Fun* (1881, re-published in facsimile edition in 1973); *The Complete Book of Games* by Clement Wood and Gloria Goddard (Garden City Books, N.Y., 1940); *Sport in England* by Norman Wymer (Harrap, 1949); *English Sports and Pastimes* by Christina Hole (Batsford, 1949); *Dictionary of Games* by J.B. Pick (J.M. Dent, 1952); *Board and Table Games I* and *II* by R.C. Bell (Oxford University Press, 1960, 1969); *Gambling* by Alan Wykes (Spring Books, 1964); *The Past of Pastimes* by Vernon Bartlett (Chatto and Windus, 1969); *Scarne's New Complete Guide to Gambling* by John Scarne (Constable, 1974; *Games of the World* edited by Frederick V Grunfeld (Holt, Rinehart and Winston, N.Y., 1975); *The Way to Play* (Paddington Press, 1975); *The Oxford Companion to Sports and Games* edited by John Arlott (Oxford University Press, 1976); *The Macmillan Dictionary of Sports and Games* (J.A. Cuddon, 1980); *The Hamlyn Book of Games* edited by Peter Arnold (1989); *Sport and the British* by Richard Holt (Oxford University Press, 1990).

Books on specific games: *The Backgammon Book* by Oswald Jacoby and John Crawford (Macmillan, 1970); *Darts* by Rupert Croft-Cooke (London, 1934); *Darts* by Tom Barratt (Pan, 1973); *Darts* by Noel E. Williamson (Elliot Right Way Books, 1973); *The Dart Player's Handbook* by George Hakim (Hodder and Stoughton, 1973); *Darts – The Compleat Book of the Game* by Keith Turner (David and Charles, 1980); *Darts – Fifty Ways to Play the Game* by Jabez Gotobed (Oleander Press, 1980); *The Guinness Book of Darts* by Derek Brown (Guinness Publishing, 1981; *Leighton Rees on Darts* edited by Dave Lanning (London, 1981); *The Crafty Cockney* by Deryck Brown (Queen Anne Press, 1985); *The Watney Book of Bowls* by C.M. Jones (Queen Anne Press, 1967); *Corner to Corner* by John D. Vose (The Strule Press, 1969); *The BBC Book of Bowls* edited by Keith Phillips (1987); *The Daily Telegraph Book of Bowls* (1990); *Early Golf* by Steven J.H. Van Heugel (1982); *The Pernod Book of Petanque* by Maurice Abney Hastings (Allen and Unwin, 1981); *Petanque* by Garth Freeman (The Carreau Press, 1984); *Domino Games and Domino Puzzles* by K.W.H. Leeflang (Hamlyn, 1976); *The Domino Book* by Frederick Bernat (Bantam, 1975); *Links with the Past* (Thurston and Co., 1942); *The Story of Billiards and Snooker* by Clive Everton (Cassell, 1979); *Billiards and Snooker Byegones* by Norman Clare (Shire Publications, 1985); *Billiards, The Official Rules and Records Book* by the Billiard Congress of America (1986); *Snookered* by Donald Trelford (Faber and Faber, 1986); *Shoot Pool* by Ian Pannell (The Apple Press, 1989); *Billiards and Snooker, a Trade History* compiled by J.R. Mitchell (British Sports and Allied Industries Federation).

Historical studies: *Popular Recreations in English Society 1700–1830* by R. Malcomson (Cambridge University Press, 1973); *Once a Year* by Homer Sykes (Gordon Fraser, 1977); *Popular Custom and Culture in Nineteenth Century England* edited by R.D. Storch (1982); *The English Alehouse – A Social History 1200–1830* by Peter Clark (Longman, 1983); *The Customs and Ceremonies of Britain* by Charles Kightly (Thames and Hudson, 1986): *Fairs, Feasts and Frolics – A Yorkshire Survey* by Julia Smith (Smith Settle, 1989).

General: *Your Local* (Whitbread, 1947); *Inside the Pub* by Maurice Gorham and H.McG. Dunnet (Architectural Press, 1950); *Pub* edited by Angus McGill (Longman, 1969); *The Pub and the People – A Worktown Study by Mass Observation* (Seven Dials Press, 1970); *Victorian Public Houses* by Brian Spiller (David and Charles, 1972); *Victorian Pubs* by Mark Girouard (Studio Vista, 1975); *The English Pub* by Michael Jackson (Collins, 1976); *A Haunt of Rare Souls* by Barrie Pepper (Smith Settle, 1990).

Index